LOOKING FORWARD

Also by John Marks Templeton

Is Progress Speeding Up? Our Multiplying Multitudes of Blessings

How Large is God? The Voices of Scientists and Theologians
(editor)

Golden Nuggets

Worldwide Laws of Life: 200 Eternal Spiritual Principles

Is God the Only Reality? Science Points to a Deeper Meaning of the Universe
(with Robert L. Herrmann)

Evidence of Purpose: Scientists Discover the Creator (editor)

Discovering the Laws of Life

The Templeton Plan: 21 Steps to Personal Success and Real Happiness
(as described to James Ellison)

The God Who Would Be Known: Revelations of the Divine in Contemporary Science
(with Robert L. Herrmann)

Riches for the Mind and Spirit

The Humble Approach: Scientists Discover God

Global Investing: The Templeton Way
(as told to Norman Berryessa and Eric Kirzner)

LOOKING FORWARD

The Next Forty Years

EDITED BY

JOHN MARKS TEMPLETON

A Giniger Book
Published in Association with

Templeton Foundation Press
Philadelphia & London

TEMPLETON FOUNDATION PRESS
Five Radnor Corporate Center, Suite 120
100 Matsonford Road
Radnor, Pennsylvania 19087

Printed in the United States of America

Library of Congress Cataloging-in-Publication Data

Looking forward: the next forty years / edited by John Marks
    Templeton.
        p. cm.
    "A Giniger book."
    Includes index.
    ISBN 1-890151-05-X
    1. Twenty-first century— forecasts.   I. Templeton, John, 1912–
CB161.L665   1993
303.49'09'05—dc20   92-55048

CONTENTS

LOOKING FORWARD

1

INTRODUCTION TO THE NEW EDITION

by John Marks Templeton

Sir John Marks Templeton has had a long career as an investment counselor. Founder of the successful Templeton group of funds, he has been a pioneer in searching out worldwide investment opportunities. He is also widely known as a philanthropist, particularly for his foundation's Templeton Prize for Progress in Religion, the world's most generous philanthropic cash award.

JUST OVER A CENTURY AGO, when Edward Bellamy penned his classic *Looking Backward,* he envisioned our globe in the year 2000 as a somewhat somber place—a world in which individualism had been suppressed and entrepreneurship vanquished, with most of its people toiling under a system of state socialism. Now, we stand poised on the brink of another new century—indeed, a new millennium—and Bellamy's predictions have, thankfully, been tested and proved wanting. Today's world is not a place of gray uniformity and institutionalized drudgery for the sake of social security and the least amount of injustice. Rather, it is a world of great hope and glorious promise—a world stepping boldly into a new golden age of opportunity.

We live in a wonderful age—a period of unprecedented discovery and opportunity, a blossoming time for mankind. It is also a world of dramatic changes—politically, economically, culturally, and spiritually.

The evolution of human knowledge is accelerating enormously. More than half of the scientists who have ever existed have lived during the twentieth century. More than half of the discoveries in the natural sciences have been made in this century. More than half of the goods produced in the history of the earth have been produced since 1800. More than half of the books ever written were written in the last fifty years. More new books are published each month than were written in the entire historical period before the birth of Columbus.

We know, in a vast and intricate cosmos, that there is still much more to be discovered. And we need to plan! Now, more than ever before, we need to try to see the future more clearly. What will the next thirty or forty years portend? From a business perspective, we must consider the types of products that we will be buying and selling. What careers will be meaningful? What will the job market be like? What types of materials and services, which currently do not exist, are likely to be commonplace by then? Will our lifestyles forty years from now be as different from our current lives as our current lifestyles are from those of forty years ago?

THE ART OF PROPHECY

This book is intended to suggest some answers to those questions—to look ahead with a sense of expectancy and hope. We will try to peek into the future through clouds of uncertainty, much as we try to watch a parade from behind a crowd of heads.

Of course, prophesying is not without its hazards. The Princeton physicist Gerald O'Neill discusses its complexities in his book, *2081.* His opening chapter, "The Art of Prophecy," notes that many writers, in addition to Edward Bellamy, seeking to anticipate the future have badly missed the mark. Rudyard Kipling wrote that war would be out of fashion by the year 2000. H. G. Wells prophesied that there would be a World State in 1977, which would suppress all religions. Kipling further believed that future travel belonged to the zeppelin; Wells was convinced that the moon would not be explored until the year 2054. Perhaps Jules Verne, the famous French science fiction author, was most accurate. He boasted that he had read a thousand scientific articles and books before he began his prophetic *20,000 Leagues Under the Sea*. And his vision was quite uncanny. He correctly anticipated the Apollo moon program—the Florida launch site, the three-man crew, the initial circumnavigating around the world, and the subsequent moon landing. And he did all of this one hundred years before the fact.

Among the scientific prophets of the past, O'Neill extols the virtues of the English biologist J. B. S. Haldane, who argued correctly that fundamental scientific advances have an enduring significance whereas the impact of military conquest diminishes with the passage of time. Thus, the generals of World War I are virtually forgotten except by a few historians. But every schoolboy knows about Albert Einstein. During the first quarter of our century, Haldane correctly anticipated the fertilization of human eggs outside the body—first carried out in 1978. In 1928, he prophesied that the world was at risk of successfully completing experiments in "induced radioactivity," the precursor to nuclear reactions.

THE STATIC SOCIETY

The idea of future threats to personal freedom was seriously discussed in sobering terms by George Orwell in his classic *1984* and by Aldous Huxley in *Brave New World*. Both authors perceived the threat of a future government's absolute control over society, the end result being a static society devoid of creative thought and expression. The ultimate objective was "social stability" at the expense of human experience. O'Neill expresses alarm that, in our contemporary world, distinguished scholars have published a book, *The Limits to Growth*, which proposes restriction of certain freedoms in order to more effectively manage a global static society. These authors, focusing on the negative aspects of our world, fear a rapid depletion of natural resources and the threat of nuclear catastrophe. The static society is not a new idea, having been proposed in the last century by Rudyard Kipling and others. But it represents a pessimistic doomsayer's approach to the future and fails to capture the energy and resources inherent in the human spirit. From my perspective, this doomsayer approach is also inconsistent with the evolutionary history of our species, which has demonstrated its resilience by creating and ever increasing its sophistication and adaptability, moving ever forward to some purpose. Indeed, the doomsayer misses the overriding fact that there is a Creator behind this drama, moving our world and us to bring an ever greater revelation of His goodness and concern for His creation.

THE INFORMATION SOCIETY

With the sheer driving force of advancing technology, it is increasingly clear that our society is moving from a material-based one to an information-oriented/knowledge-intensive base. John Naisbitt pointed out in *Megatrends* that, in 1950, only 17 percent of us worked in information-related occupations. By 1982, that figure had soared to 65 percent. Teachers, computer programmers, clerks, secretaries, accountants, stockbrokers, and so on, all saw their relative numbers increase, and the knowledge and information content of their jobs explode.

Today, most Americans spend their time creating, processing, or distributing information. In 1980, more than a decade ago, American companies generated $60 billion in revenues from selling goods and services overseas. That represented about 20 percent of the world's share of trade. Since that time, America's trade deficit has been the subject of widespread political and social debate; indeed, trade negotiations between the U.S. and some of its key trading partners have resulted in serious shifts in trading practices such as the North American Free Trade Agreement. But in *Megatrends 2000,* Naisbitt and his co-author Patricia Aburdene suggest that the deficit problem is overstated because conventional trade accounting focuses primarily on the output of manufactured goods and fails fully to account for trade in information and knowledge. Indeed, after accounting for our heavily information-oriented intangibles, America may be experiencing a significant trade surplus.

A second distinction of the information economy is that it is based upon renewable and self-generating resources—knowledge and information. It is thus inherently less dependent upon material resources such as oil, coal, or nuclear energy. Consequently, we have another reason to reject the static society doomsayer. As we become more of an information-oriented society, we require fewer material inputs to create additional economic output. We are essentially substituting knowledge for physical capital and unskilled labor.

The major challenge to be faced by the new information economy is to find faster and more efficient ways to process the enormous amount of technical data accumulating in our society. In the mid-1980s, scientific and technical information was doubling every twenty months. Now it is doubling in less than nine months. This extremely valuable resource must be organized and made accessible. Consequently, the focus of current efforts should shift away from the gathering of information and move toward analyzing, evaluating, and selecting the relevant segments of this information tidal wave. On-line databases and wide-spread access to the information superhighway via the internet give the user direct access to resources such as special libraries, indexes, and information once available to a very few. Such "democratization" of information gives individuals access to this wealth of information at only nominal cost. As this process continues, and the technology for providing information evolves, the balance of power will shift from those who excel at providing information toward those whose strength lies in analyzing the data and inferring superior insights from it.

With power shifting toward those who excel at analyzing data, we must become concerned with the ability of our workforce to successfully access information, analyze it, and draw valid conclusions from that analysis. This, in turn, requires an educational structure which will train our citizens to meet these knowledge-intensive tasks. There continues to be an acute shortage of high school and college science and math teachers, which has already adversely affected the entry-level competence of new workers. Perhaps just as important, there seems to be a failure in American society as well as in many other societies to cultivate the intellectual skills required for critical thought and analysis. Academics have bemoaned the deterioration in writing expository skills, necessary tools for the critical thinker. In consequence, we have a powerful anomaly developing. As our society becomes more information- and knowledge-oriented, our schools are providing us with graduates unable to meet the requirements of our evolving society. In Naisbitt's words,

> without basic skills, computer illiteracy is a foregone conclusion. In the new information society, being without computer skills is like wandering around a collection the size of the Library of Congress with all the books arranged at random with no Dewey Decimal system, no card catalogue—and of course no friendly librarian to serve your information needs.

And we would take his analogy one step further. Access to that great library is not enough. Without the ability to read, comprehend the ideas, and utilize them, the benefits associated with entry to that tremendous library would be lost.

To meet the predicament, corporations are going into the education business. Many of the nation's largest companies are operating remedial courses in basic math and English for new employees. And, of course, the opportunities for science, math, and English teachers to consult and to tutor in these areas are widespread. But, interestingly, the "invisible hand" of the market may be aiding us as well. Preschool students are successfully being introduced to our information society through a wide variety of computer games, video arcades, and a host of child-oriented products. While these products have been criticized (perhaps rightly so in many cases), today's youth are far more computer-literate than most of their parents. Indeed, many young people are computer-literate before they are book-literate. In every generation, we tend to underrate our youth. Perhaps we are doing the same now. Watching a preschooler successfully operate a computer beyond my capabilities leads me to conclude that our youth, as historically has been the case, will rise to the needs of society.

As I look out over the next forty years, I am watching a swiftly moving cavalcade of progress. The technology to access and deliver unfathomable amounts of information is evolving rapidly. Increasingly sophisticated and accessible technologies allow for real time/high-resolution audio and video access between individuals with personal computers, and transfer of information to and from the great libraries of the world.

The same technological innovations will allow individuals access to video/audio/written information between virtually anyone located anywhere on the earth. A child with moderate computer skills can log on to the internet today and converse in real time with another youngster thousands of miles away. Companies that were once limited in their expansion capacities by distance and travel time to foreign locations can now carry on virtually every facet of business without leaving their home turf. Extrapolating into the future, I expect that one day soon, today's fax machine, overnight delivery, and internet services will seem as primitive to our grandchildren as the telegraph key and the Pony Express are to us today.

In practical terms, sitting in my home in Nassau in the Bahamas, I have immediate real time high-resolution multimedia access to virtually any information source. Information sources include not just books and library documents, but also video, radio, and theatrical broadcasts, great symphonies, moving operas, recorded speeches, and conventional data. Moreover, it is all available not only from my office, but from the pool side or the beach!

Perhaps I can provide a helpful example of why critical analytical skills will become increasingly important with time. Allow me the liberty of using the investment management business, a business with which I was associated for over fifty years. As information technologies evolve, the transaction costs involved with buying and selling stocks should decline sharply. In today's world, expensive brokers take the orders to expensive stock exchanges to process the buys and sells. However, as technology continues to develop, we are increasingly able to cut through those two layers to effect a transaction. Investors from anywhere in the world are already able to enter orders on several automated trading systems, and this will accelerate over time. The democratization of information, coupled with the ability to implement decisions based on that information instantaneously and inexpensively, will mean that markets are likely to become increasingly efficient. Consequently, those who seek to benefit from short-term trends will find the opportunities increasingly elusive. I have seen this process developing in the United States, where index arbitragers, using the more common models, are unable consistently to generate profits above their costs of capital.

Those who are successful today are employing increasingly complex computer algorithms and more expensive computer networks. Such complex investing systems require immediate access to information and computer power. However, within the next forty years, the sophisticated systems of today will look crude, and technologies for developing even more sophisticated computer trading models are likely to be widely disseminated. Consider the following analogy. Fifty years ago, computers costing millions of dollars and occupying whole rooms were used for calculating missile trajectories—the important state secrets of the day. Today, the same computer power can be found in a notebook-sized computer and the software can be written by a precocious junior high school student. The diffusion of the technology has been widely disseminated.

Increasingly, there will be little value added to following short-term investing strategies that rely on mere computer power. The computer systems required to do the job and the information required to be processed are readily available to a wide spectrum of users. While those with the most money available will do what they can to push the envelope of investment technology further along, additional gains will be difficult to achieve as the costs of accessing the information and applying advanced computer techniques to the information continue to decline. Computers and internet access have made special trading strategies such as "index arbitrage" possible. But, as the costs of these computer systems have dropped, and the computer programmers who know how to execute these strategies have multiplied, the markets have become more efficient and profits using these strategies have become increasingly difficult to achieve. Over the next forty years, these trends will continue, forcing the global markets to become increasingly efficient. This efficiency will make it difficult for even the best traders to consistently profit from their short-term trading techniques.

But despite the development of neural networks, expert systems, and other forms of exotic computer systems, it is unlikely that the component of human wisdom will be replaced in the investment process. Machines can be used to process hard data, but not human qualities such as greed, fear, or creativity. If we reflect on the fact that companies are really groups of people who manage assets and work with each other to create wealth; that they are intimately affected by other complex groups, politicians, local citizens, belligerent militarists, and so on; then it is clear that machines cannot adequately capture the complexity of these human conditions. Nor do we expect them to be able to do so within the next forty years. But the human mind obviously can. Through accumulated wisdom and experience, the human mind can integrate the almost infinite dimension of a corporation and use that process to develop long-term investment-oriented insights. As technology strips out the purely objective aspects of the investment process, the remaining subjective nature will become the fulcrum around which investment decisions will be made. And the value of wisdom will ascend.

THE GLOBAL ECONOMY

The 1990s presented us with a new world view that will play a major role in the way we move into the next millennium. As Communism collapsed with the Berlin wall in the 1980s, free market theories and practices became the prevailing force in the global economy. China and the former Soviet Union experimented with private enterprise in the 1980s and early 1990s, and after experiencing initial bumps and pangs which come with market transitions, both have begun developing market economies. The transfer of ownership of Hong Kong from Britain to China, in 1997, and China's subsequent adherence to Hong Kong's long-standing free-market practices, demonstrates a substantial shift in global thinking about economies. Many pundits predicted that China would force Hong Kong to convert to a communist economy, but as the global situation changed in the early 1990s, China saw the benefits of leaving Hong Kong's market system intact, and had even begun assimilating some of its practices into its own economy. In England, Prime Minister Margaret Thatcher's promotion of privatization of state-owned enterprises such as gas and electric utilities, the Jaguar automobile company, and British Airways, set a precedent for the world. From Chile to Turkey, Brazil to Bangladesh, and even in the socialist Scandinavian countries, tax reform and privatization became the torch of political reformers and bureaucrats alike.

The dramatic shift toward free enterprise and away from state control has affected the American economy as well. During the Reagan, Bush, and Clinton administrations, tax rates were dramatically lowered and the balance of power moved away from the central federal system toward the state and local communities. As the decision making moved increasingly into the hands of local decision makers, they became responsible, at the local level, for improving the health, education, and welfare systems of their communities. The positive benefits of this shift in the economic trends in the U.S. were evidenced in the substantial surplus in the federal budget in 1997.

The continuing movement of the global economy toward free market systems as we enter the new millennium will generate new economic forces unseen in world history. The benefits of free markets have become evident during this century, and the world has only just begun to reap the rewards that free markets can afford us.

THE NEW WORLD STRUCTURE

As a result of successful United States post-World War II policy, the very dominant economic position which the United States has maintained for many decades is becoming less pronounced. Japan has enjoyed a phenomenal rate of growth, initially in the manufacturing sphere, but also in the information sector, and has challenged, and in some cases exceeded, the United States for world leadership in several technology-intensive industries. Japanese economic strength is weakening as we approach the new millennium, perhaps in part due to pressure to lessen their restrictions on foreign trade. Western European countries have united in the European Community, removing more barriers to the flow of people, goods, services, and money. The efficiencies that the E.C. has afforded the countries under its auspices has helped make these nations participants in world prosperity. And, finally, a host of new players have joined the drama—the rapidly developing countries of the Pacific Rim: South Korea, Taiwan, Hong Kong, Singapore, Indonesia, Thailand, and China. In fact, though the Europeans will be a prosperous economic power, the Asian countries will probably be the linchpins to growth in the next few decades. The reason for this, as argued in *Megatrends 2000,* is that the Pacific Rim region is twice the size of Europe and the United States. It contains half the world's population at present and this will likely increase to two thirds of the world population by the year 2000. This represents, in a growing economy, an enormous number of consumers with money to spend.

Of course, the United States also borders the Pacific Rim, with its West Coast states ideally situated for trade and cultural exchange. In fact, California, with its huge economy, is like another Pacific Rim country. Measured apart from the rest of the United States, it has one of the world's largest economies. Furthermore, its economy is growing about eight percent per year, significantly more than the average U.S. rate, in part because of its position as the gateway to the Pacific Rim markets. California has already become the focal point for Japanese investment in the United States; it has more than 1,000 subsidiaries of Japanese firms. Taiwan has major investments in Silicon Valley, and also in a dozen U.S.-based plastics plants, a textile factory, and a computer plant jointly operated with Texas Instruments. More than 500,000 Americans work for Japanese companies in the United States. But there are more than 100,000 Japanese who work for American companies in Japan. And the United States has heavy investments throughout the Pacific Rim. For example, American-owned firms in Singapore account for more than half of that country's exports to the United States.

If the Japanese appetite for American goods—Coca-Cola, Levi jeans, Schick razors, American food, etc.—is shared by the other Asian countries, then the future consumers of the developing Pacific Rim nations offer exciting business opportunities for the United States. And that seems to be occurring. During the past several years, trade barriers between the U.S. and the Asian nations have been steadily diminishing. This has stimulated dramatic increases in exports to Japan, China, and the "Four Tigers" (South Korea, Taiwan, Hong Kong, and Singapore).

THE GLOBAL LIFESTYLES

The explosion of international trade, sources, and information will increasingly influence the way we live. Because we buy and sell not only raw and manufactured materials globally but also stocks, bonds, currencies, clothing, food, and entertainment, the lifestyle images now come to us rapidly from every port of the world. This leads to a certain "sameness" in what *Megatrends 2000* refers to as a code of international fashion. Nike footwear, Louis Vuitton luggage, and Japanese Toyotas are all high on the consumer's wish list around the world. America has been exporting its culture through the medium of film for a long time. In more recent years the U.S. share of the foreign film market has increased and its quality improved dramatically, with Italy, Germany, the United Kingdom, and Japan as the best customers.

More recently the television market has been growing tremendously. With the development of international cable and transnational satellite broadcasting there has been a spate of interest in American programs. Even China has entered the media market, with MGM/UA Communications, Paramount Pictures, and Universal Studios distributing movies and television programs under contract to the Chinese government.

While we are increasingly embracing each other's cultures, there are elements of "cultural nationalism" that are highly sensitive to local tastes and customs. The clash between international culture and local custom has raised concerns about "cultural imperialism," the importation of ideas that undermine long-cherished domestic ideals and customs. Examples of the backlash against perceived US cultural imperialism include recently instituted laws in France requiring the use of the French language as the language of trade. Other strong expressions of cultural nationalism are occurring, for example, in Scotland, Quebec, and Spanish Cataloña, where there are fears of transnational cultural rejection. In those areas, native language and customs are being emphasized, sometimes militantly. This conflict between local and transnational cultures reflects the increasing integration of the world.

All of this underscores the need for increased understanding and dialogue. Of special concern should be the discussion of shared moral and ethical values, and the development of an ecumenical moral-ethical climate throughout our societies. We do not service a country by undermining its standards of behavior. If you share this concern, you may wish to receive a copy of the John Templeton Foundation's *Honor Roll for Character Building Colleges,* a nationwide rating based upon the moral climate of academic institutions (free from The John Templeton Foundation, P.O. Box 8322, Radnor, Pennsylvania 19087-8322).

DIVERSITY AS A GENERAL TREND

Not only are our tastes becoming international, but they are also expanding in terms of the arts, our personal relationships, and our spiritual values. Future careers will favor the generalist, the broad thinker, the eclectic individual who is comfortable in several areas of knowledge and has broad-based experience. In a society where the expert has been regarded so highly, the generalist's talents have not been highly valued.

As our culture becomes increasingly global in scope, there is a parallel expansion of interest in the arts. *Megatrends 2000* predicted a veritable renaissance in the arts in the 1990s, reasoning that wherever the affluent information economy has spread, the need for examining the meaning of life through the arts will follow. Indeed, this prediction has proven correct. The growth in attendance and in the numbers of museums has been dramatic, not just in American museums, but in Japan, West Germany and Britain as well. In the United States, funding for the arts will increasingly come from corporations, some of whom are abandoning sports for the arts as a preferred way to define their images in the marketplace. The arts explosion is a global phenomenon. Not only is it occurring in the major cultural centers—Paris, London, New York, Tokyo—but it is flourishing in small towns and villages. Ninety percent of American theater now takes place outside of New York City.

The burgeoning interest in theater is also matched by opera, symphony, and dance. Opera audiences have tripled in a decade and a half. There are hundreds of small opera companies which are meeting in such places as veteran's halls and civic auditoriums across the country. Classical music has also become far more popular in the United States. Regional orchestras have grown from sixteen in 1975 to more than 100 in 1997. Chamber music is booming; the number of ensembles increased from 393 to more than 5,500 between 1985 and 1997. And new dance companies are appearing all across the country, often with sponsorship shared between two cities. For example, the Cincinnati Ballet became the Cincinnati/New Orleans Ballet, and New York's Joffre Ballet now has a second home in Los Angeles. Perhaps the Cleveland-San Jose Ballet is the new archetype. Cleveland was seeking a joint sponsor for its well-established group. San Jose was able to enlist support for joint sponsorship from E. F. Hutton and Apple Computer founder Steven Wozniak, who matched the Hutton gift.

The boom in art collecting also represents a trend that will continue into the next century. Sales of limited edition lithographs have increased by 80 percent. Sales of original art have reached manic proportions. Total sales at two of the largest auction houses, Sotheby's and Christie's, each broke the $1 billion barrier in 1987, and have continued to grow with celebrity auctions from the estates of Jacqueline Kennedy Onassis and Princess Diana.

The dimensions of this art renaissance are encouraging. More than 8 million visitors each year visit the Centre Georges Pompidou, France's treasure of modern art and architecture—twice the number who visit the Eiffel Tower. The next few decades may see the arts replace sports as the primary amusement. This accelerated search for intellectual nourishment, especially for the spiritual side of life, is a primary characteristic of our new era, represented by the most affluent and highly educated population in history. The "baby boomers" who were born in the decade after World War II are leading this new trend.

Another phenomenon has been the "democratization of the genders." In the last two decades, U.S. women have taken two thirds of the millions of new jobs created in the information society, jobs where intellect is more important than physical brawn. As part of this gender democratization, parenting has become a shared and savored experience for both parents. A large number of the nation's adults are entering two of life's passages simultaneously; middle age and parenthood. To enter middle age is to realize that time is short. That in turn creates a critical need to reevaluate goals and accomplishments, and to concentrate one's remaining energies on the most productive aspects of life.

Charles Reich's book *The Greening of America* expressed in a powerful way the reaction of people—this time college students—to the rigidity amid apparent meaninglessness of the workplace. Reich described a new information-age phenomenon, "Consciousness III," a thought framework for a person who assigns low priority to the materialistic aspects of society, instead placing primary emphasis on the intrinsic value of the human being ("Whatever I am, I am") and the ideal of personal freedom. What a joy it is to encounter this non-conforming, open, friendly, inquisitive person, who loves nature and experiences "the sense of God in everything." Reich hoped that this vision of humanity, first appreciated by those young adults, would diffuse through the older generation and so spread throughout society. Thirty years later, it seems not to have done so. The sense of alienation has tended to be a negative effect of this transition of our society in the post-industrial age. With our information-rich global society comes an unsettling insight into a truth which recognizes the enormity of the universe of which each of us is a tiny part.

Constant change increasingly seems to be the character of our universe. Despite the cycles of day and night and the seasons, we may be learning that nothing really repeats, but evolves instead. The universe seems to be vast in its conception, yet its evolution seems curiously experimental and tentative, a truly creative work in progress. Perhaps human beings, so late in appearance in this evolutionary process, have been given some creative role in seeking to understand and interpret awesome and mysterious processes which science only now begins to fathom. Perhaps the new wisdom of this new era of information will be that we can conceptualize and experiment over a wide diversity of possibilities in the physical and spiritual worlds.

Since Copernicus, it has been assured that we could hardly be the center of such a universe, or even the total fulfillment of God's plan for this world. In whatever way we relate to these cosmic concepts— and the great religious traditions have contributed much, as far as they go—we believe that we must expand our efforts to comprehend our Creator's purpose. Indeed, it is our responsibility to explore the universe's spiritual dimension as earnestly as we have been exploring its physical aspects. For this reason, I have encouraged the John Templeton Foundation's formation of new centers for the study of the spiritual aspects of health and healing, and for the interpretation of our new scientific knowledge of the universe in theological terms.

In much the same way that *Megatrends 2000* sought to prophesy the state of humanity in the last decade before the new millennium, the authors in this book look to the next few decades in an effort to predict our progress. Enormous advances in technology, ever-increasing access to information, and shifting demands on our time, make forecasting changes, as we look forward to our next thousand years, even more important. It is crucial that we assess our current situation and look to the future with a proper understanding of our past, and deference to the spiritual power that allows us to be poised on the brink of a new millennium with such promise.

To enjoy the fruits of our discoveries, we must allow time to educate our spirits as well as our bodies and minds. The spirit can be nourished by authors like the anthropologist Loren Eiseley and the poet and writer Annie Dillard, who capture the wonder of our world in a remarkable way. To their works I would add Ralph Waldo Trine's *In Tune with the Infinite* and Paul Davies' *The Mind of God*. And, if you are unfamiliar with the more recent translations of the Bible, such as the New International Version, I believe you will find them very readable.

This book can begin with a few of Annie Dillard's words:

Einstein said that "nature conceals her mystery by means of her essential grandeur, not by her cunning." It could be that God has not absconded but spread, as our vision and understanding of the universe have spread, to a fabric of spirit and sense so grand and subtle, so powerful in a new way, that we can only feel blindly of its hem. In making the thick darkness a swaddling band for the sea, God "set bars and doors" and said, "Hitherto shalt thou come, but no further." But have we come even that far? Have we rowed out to the thick darkness, or are we all playing pinochle in the bottom of the boat?

January 1998

2

THE ENVIRONMENT

by Ghillean T. Prance

Professor Ghillean T. Prance is the director of the Royal Botanic Gardens at Kew, England. He has been a senior vice-president at the New York Botanical Gardens and a visiting professor at the City University of New York, Yale, and Reading. A specialist in tropical botany, he has made fourteen botanical expeditions to Amazonia and written numerous books and articles.

I. INTRODUCTION

The energy crisis of the 1960s brought with it a special awareness that energy and other resources were running out. Much alarm was raised, which helped to stimulate concern about the finite nature of our resources and the carrying capacity of our planet. The fact that oil and minerals are not being depleted as quickly as the prophets of doom of the sixties predicted gives no room for complacency in the nineties. We may have a 3,000-year supply of coal, but it is still a finite resource and its use should be planned. The rate of supply of petroleum and coal has not diminished in the last three decades, but through their use the environment has deteriorated more rapidly than during any other similar period in human history. In the four weeks during which I prepared this essay, articles in scientific and environmental journals have carried such headlines as: "Scientists Fear Gaia Is Heading for a Breakdown" (the opinion of a group of scientists that met in Rhode Island in 1991 to discuss the increase in algal blooms in our oceans); "Mystery of Florida's Dying Coral" (based on a fifteen-year monitoring of Florida's Keys, where reefs are shrinking and species are disappearing); and "Water Crisis Looms" (based on the destruction of watersheds and the depletion of aquifers). As a biologist studying the vegetation of the world during the same period, I have observed an unprecedented rate of destruction of natural environments and an increase in the rate of species extinction far beyond any natural rate. We are now seriously eroding our options for the future.

As population multiplies, the demands for resources and the amount of pollution both increase. There is a limit to how much we can pollute our planet without causing a breakdown to the functioning of our biosphere. The signs of such a breakdown are apparent now: increased carbon dioxide in the atmosphere, an ever-enlarging hole in the ozone layer of the upper atmosphere, acid rain destroying the forests of Europe, North America, and China, declining supplies of cod in the North Sea because the catch is beyond a sustainable rate, and many other obvious examples. The future quality of life will depend upon the actions that are taken during the next few decades; and so, from an environmental point of view, it is essential to look ahead and to plan ahead. We are living off our capital as regards the environment and that is as unsustainable in the environment as it is in our bank accounts. We cannot continue using up capital for ever. The next few decades must be the time of adjustment when we learn to conserve our capital, whether it be energy, biological species, water, atmosphere, or food supplies. To live off the interest rather than the capital requires a change in global attitude that bases policy on the long-term future and sustainability rather than on quick profit and growth, which in turn will require a new approach to calculating gross national product and to auditing the value of environmental resources. We need to listen to the wisdom of some groups of North American Indians who judge their actions by the effects they will have on the seventh unborn generation. If we thought about the effects we are having on our

5 × great-grandchildren, we would regard our environment differently.

I will consider here some of the most important aspects that must be addressed over the next few decades if our race is to have a long-term future. The warning lights are flashing now and to ignore them will lead to disaster. The head of the United Nations Environment Program, Mostafa Tolba, recently declared that the United Nations Conference on the Environment and Development which took place in June 1992 was "our best chance, perhaps our last chance, to save the planet." He is correct. We have no time to lose.

II. POPULATION

I address the issue of population first because it is at the root of the environmental crisis and the most important factor if the future of humankind is to be secure. The statistical facts about population are simple and obvious, but the consequences of ignoring them are dire. It took approximately 2 million years from the origin of the human species in the savannas of Africa for the worldwide population to reach 1 billion in about 1830. Over the next century this figure had doubled to 2 billion in 1930, but by then growth was exponential. Our population reached 4 billion in 1970, and it is currently well over 5 billion because that number was reached in 1987. The growth rate has fallen in recent years from 2.1 percent to 1.7 percent, which is still exponential and gives a forty-year doubling time. Therefore, we can expect a population of around 10 billion in the year 2030 unless drastic measures are taken to slow down the growth rate (see Table 1). Between 7 and 8 percent of all human beings that ever lived on this planet are alive today. In many developing countries, 50 percent of the population is under reproductive age, which will lead to a future burst in population growth; and in Africa, 60 percent is younger than twenty years old and half are unemployed, with no future job prospects. There is considerable disagreement about the future growth of human populations and about when and what will stop it growing, but it is generally predicted to stabilize soon after the year 2100.

Apart from the sociological, political, economic, and environmental consequences of excess population that are discussed later in this essay, what worries me is the apparent ignoring of the basic

TABLE 1. WORLD POPULATION AND ESTIMATED GROWTH

	Population mid-1984 (millions)	Natural increase (Annual %)	Population under age 15 (%)	Population 2020 (est.) (millions)
Africa	583	2.3	45	913
Latin America	419	2.3	38	736
Southeast Asia	408	2.2	39	664
Brazil	138.4	2.4	38	242
Mexico	81.7	2.6	42	147
Kenya	21	4.2	53	73.7
Nigeria	105.4	3.0	48	298.7
Europe	493	0.3	22	523
United States	241.0	0.7	22	305.3
World	4,942	1.7	35	7,731

SOURCE: Population Reference Bureau, Inc.

biological fact that any organism whose population rises above its resource capacity is bound to crash. Many studies of population biology—whether it is with single-celled paramecium, fruit flies, rats, or deer—have repeatedly shown that species whose population increases with excessive rapidity are also subject to rapid declines or crashes in their numbers—see, for example, Rasmussen (1941) for Kaibab deer, or Davidson and Andrewartha (1948) for thrips, or MacLulich (1937) for a fascinating study of the oscillations of snowshoe hare and Lynx populations, depending on the ratio of predator versus prey. We know that the human species is subject to most of the same constraints and biological rules as these other species. We have the power of reasoning that invented agriculture and the industrial revolution, the main causes of growth, and our intellect should also enable us to control our destiny and avoid a population crash. The greatest challenge of the next forty years is the stabilization of world population. This is often an unpopular subject with governments and religions, but it is vital that we address it.

Increased population leads to the shortage of resources, and hence to social unrest and fighting over their distribution, to destruction of the natural environment through the greater demand for food and other products, to more use of energy and consequently greater pollution, to increase in carbon dioxide and loss of the ozone layer that protects us from excess ultraviolet radiation, and finally to the extinction of many species.

I have spent considerable time amongst the Yanomami Indians and have personally observed the truth of Napoleon Chagnon's study (1968). When a village is small, with a population of around eighty people, it is quite peaceful. By the time there are 120 people, there are many disputes and fights; and when the population reaches 180 to 200, there is usually a huge fight that ends up with the village splitting into two. In the vast Amazon rain forest there is still room for this group fission and population increase, but this is a microcosm of what could happen today as the world's population and individual countries expand beyond their resources.

Already life in many of the large cities of the world is deteriorating badly because they are just too large to manage ecologically. São Paulo in Brazil had 20,000 inhabitants in 1818 and currently has 17 million. The 19 million inhabitants of Mexico City now live in one of the most polluted atmospheres in the world, and misery is on the increase in Calcutta, Lima, and many other large cities. El Salvador is the most overpopulated and environmentally degraded country in Latin America (see Anderson, 1981). It is not surprising that this country has been in a continual state of strife since 1969. Despite the current signs of the end of a period of Cold War, local and regional warfare and environmental deterioration will continue if we have not resolved the issue of population growth within the next twenty years. Is it beyond hope that we could achieve a stable population of 9 billion by the middle of the twenty-first century? It is a proven fact that education, the employment of women, and increased life expectancy so that more children are not needed as a means of social security are all factors that lead to a reduction in population growth. These are the areas upon which we should concentrate over the next few decades. The problems of overcrowding can also be reduced considerably if there is a much more equitable distribution of wealth and if we can address the issues of social justice.

III. THE GREENHOUSE EFFECT AND THE OZONE LAYER

Although there are conflicting reports about the extent of the greenhouse effect, its reality is beyond doubt. The increase of the so-called greenhouse gases in the atmosphere are causing a definite warming trend in the earth's atmosphere. Like the panes of glass in a greenhouse, gases such as carbon dioxide, halocarbons, methane, and nitrous oxide allow most solar radiation to enter the earth's atmosphere, but prevent part of the heat being reradiated back into space. The trapped heat then causes a gradual warming in the atmosphere. Whether the climate change over the next century is 1.5°C or 4.5°C is academic; even a change of 1.5°C—the estimate of the more conservative scientists—will have serious repercussions for the future. The decade of the 1980s was 0.2°C warmer than the average for 1950–80 and 0.5°C warmer than a century ago. The year 1990 was the warmest on record, and 1991 second just behind 1988 and 1987; therefore, 2030 is likely to be at least 0.5°C warmer than 1990. In spite of these clear warnings of the future, politicians are still complacent about addressing the issues because of the cost of correction.

Table 2 shows the increase in atmospheric concentrations of the principal greenhouse gases since pre-industrial times. Carbon dioxide concentration has risen from 280 parts per million by volume to 354 ppmv. The rate of emission continues to rise—principally from the burning of fossil fuels. Half of the carbon dioxide content added to the atmosphere during the entire human history has been added during the past thirty years. This great increase in rate is why the greenhouse effect is upon us so suddenly and requires such urgent action. The table also shows

TABLE 2. ATMOSPHERIC CONCENTRATIONS OF GREENHOUSE GASES SINCE PRE-INDUSTRIAL TIMES (= 1750)

Gases	Pre-industrial	Unit (1)	Present day	Current rate per year		Relative greenhouse effect per molecule	Atmospheric lifetime (yr)
Carbon dioxide	280	ppmv	354	1.8	(0.5%)	1	50–200
Methane	0.79	ppmv	1.72	0.015	(0.9%)	30	10
Nitrous oxides	288	ppbv	310	0.8	(0.25%)	160	150
Tropospheric ozone	?	ppbv	60	0.9	(1.5%)	2,000	very short
CFC-11	0	pptv	280	10	(4%)	21,000	65
CFC-12	0	pptv	484	17	(4%)	25,000	130

ppmv: part million by volume (10^{-6}); ppbv: part per billion by volume (10^{-9}); pptv: part per trillion by volume (10^{-12}).

SOURCE: J. T. Houghton, G. J. Jenkins, and J. J. Ephraums. *Climate Change, the IPCC Scientific Assessment* (Cambridge, Engl.: Cambridge University Press, 1990), p. 7.

the relative greenhouse effect per molecule of different gases. CFC-12 is 25,000 times more serious than carbon dioxide, and is therefore essential to control, not only because of its effect in the ozone layer but also because of its role in the greenhouse effect. Methane is thirty times more effective as a greenhouse gas. It is therefore necessary to curb the percentage of natural gas that escapes into the atmosphere through leaks in the gas piping of the United Kingdom, and even more important to address this issue in Russia and Eastern Europe.

If the causes of the greenhouse effect are not corrected within the next forty years, the consequences for global ecology will be serious. Not only will climate continue to warm but the pattern of climates in the world will alter. For example, it is predicted that the breadbasket of the United States, the Midwest, will become considerably drier. Changes in climate pattern would also cause extinction of many plant species because they would be unable to migrate at the speed of these man-made climate changes, which are far more rapid than natural climate cycles. Warmer climate is already causing the sea level to rise through the thermal expansion of the water and partial melting of the polar ice caps. Within the next forty years, sea level could rise by as much as 20 centimeters, causing huge problems in low-lying areas where many of the world's major cities lie. For example, it could render the Thames Barrier outside London ineffective, flood large areas of Bangladesh and Florida, and submerge many Pacific islands. Since warming is likely to be much greater at higher latitudes than the average increase for the whole globe, the danger of melting of the polar ice caps is very real.

Some action is already being taken to slow down the greenhouse effect, but much more is needed. Already a certain amount of warming is inevitable, and whatever corrective measures we take today, the warming trend will continue over the next forty years. The actions we take during this period will be crucial for the future and will determine the total extent of the greenhouse effect. This is the time in which the corrections must be made. Seventy-eight percent of the world's energy is derived from the burning of fossil fuels, and the United States is by far the largest consumer, followed by Russia and Eastern Europe. The developing countries presently use less, but their plans for development predict a considerable increase. They regard energy use restrictions as another way for the developed world to maintain its dominance over the less developed world, adding to North/South conflict. However, the entire globe is in this crisis together, and global action will be needed that encourages the developed world to reduce consumption and the developing world to develop in energy-efficient ways. It is unreasonable to request that the Amazon countries halt deforestation if developed countries refuse to reduce their emissions of greenhouse gases.

Actions that are needed to slow down the greenhouse effect are numerous; in addition to population control, the following steps are needed:

1. A complete ban on the use of chlorofluorocarbons (CFCs), because of their dual role as the most powerful greenhouse gases and destroyers of the ozone layer.

2. A rapid switch to greater use of energy sources that do not emit greenhouse gases, such as solar, wind, hydro, and tidal power, and perhaps even a new generation of safer nuclear reactors. The use of methane for power plants emits much less CO_2 than coal, and methane from landfill sites could be used more rather than allowing it to escape and increase the greenhouse effect.

3. The reduction of emissions of CO_2 through energy conservation and filtering. Thirteen percent of the gas going up the chimney of a coal-fired power station is CO_2. This could be removed by some type of filter, as sulfur dioxide is removed in many chimneys. The installation of such CO_2 filters could add 30 percent to our power bills. Energy is currently too cheap in most countries, and its cost must pay for the necessary environmental controls. Petroleum costs more in Japan; as a result, cars tend to be small and efficient, public transport is used more, and less CO_2 is sent into the atmosphere per person transported. In the future, energy must cost more.

4. The halting of deforestation and the encouragement of replanting of forests in both tropical and temperate regions (see section V on biodiversity).

5. In future, the idea of a carbon tax against producers of CO_2 emissions should be taken seriously and the funds raised used to promote CO_2-free energy—particularly for the developing world, which must not be too constrained by the system. The living stan-

dards of developing countries could be raised without large increases in energy consumption, but it will cost the developed countries in technical aid to implement such energy-efficient economies.

6. Energy conservation is essential through the use of smaller, fuel-efficient cars, well-insulated buildings, more public transport, and passive solar energy in buildings.

We would do well to heed the words of U.S. Secretary of State James Baker 3rd, who in his maiden speech to the International Panel on Climate Change (IPCC) said that "We face the prospect of being trapped on a boat that we have irreparably damaged— not by the cataclysm of war, but by the slow neglect of a vessel we believed to be impervious to our abuse. . . . The political ecology is now ripe for action."

If we are to survive as a species, the political aspects of the greenhouse effect must be resolved during the next decade.

In the lower atmosphere, ozone is known as a harmful industrial pollutant that is a component of smog, which causes difficulty with breathing and reduces the growth of trees. However, in the upper atmosphere, ozone is an essential component that protects life on earth by reducing the amount of ultraviolet radiation. In 1985, scientists from the British Antarctic Survey discovered a large hole in the ozone layer over Antarctica. Three years later they traced the cause to chlorofluorocarbons (CFCs), which are the gases used in refrigeration, air conditioners, aerosols, and various foam materials. Since this discovery, the news has become progressively worse. In October 1991, the ozone hole reached a record depth extending over 21 million square kilometers, an area four times the size of the United States, and allowing twice as much ultraviolet light to reach the earth's surface. It is already seriously affecting the countries of Argentina, Australia, Chile, and New Zealand. It is well known that ultraviolet radiation causes skin cancer, but now reports are beginning to come in from Chile of blind rabbits and salmon, and deformed tree buds. Also in 1991 the United Nations' Environmental Program and the World Meteorological Organization announced that for the first time the ozone shield is thinning over temperate latitudes in summer (Appenzeller, 1991), exposing people and crops to a larger dose of ultraviolet light just when they are most vulnerable.

Fortunately, governments have been rather responsive to the ozone crisis and the U.N. Environmental Program helped to formulate the Montreal Protocol of November 1987, which will halve CFC use by 1999. Yet the most recent evidence for 1991 indicates that this is not nearly enough and we must strive for a global ban of CFCs by 2000. CFC substitutes are more expensive, but in future we cannot continue to live at the expense of our environment.

IV. POLLUTION

There are numerous other pollutants besides the greenhouse gases, and we have been so careless with our waste products that they are encountered wherever we go on land, in the air we breathe, and in our rivers and oceans. I remember my surprise on a visit to Palmer Station in Antarctica on encountering scientists working on pollution. They were finding industrial pollutants from São Paulo, Brazil, in the air, and penguins with large quantities of mercury in their bodies in what appeared to be one of the most pristine, beautiful, and untouched habitats remaining on earth. By contrast I expected pollution when, out of curiosity, I visited Cubatão, in São Paulo State—allegedly the most polluted city in the world. I could not believe that humans could live in that atmosphere where it was painful to breathe the cocktail of noxious chemicals mixed with cement dust.

Contemporary society has been quick to react to some of the most toxic pollutants to health, such as DDT, dioxin, and PCBs, but much slower to control the emissions from cars and factories that belch out huge quantities of carbon dioxide, and the oxides of sulfur and nitrogen.

The U.S. government has been slow to acknowledge the reality of acid rain, but its existence and its harmful effects can no longer be disputed. "Forest death," or *Waldsterben*, is a familiar term in Germany, where thousands of conifers are dying as a result of acid rain caused mainly by sulfur dioxide and nitrogen oxides. The sterility of the Swedish lakes has been known for several decades. The effects of acid rain on the forests of the eastern United States and Canada are well documented, and clouds in the eastern United States sampled by the New York Botanical Garden Institute of Ecosystems Studies were more acid than lemon juice.

Air pollution is already a costly matter because of its damage to forests, crops, water quality, and human health. The expense needed to control emissions of sulfurous gases could be compensated for by the reduction in medical bills and the increased agricultural productivity. It has been estimated that acid rain will cost Europe 118 million cubic meters of wood, worth £16 billion annually (Brown, 1990). It would be better to invest £16 billion in pollution control than to reduce tree growth so drastically.

During the next few decades we need to reduce the emissions of sulfur dioxide and nitrogen oxides considerably through greater use of scrubbers on factory chimneys, worldwide use of catalytic converters on cars, greater use of cleaner fuels, and improved public transport.

Pollution is not confined to acid rain and the atmosphere. Wherever we go, we encounter its effects. Rivers and seas are polluted with sewage and industrial effluents, agricultural land and water tables are polluted by chemical fertilizers, pesticides, and radioactive fallout, oceans are polluted by oil slicks; even outer space is polluted by satellite debris to such an extent that it is a hazard to U.S. Space Shuttle flights.

Two recent events have drawn attention to pollution: the Gulf war, with the blowing up of hundreds of oil wells; and the opening up of Eastern Europe to reveal the consequences of the complete lack of pollution control by industry there. The latter has shown that the regulatory procedures of the Western industrialized countries have had a considerable effect. The next forty years must include a strengthening of the legislative effort to control pollution. Lead emissions in the United States have declined impressively as a result of a legislated transfer to unleaded petrol since 1970. This is just beginning in the United Kingdom, and in the United States motorists are paying more to have catalytic converters on their vehicles. We must learn the lesson that it is usually cheaper to prevent pollution than to clean it up.

As we in the developed world apply this lesson and clean up our act, we must also transfer our technology freely to the Third World, Eastern Europe, and anywhere else that needs assistance. Future costing must include disposal of waste, and the control of pollutants in the cost of products. As population inevitably continues to increase for the next forty years, the future of our biosphere will depend upon the reduction of poisonous emissions.

We have got away with a lot because of nature's extraordinary capacity to act as a sink for unwanted products. Today, we have reached the limits of this natural sink, and in future we must insist that the polluter pays for control of pollutants. We will see legislation that is unpopular because of its cost and its effect on lifestyle, but this is a small price to pay for survival.

V. BIODIVERSITY

Biodiversity has become a buzz word in recent years. It is a term that includes the diversity of species of living organisms on earth, the genes or genetic information which they contain, and the complex ecosystems in which they live. Biodiversity is the result of 4 billion years of evolution; the human race is a recent newcomer that is seriously altering this process. Estimates range from 5 to 50 million species on our planet, but only 1.5 million have been named and classified. All species interact with others in an intricate network of predator/prey relationships, the pollination and dispersal of plants by animals, the attack of and resistance to diseases, the competition for a niche, and in many other ways. Species are not autonomous; they interact with others in some way and together form the ecosystems of the world, such as tropical rain forests, tundra, even deserts. Each ecosystem is held together by a delicate web of interdependence. Remove certain keystone species and the whole system can break down.

We need to maintain biodiversity into the future for many reasons. The living organisms of the earth maintain our atmosphere and our climate. Without forests and the organisms in the oceans, the life-support system will break down. Yet at present we are still cutting down tropical rain forests at the rate of fifty-four acres a minute. A tropical forest area the size of Kew Gardens disappears every six minutes! In future an economic value must be placed on forests, both tropical and temperate, for their role in preserving world climate and acting as a store of carbon. This type of economic thinking is only just beginning.

Humankind depends upon biodiversity for food, medicines, shelter, clothing fibers, and industrial products such as rubber, starches, and oils; yet at present we are still prepared to allow the extinction of species in such places as Madagascar, Hawaii, and Atlantic coastal Brazil. Modern agriculture and forestry favors monocultures with little genetic diversity, which encourages susceptibility to disease and pests. The Irish Potato Famine of the 1840s was caused by cultivation of a single variety of potato. In contrast we find in the Andes, where the potato is native, that any Peruvian market will have twenty to fifty different varieties available. To maintain their crops, plant breeders must return to the wild species for disease-resistant species, for new properties such as sweeter tomatoes, or for drought resistance. As the world climate changes, the need for varieties of crops adapted to different climates, pests, and diseases will increase. We will have this flexibility only if genetic diversity is preserved.

At Kew we now control pests in our greenhouses by using ten species of insect predators, two fungi, and a bacterium. This avoids the use of toxic pesticides. Biological control of this sort is on the increase, but will only be possible if we can preserve the insect species, the fungi, and the bacteria that are needed. In California, the wild brambles harbor a species of wasp that controls a major pest of grapes. It has been estimated that this saves farmers $125 per hectare in pesticide costs (Office of Technology, 1987). So many wild species other than this wasp and bramble have an economic value, yet we still destroy them.

Each time a species goes extinct we narrow our options for the future in some way. Only 5 percent of the world's plant species have been properly tested for their medicinal properties. How many potential cures for cancer or AIDS are we losing as extinction progresses? Global extinction rates could already run as high as twenty to fifty species a day (Myers, 1990), representing an irreplaceable loss of potentially useful natural resources. Human-caused extinction now exceeds the natural rate of extinction by over ten thousand times.

We have already lost half of the tropical rain forests of the world, which harbor perhaps 70 percent of the species. We have therefore little time to save the species that remain. If there is to be a future for the human species, it is essential to preserve all three aspects of biodiversity: large areas of natural habitat that preserve the species and maintain climatic stability of our planet; as many species as possible because of their roles within ecosystems and because of their potential uses; and as much of their genetic diversity as possible because the future use of many of our crops depends upon the genes of their wild relatives.

The biodiversity issue is absolutely international. The corn crop of the United States depends upon wild species of maize in Mexico. The coffee crop of Brazil depends upon the wild species of *Coffea* in Ethiopia and Madagascar. The world climate depends as much on the forests of the boreal zone in Canada and Siberia as upon the rain forests of Brazil or Zaire. Our future needs more concerted international efforts, without which we are narrowing the options for our descendants and will become known as the generation who diminished biodiversity. It is almost too late, but by turning to sustainable use there is time to reverse the trend and slow down extinction. However, there is no room for complacency. The actions of the next forty years regarding biodiversity will determine whether or not human life will survive on earth. If we continue at the present extinction rate of between 4,000 and 6,000 species a year, by 2030 there will be between 160,000 and 250,000 less species to hold our biosphere together or for us to use.

VI. TOWARD SUSTAINABILITY

Sustainable development is another current catchword within the environmental movement and was the focus of *Our Common Future,* the report of the World Commission on Environment and Development (1987). It is the failure of humankind to utilize natural resources in a sustainable manner which has led to the gravity of our current ecological crisis. A seminal document in changing attitudes was the 1980 *World Conservation Strategy* of the World Conservation Union, the United Nations Endowment Program, and the World Wildlife Fund. For the first time on an international scale, this publication brought together development and conservation, and showed that the two could be interdependent rather than exclusive. The strategy document led to the formation in 1983 of the World Commission on Environment and Development by the United Nations, whose report, usually named after Chairman Gro Harlem Brundtland, had the specific goal of proposing long-term environmental strategies for achieving sustainable development by the year 2000 and beyond. The commission's definition of the subject was "development that meets the needs of the present without compromising the ability of future generations to meet their own needs." The Brundtland

Report has been a catalyst for many organizations and governments to begin thinking in sustainable terms. *World Conservation
Strategy* has also been updated in 1991 by a new document issued
by IUCN, UNEP, and WWF, entitled *Caring for the Earth,* which
places an even greater emphasis on sustainable living. In fact, the
number of reports alone indicates that sustainability is firmly on
the agenda for the future.

The quality of life on earth will depend upon how much these
ideas are implemented, rather than discussed in the halls of the
United Nations, the parliaments of the world, and at environment
conferences such as the United Nations Conference on Environment and Development, and so I will concentrate next on some
points of the pathway to sustainable living rather than on analysis
of reports. The issues of population control and pollution already
addressed are basic to sustainable living; but many other aspects
are involved.

Energy

The availability of energy is an essential of human life, and development is impossible without energy. Seventy-eight percent of
current energy comes from the burning of fossil fuels, coal, petroleum, natural gas, and peat, which by definition are non-
renewable resources; 80.6 percent is consumed by the developed
world, 7.3 percent by China, and only 12.1 percent by the less
developed world. The energy consumption of a resident of the
United States is 297 times greater than one of Rwanda, 37 times
greater than that of an Indian (Mathews and Tunstall, 1991).

There is therefore a great inequity of distribution of energy
around the world. If per capita use remained the same as today,
by 2030 we would need an increase of 50 percent over 1990
consumption just to allow for population growth. The less developed world, which presently uses so little energy, contains 75
percent of the population and obviously needs more energy in
order to develop a reasonable standard of living. It is therefore
likely that energy consumption will increase far beyond the level
per capita 50 percent rate. The more we use from the present
sources, the more we contribute to the greenhouse effect, acid
rain, and pollution. The future pathway is clear. The developed
world must become much more energy-efficient in order to allow

for development elsewhere, and everywhere we must seek to use more renewable, non-polluting sources of energy. Within the next decade we need long-term energy strategies for all countries. This will include carbon taxes so that polluters pay for their cost to the global environment.

In forty years' time the supply of oil will have leveled off, but supplies of natural gas, which is cleaner, will last at least two hundred years. Since coal reserves are the greatest and are a 3,000-year supply, the way in which they are used without polluting the atmosphere is crucial. Energy conservation will take many forms, but will only really be effective if energy is fully costed. Japan produces twice as much GNP per unit of energy as the United States. That island nation has to be much more energy-conscious because energy costs a lot more. In forty years' time, vehicles will be much more energy-efficient and not all will run on petroleum. Electric, gas, and alcohol-fueled cars are already being used to a small extent, and over 50 percent of Brazil's vehicles are fueled by alcohol. All of these sources of power and others such as hydrogen will increase over the next few decades, and all are less polluting than the conventional petrol engine. In addition, public transport needs much attention. In many large cities of the world, such as New York and London, public transport is deteriorating rather than improving at a time when we should be encouraging people to ride together to work rather than drive alone in a car.

In cooler climates, building codes need to be strengthened to enforce better insulation and the use of passive solar energy, and to reduce the need for air conditioning in warmer climates. The type of building can make a measurable difference to the amount of energy needed for heating, cooling, and lighting. The earth shelter building at the Cary Arboretum of the New York Botanical Garden was so well insulated that the solar collectors were an unnecessary boost to the heating and had to be removed to avoid extra cooling costs. The same energy efficiency is being shown by the earth shelter Sir Joseph Banks Building at the Royal Botanic Gardens, Kew. However, so far comparatively few earth shelter buildings exist. The placement of windows in a building makes a vast difference to the energy needs for lighting. Energy considerations will be much more part of standard building practice by 2030. The developed world could halve its energy consumption without seriously reducing the standard of living.

The use of clean and sustainable sources of energy is only just beginning, and it receives very little encouragement from the governments of the developed world. There are numerous possible sources of renewable energy, including hydropower, solar energy, and solar photovoltaic cells (which are becoming increasingly more efficient), tidal, wind, and geothermal energy, the use of biomass and municipal waste to produce methane and alcohol. Most of these renewable sources of energy are more suitable for small-scale use in rural and suburban areas, and they have a distinct advantage in developing countries because they are far less susceptible to price fluctuations and to the vagaries of foreign exchange rates.

The Chernobyl disaster has heightened awareness of the dangers of nuclear power. The disposal of nuclear wastes remains a major problem, but further research into both safe nuclear power and waste disposal should continue. Despite the critics, it is probable that nuclear energy will be in much greater use by 2030. It has the as-yet-unrealized potential of being the environmentally cleanest source of energy.

Some signs of the future of energy are indicated by the fact that Brazil runs many of its motor vehicles on alcohol; rural areas in India are increasingly using biogas derived from plant material and animal wastes; California, Denmark, and Britain have all installed experimental wind farms; and sunlight powers 150,000 homes in California. These are all sustainable, non-polluting sources of power preparing the pathway for the future, which must be based on energy efficiency, correct costing, low pollution, and sustainability.

Soil and agriculture

The ability to feed the world population depends upon the quality of the soil. During the past four decades the world's agricultural production of food has outpaced population growth, but it is gradually leveling off and the growth in production has been at the expense of topsoil. Topsoil is the precious few inches of soil near the surface that contains much organic matter, billions of living organisms—and is well aerated. It forms a fertile carpet over the less productive subsoil. When erosion exceeds the natural rate of soil formation, one is living off one's capital. In the

United States, 2 billion tons a year of soil are lost by water erosion, but only 1 billion is formed. Natural annual replacement is about 5–12.5 tons per hectare, but topsoil loss in Tennessee was estimated to be 35 tons per hectare and in Iowa 25 tons. Seriously affected areas of India lose 75 tons per hectare per year, and in Zimbabwe the figure is 50 tons.

Topsoil is being lost faster than replacement agriculture in the United States because of the use of high amounts of synthetic fertilizer, mainly made from petroleum, and the use of large quantities of pesticides, as well as capital-intensive machinery. In less developed countries where this is not feasible, soil erosion is greater, and new land must be continually found by incursions into natural ecosystems. Food production kept up with population growth in the last decade because of increased productivity in Asia, Europe, and the USSR. Africa's per capita food production has dropped by 8 percent over the past decade and South America's per capita food production remained stagnant (World Resources Institute, 1990). The warning bells about soil and food production are sounding. Production is leveling off. To increase production significantly using current agricultural methods would lead to a massive destruction of natural ecosystems, species extinction, and intolerable soil loss. This is yet another indication that population control is essential.

A study by the Missouri Agricultural Experiment Station showed that when a corn–wheat–clover rotation is used, topsoil loss is about 6.75 tons per hectare, which is well within the limits of natural replacement. When corn is grown continuously, the loss is 49.25 tons (National Agricultural Lands Study, 1980). Because there is the need for corn to feed the world, farmers do not use the simple remedy of rotation, and indeed, to do so in the short term would increase famine. We already have this dilemma in 1992, so what of the future? The concept of regenerative agriculture developed by the late Robert Rodale at his Rodale Institute Research Center, Maxatawny, Pennsylvania, is needed, whereby soil is allowed to regenerate as fast as it is used by the use of organic techniques rather than chemicals. Farms that have converted to this system have been shown to be just as productive, but they can't produce grain on the same land continuously. The future will see a move away from grain toward a greater diversity of crops. Today, we are beginning to see crops that are not soil-dependent grown by hydroponics and in vitro in large flasks. The use of such techniques that employ carefully controlled amounts of both water and nutrients is likely to increase greatly over the next decades. They could be employed on a sufficiently wide scale to allow the soil to be used as a sustainable resource rather than as something that is lost to erosion.

Fresh water

Earth is the only planet with large volumes of free water. This is an essential to sustain life and is the reason for the existence of life on our planet. Water is another easily renewable resource because of the way in which it is cycled through plants and through the process of evaporation and precipitation. However, our attitude to water needs a critical review, since use has increased thirty-five-fold over the last three hundred years and is projected to increase 30–35 percent more by the year 2000. People living in arid regions are well aware of the value of water, but people in other parts of the world are as profligate with water as they are with energy. A population of 10 billion in 2040 could not sustain the current pattern of water use, so we would do well to begin adjusting now.

The principal problem with our fresh water is pollution—especially from agricultural and industrial pollutants. Even as I write this, we are advised not to drink the water in Richmond today because of bacterial contamination. Events of this sort are on the increase. We are also mining rather than using sustainable supplies of water in many parts of the world where irrigation is used. The Ogallala aquifer in the northwestern United States is becoming depleted and Saudi Arabia's remarkable success with agriculture can only depend on underground water for another twenty years. Since 70 percent of the fresh water we use is for agriculture, water-efficient systems of crop production are essential for water conservation as well as soil protection. This is a strong argument for greater use of hydroponic and in vitro agriculture for the future.

River quality and flood control are closely linked to the preservation of natural vegetation. In Amazonia, 25 percent of the rainfall evaporates directly from the tree leaves into the atmosphere, and another 50 percent is absorbed by the trees and pumped back into the atmosphere through the process of transpiration, leaving only 25 percent to run off into the rivers. When the forest is cut down, it is no longer there to hold all of this water, and flooding and a huge amount of erosion takes place. Recent floods in Bangladesh and the Philippines have been linked to the loss of forest.

Each of the factors treated here is in some way linked to the others. The future solutions for the environment have to be holistic and to consider water, air, vegetation, soils, and all other factors together. Sustainable use of fresh water involves not only the quantity we use but the preservation of watersheds upon which the rivers depend. Unlike oil, water is not running out. There is enough to go round for more than forty years ahead, but only if we do not ruin the quality by pollution and do not break down the natural processes that maintain the water cycle.

The use of forests and other natural ecosystems

We have already considered the importance of biodiversity that makes up the natural ecosystems of the world. In many parts of the world the natural vegetation is still disappearing because we are not using it in a sustainable way. Most of the deforestation of the Amazon rain forest has been for short-term profit, with no consideration of sustainable use. Tax incentives have been given to farmers to create cattle pasture that either never produces cattle or that lasts for only a few years. Timber and rubber plantations have been planted that quickly failed, and some of the most useful resources, such as mahogany or Brazilian rosewood, have been mined out of the forest rather than managed. The most conservative estimate for future deforestation in Amazonia of a 3.5 percent annual increase in deforested areas would mean that 22 percent of the forest was felled by 2030, releasing 10.5 billion tons of CO_2 into the atmosphere (Reis, 1991). But at the present rate of a 4.6 percent increase in deforestation, 32.9 percent of the region would be destroyed, contributing 18.2 billion tons of CO_2 to the greenhouse effect.

The 1990s will decide the future of Amazonia—and of many other natural ecosystems. There are now many people, including high government officials of the Amazon countries, who are looking for alternatives to deforestation. On the other hand, there are also many politicians exploiting the desires of the wealthy landowners to oppose anything that slows down deforestation.

Sustainable use of the forest will involve exploitation without deforestation. In a small way, this has been carried out for many years by the extraction of forest products such as rubber latex, Brazil nuts, and other commercial products that can be collected without cutting down the forest. Brazil has recently set up a number of extraction reserves to allow this process to continue. Extraction of this sort is a small part of the answer to sustainability and it will depend upon a stable market for a large variety of forest products. However, it is possible to extract a limited amount of timber without destroying the forest. It is a tragedy that according to estimates of the International Timber Trade Organization, less than one-half percent of current tropical timber production is extracted in a sustainable way.

A good example of overexploitation is that of the timber Virola, which is extracted in great quantities in the lower Amazon. This is a fast-growing and abundant tree of the flooded forests of the Amazon estuary. Many sawmills are exploiting Virola, and they send out groups of men to fell the trees and float the logs to the mills. The correct laws already exist, prohibiting the use of trees under 50 centimeters in diameter, but they are ignored and even the small trees are felled. As a result, Virola is becoming rarer and rarer, and the fellers are having to go further and further away from the mills. Since Virola is fast-growing and easy to extract because it grows beside the rivers, it is an ideal candidate for sustainable management. Yet today's lumber merchants would rather extract every tree to make a quick profit for themselves and forget tomorrow and their grandchildren. This trend has dominated tropical timber extraction for many years, but I believe that there is now some hope for the future, since the tropical timber industry itself is concerned, and governments such as those of Brazil and Indonesia are beginning to take action to control the exploitation of the remainder of their forests.

The rain forest is but one example of the need to switch from destruction to sustainable use of natural ecosystems. Equally alarming examples could be given for the wetlands of the world being eaten up for waterfront development, for the vegetation of arid regions that are particularly easily destroyed, or even for the forests of the Pacific Northwest of the United States, where the same trend of overuse is taking place.

Recycling

The process of recycling resources is an obvious part of sustainable living. Recycling is in its infancy at present, but fortunately it is on the increase and already quite advanced in a few cities. Whether it is minerals such as aluminum—currently one of the most economical materials to recycle because that process uses far less energy than smelting the ore—or paper pulp derived from trees, recycling helps to maintain environmental quality. By 2030 we will not be able to afford not to recycle and it will no longer be regarded as an inconvenience to separate our garbage into several different categories. Manufacturers will also make this process easier by producing more readily recyclable containers. At present, plastic is the greatest problem because of the numerous types which do not mix and are not identified on containers.

A few pilot plants use garbage to generate energy. In future this will increase, both to fulfill energy needs and to reduce the ever-mounting piles of waste that often contribute to the greenhouse effect by the amount of methane they produce. Hopefully, garbage treatment will be much more scientific and our waste much more useful within the next forty years.

The global commons

Certain areas of our globe and its surroundings fall outside the traditional boundaries of sovereignty and have been termed "the global commons." These shared ecosystems are the oceans, space, and Antarctica. Nowhere calls more for a concerted international effort than the global commons. Without international agreement, life-dependent quality cannot be maintained.

The Antarctic Treaty of 1959, signed by seven states that claimed territory there, has been an example of success. The treaty banned military and nuclear activity in the area, suspended territorial claims, and established rules for scientific research. There is hope for the integrity of Antarctica forty years hence because in October 1991 an agreement signed by twenty-four nations banned mineral and oil exploration for at least fifty years.

This agreement also included new additional regulations for wild-life protection, waste disposal, marine pollution, and continued monitoring. This great wilderness which covers almost a tenth of the world's land surface has been protected for the future. The challenge for the next decades is to avoid pollution, oil spills, and a breakdown of the oceanic and atmospheric conditions that maintain Antarctica.

The problems of the oceans are much greater than those of Antarctica because the oceans are a vital part of the life-support system of our planet. They affect climate, act as a major sink for gases such as carbon dioxide, and provide the habitat for many species of organisms. Coral reefs are second to rain forests in their level of species diversity. Ocean fish are an essential part of a complex food chain and of human diet, and minute phytoplankton play a vital role in the production of oxygen.

In spite of the human value of the oceans for their ecological and commercial role, we are still grossly mismanaging them. They are a dump in which to place our toxic wastes and effluents. A walk along any coastline will show how oceans are still regarded as a huge garbage pit. In 1991, algal blooms in the Mediterranean virtually destroyed the Italian tourist season. Oceans have already been subjected to many major oil spills, and the risk increases as offshore oil wells proliferate. Most major fishing areas of the world such as the North Sea and the Northwest Pacific are suffering from overfishing. As supplies of one fish diminish, the fishing industry turns to other species that were formerly ignored, and these "trash fish" are often the species upon which the more useful ones feed. The annual marine catch of fish has increased by 30 percent over the last decade, mainly because of increased activity by Japan and the Soviet Union, which together now account for one fourth of the world's catch.

This increase cannot continue because it is no longer sustainable. We have now reached the limits of a sustainable catch from the sea at the 80 million tons of fish that are taken today. This leaves no room for growth in the future, indicating that our population has reached the carrying capacity of the oceans and should not be allowed to increase. Any increase in fish production will come from fish farming rather than from the natural stock of the oceans, so we can expect a rapid increase in fish and shrimp farming. Better success has already been reached in the control of whaling. After many years of overexploitation, the International Whaling Commission has brought about a moratorium that has almost banned whaling. A good prospect in forty years' time is the probable increase in numbers of these magnificent marine animals.

The oceans have been the subject of various conventions to control their use, the most comprehensive of which is the convention resulting from the United States Conference on the Law of the Sea, which was signed by 159 nations in 1987. The future must see stricter conventions and stricter control both of the way in which we use the sea as a dump and of the rate at which we exploit it for food.

The third global common—space—has not been subject to sovereignty claims because of the 1967 Outer Space Treaty that banned such action. Since the first rocket was launched beyond our atmosphere, space has become a much-used area for communications, remote sensing, and the monitoring of climate, natural phenomenon, and man-made destruction of natural ecosystems. It has also been much used for the military purpose of spying. The most serious problem, which is likely to increase as more nations send rockets into space, is pollution.

Space is now cluttered with spent fuel tanks, rockets, satellites that have ceased to function, and many fragments from explosions. A recent flight of the U.S. Space Shuttle had to change course to avoid space junk. The future calls for reusable equipment in space so that the entire vehicle returns to earth. If we continue to litter, space flight will no longer be safe. There is an immediate need for the regulation of the earth orbit part of space; it is likely that by the year 2030 space will be regulated in a controlled way, much as our airplanes are subject to airport control towers within the atmosphere.

VII. CONCLUSION

Control of population growth and sustainable development must be the main goals of the next two decades. What the world is like in forty years' time will depend on our ability to agree internationally to the major changes in attitudes which are required to achieve these objectives. They involve looking ahead to the long term rather than being governed by short-term profits or the time period between political elections. The environment cannot be thought of or planned for in the short term. Of all the subjects in this book, the environment is the most in need of planning, and of corrective measures that are required at present.

In spite of the environmental difficulties we are already facing, I am much more optimistic about the future than I was a few years ago. The environmental movement of the last few decades has been successful in heightening awareness to such an extent that it is now part of the political agenda of all major parties in the United States, Europe, and many other countries of the world. Industry knows that it cannot get away with the environmental neglect of the past; it is becoming much more approachable and is doing much more for the environment. But it is essential for scientists with accurate information to keep up the pressure for change. The end of the Cold War has shown us the extent of pollution behind the former Iron Curtain, yet it has also enabled us to work in collaboration to improve environmental conditions. Our ability to use this opportunity to take advantage of this so-called new world order and work together will determine the quality of life in forty years' time. The new world order should enhance the ability to negotiate international conventions to improve our environment. The Rio de Janeiro United Nations Conference of 1992 is considering conventions on global climate change and also on biodiversity. This is a start. Forty years hence, we will necessarily be governed by a whole host of international conventions and national laws that would be considered over-restrictive today. However, the need to control the major issues considered here and to accurately cost the value of the environment or the price of pollution will have become standard practice by 2030.

Above all, we must realize that our planet is of a finite size, with a finite carrying capacity, and a finite ability to act as a sink for pollutants and to make adjustments to the atmosphere as abnormal amounts of CO_2 and other gases are pumped into it. This means that there is truly a limit to the capacity for growth. The next few decades will be the period in which we adjust our thinking from growth and short-term profit to stability and sustainability. The survival of our race will be determined within the next forty years.

*   *   *

(*I thank Anne E. Prance and Dr Charles Stirton for reading an earlier draft of this essay.*)

REFERENCES

T. P. ANDERSON. 1981. *The War of the Dispossessed* (Honduras and El Salvador, 1969; Lincoln, NE: University of Nebraska Press).

T. APPENZELLER. 1991. "Ozone Loss Hits Us Where We Live." *Science,* 254: 645.

W. BROWN. 1990. "Europe's Forests Fall to Acid Rain." *New Scientist,* 11 (August 1990), 17.

N. A. CHAGNON. 1968. *Yanomamö. The Fierce People* (New York: Holt, Rinehart & Winston).

J. DAVIDSON, and H. G. ANDREWARTHA. 1948. "Annual Trends in a Natural Population of *Thrips imaginis* (Thysanoptera)." *Jour. Animal Ecol.,* 17: 193–99, 200–22.

J. T. HOUGHTON, G. J. JENKINS, and J. J. EPHRAUMS. 1990. *Climate Change, the IPCC Scientific Assessment* (Cambridge, Engl.: Cambridge University Press).

IUCN, UNEP, WWF. 1980. *World Conservation Strategy* (International Union for Conservation of Nature and Natural Resources, Gland, Switzerland).

———1991. *Caring for the Earth: A Strategy for Sustainable Living* (Gland, Switzerland).

C. D. KEELING, R. B. BACASTOW, A. E. BAINBRIDGE, C. A. EKDAHL JR., P. R. Guenther, L. S. Waterman, and J. F. S. CHIN. 1976. "Atmospheric Carbon Dioxide Variations at Mauna Loa Observatory, Hawaii." *Tellas,* 28: 528–51.

C. D. KEELING. 1986. "Atmospheric CO_2 Concentrations—Mauna Loa Observatory, Hawaii, 1958–86." *CDIAC NDP-001/RI* (Rev. 1986). Carbon Dioxide Information Analysis Center, Oak Ridge National Laboratory, Oak Ridge, Tennessee *CDIAC* (Spring 1990).

D. A. MACLULICH. 1937. "Fluctuation in Numbers of the Varying Hare (*Lepus americanus*)." *University of Toronto Studies,* Biology Series no. 43.

J. T. MATHEWS, and D. B. TUNSTALL. 1991. "Moving Toward Eco-Development: Generating Environmental Information for Decision Makers." *World Resources Institute: Issues and Ideas* (August 1991).

N. MYERS, 1990. *Deforestation Rates in Tropical Forests and Their Climatic Implications* (London: Friends of the Earth).

NATIONAL AGRICULTURAL LANDS STUDY. 1980. *Soil Degradation: Effects on Agricultural Productivity.* Interim Report no. 4 (Washington, D.C.: USDA).

OFFICE OF TECHNOLOGY ASSESSMENT, U.S. CONGRESS. 1987. *Technologies to Maintain Biological Diversity* (Washington, D.C.: U.S. Government Printing Office).

D. I. RASMUSSEN. 1941. "Biotic Communities of Kaibab Plateau, Arizona." *Ecological Monographs,* 11: 230–75.

E. REIS. 1991. Cited in *The Economist,* December 7, 1991, p. 8.

WORLD COMMISSION ON ENVIRONMENT AND DEVELOPMENT. 1987. *Our Common Future* (Oxford: Oxford University Press).

WORLD RESOURCES INSTITUTE. 1990. *World Resources 1990–91* (Oxford & New York: Oxford University Press).

3

THE PHYSICAL SCIENCES

by Owen Gingerich

Dr. Owen Gingerich is Professor of Astronomy and History of Science at Harvard University and a senior astronomer at the Smithsonian Astrophysical Observatory. He has written and lectured extensively on the history of science.

A FEW MONTHS AGO in a large New England barn that serves as a second-hand book shop, I stumbled onto a long shelf of old books on futurology. For someone who had just agreed to write on the coming decades of physical science, it was both a humbling and disconcerting experience to see how badly our predecessors had missed the mark.

A 1962 book that looked a mere fifteen years ahead predicted disposable paper clothing, automatic plastic dishmakers for your kitchen, electronic highways with driverless cars, and inoculations to prevent tooth decay.[1] Before and after pictures of Boston's elevated expressways lauded the replacing of antiquated, narrow streets with modern highways to handle tomorrow's traffic. Would its authors, the editors of *Kiplinger's Newsletter,* have guessed that the same expressway is now considered poorly designed and due for replacement?

Here's another, a 1968 volume focused on the year 2018 whose jacket proclaims: "More amazing than science fiction."[2] The upbeat chapter subheadings indicate that the world population will triple, but that people won't go hungry, and that ample energy resources will supply the rising demand; plenty of nuclear power was the key. Superjets will further close the gap between nations (not very wide of the mark!), face-to-face mass communication will become worldwide, and humankind will control rain, fog, and possibly even the climate.

Back in 1923, the distinguished biochemist J. B. S. Haldane told us more about himself than about today's science when he wrote *Daedalus or Science and the Future*. He in turn looked back to H. G. Wells, who in 1902 in a book called *Anticipations* ventured the opinion that by 1950 there would be heavier-than-air flying machines capable of practical use in war. Haldane promised nothing rasher than that, and in his essay there are a few gems worth noting. He envisioned that four hundred years hence England would have solved its energy problem by covering the countryside with rows of metallic windmills. He proposed that the surplus energy could be stored in the form of liquid hydrogen gas obtained by the electrolytic decomposition of water. This is not a silly idea, just one whose time has not yet come.

Haldane must have been one of the first to mention what has now become a science fiction commonplace: "looking at a great new star in the Milky Way. . . . Perhaps it was the last judgement of some inhabited world, perhaps a too successful experiment in induced radio-activity on the part of some of the dwellers there."[3] Could Haldane have extrapolated the idea from Arthur Eddington, who just three years earlier had written that subatomic energy gave us the promise "of controlling this latent energy for the good of mankind, or for its suicide"?[4]

In 1936 C. C. Furnas, a professor of chemical engineering at Yale and frequent science popularizer, dared to write a 400-page book on *The Next Hundred Years, The Unfinished Business of Science*. Inspired by the recent Chicago Exposition, the "Century of Progress," he wrote about automobiles running sixty miles to the gallon and built to last, coal smoke gone from cities, the origin of life discovered, and a vast reservoir of minerals made available from the ocean. But he also warned of war, of a public tearing the gifts of science to tatters in a quarrel over the loot. His generalizations were astutely made, but on the specifics of the physical sciences, his crystal ball was rather foggy. "I am waiting for my television," wrote the thirty-six-year-old Furnas, "but I cannot live forever."[5] He mentioned smashing atoms, and quoted Francis Aston to the effect that half a pound of matter would contain enough energy to drive a 30,000-ton vessel from New York to Southampton and back at 25 knots. But, more impressed by Harold Urey's recent isolation of deuterium, Furnas imagined a multitude of new dyes, pharmaceuticals, and vitamins made with deuterium instead of the lighter hydrogen. "What would be the effect of a deutero-aspirin tablet?" he asked.[6]

Closer to our own time, Nobel Laureate Sir George Thomson considered *The Foreseeable Future* in a short book of that title. Guided by sound, known physical principles, he wrote thoughtfully about coming energy problems in the face of an expanding world population. He forecast improvements in strengths of materials and in speed of transport, and envisioned the cellular telephone. But, "the possibilities of travel in space seem at present to appeal to schoolboys more than to scientists. . . . The conception of a satellite station should not be dismissed as wholly fantastic, though it bristles with technical difficulties. What I personally regard as absurd is the emphasis [Werner] von Braun lays on the satellite station as an instrument of war, to be used for observation and presumably to direct guided missiles."[7] Sir George lived long enough to witness the moon landings and the first spy-in-the-sky satellites, though not the absurd implementation of Star Wars and space stations.

What seems notably lacking from all these visions of the future are specific predictions of the state of the physical sciences themselves, but of course every visionary has the shadow of the two biggest nineteenth-century gaffes falling across his path. In 1835 the great French positivist philosopher, August Comte, wrote that man could never encompass in his conceptions the physical and chemical nature of stars. They "must ever be illimitable to our successors of the remotest generations," he declared.[8] Within a quarter century, the German physicist Gustav Kirchhoff, together with his colleague, the chemist Robert Bunsen, had discovered the science of spectral analysis, and had learned how to use the detailed spectra of starlight to deduce their atomic compositions. By the first decades of this century, astrophysicists could establish not only chemical abundances in the remote stars but also the physical conditions of their atmospheres.

The second, oft-quoted blunder of prognostication is the statement that the future of physics lay in the next decimal place of physical constants. At the dedication of the University of Chicago's Ryerson Physical Laboratory in 1894, Albert A. Michelson remarked:

> While it is never safe to affirm that the future of Physical Science has no marvels in store even more astonishing than those of the past, it seems probable that most of the grand underlying principles have been firmly established and that further advances are to be sought chiefly in rigorous application of these principles to all the phenomena which come under our notice.
>
> It is here that science of measurement shows its importance— where quantitative results are more to be desired than qualitative work. An eminent physicist has remarked that the future truths of Physical Science are to be looked for in the sixth place of decimals.[9]

According to Michelson's younger colleague, Robert A. Millikan, the "eminent physicist" was probably Lord Kelvin. In a wide-ranging investigation of the idea of completeness in nineteenth-century science, Lawrence Badash was unable to pinpoint such a quotation from Lord Kelvin, but he did convince us that the general notion was widespread well into the 1890s. Within the decade, however, the qualitative discoveries of X-rays and of radioactivity were to begin to transform the face of physics, and relativity and quantum mechanics came not long after.

Another magnificent example of the cloudy crystal ball, just a few years later, was a series of popular articles by the distinguished celestial mechanician Simon Newcomb, on the improbability of heavier-than-air flight. In 1903, he carefully analyzed the prospects for the flying machine. The whole problem, he wrote, was getting a heavy metal contraption with an engine up to the requisite speed. "And, granting complete success, imagine the proud possessor of the aeroplane darting through the air at a speed of several hundred feet per second! How is he ever going to stop? Once he stops he falls a dead mass. How shall he reach the ground without destroying his delicate machinery? I do not think the most imaginative inventor has yet even put upon paper a demonstratively successful way of meeting this difficulty."

Newcomb concludes his article by saying that "if any hope for the flying machine can be entertained, it must be based more on general faith in what mankind is going to do than upon either reasoning or experience. . . . We have every reason to believe that mere ingenious contrivances with our present means and forms of force will be as vain in the future as they have been in the past."[10]

Need I remind you that the dramatic flight at Kitty Hawk took place that very year?

Forty years ago, in 1950, the newly revitalized *Scientific American* devoted an issue to a review of the past half century of science and a preview of the fifty years to come. Distinguished practitioners held forth on astronomy, chemistry, geology, and physics, as well as the life sciences. What all of them missed was the enormous development of electronics and computing power, and the transformation that it would effect in all the sciences in the next four decades. Between 1950 and 1990, sheer raw available computing power multiplied by eleven orders of magnitude.

In 1950, as had been the case for some centuries, astronomers were the principal consumers of numbers. Theirs was the first exact science, and the demands of celestial mechanics—planetary ephemerides, comet orbits, star catalogues—had moved from logarithms, the arithmometer, and the direct-multiplying Millionaire electric calculator to punched cards, vacuum tubes, and mercury resonance storage lines.

Classical astronomers soon had to share their new computing power with astrophysicists, who began to use massive number-crunching to model the internal structure of stars and to explore their evolution. Princeton's Martin Schwarzschild has described his frustration with these early calculations when he came to a point where the interior of a red giant star changed more rapidly than the IBM 650 computer could actually compute it. I can recall my own computations on the outer layers of stars—made in 1959 with an IBM 704, where the core storage was so restricted in capacity that the machine could hold only a part of the program at any one time. In those days a FORTRAN program whose logic led to the "END" statement was automatically coded to activate the card reader at that point. Hence it was possible to have the next segment of the program in the card reader ready to carry on the computation, and the computation could be made to work iteratively by standing next to the card reader and manually recycling the cards from the output back into the input stack.

I can remember telling my classes just three decades ago that computing speed had an essential limitation: the speed of light. Computers were then running with cycle times measured in microseconds, and a so-called floating-point multiple took roughly ten cycles or twenty microseconds. "It will be hard to compute more than a thousand times faster than this," I asserted, "because in two nanoseconds an electric signal travels only two feet, which isn't enough to get from the core storage to the central processor of a computer." In those days, a monster assembly of vacuum tubes in a large air-conditioned room had less computational capacity than today's advanced pocket calculators. Needless to say, the whole notion of an integrated circuit on a chip was outside my vision. Last year's personal computer already far outstripped the giant IBM 704 in both speed and storage, and today state-of-the-art computers process floating-point numbers about one hundred thousand times faster than the 704. Nevertheless, the speed of light is a fundamental limit, and for still higher speeds computer architecture has to be increasingly sophisticated. Massive parallel computing represents the wave of the future, according to many of today's computer pundits.

Back in the 1950s and 1960s, astronomers and astrophysicists lost their monopoly as the major number-crunchers. Strong competition developed for rapid, massive calculating. Meteorologists, physicists, and rocketeers all demanded the new computing power, for practical weather prediction, for studies of neutron diffusion for the theory of nuclear weapons, and for ballistic trajectories. In retrospect, the development of space science would have been unimaginable without it. Clearly, electronic control and high-speed computing not only made possible the astonishingly precise trajectories of modern spacecraft, but their complex data-gathering capacities as well. The magnificent "postcards from space"—views of the far side of the moon, of Jupiter's Io and Saturn's braided rings, or of the earth's tropical storms and the cloudless western slopes of the Andes, so beckoning to astronomers—have all been collected and transmitted back to us through the development and miniaturization of electronic logical circuitry. None of this was envisioned by *Scientific American*'s 1950 forecasters.

Nor have the chemists been unaffected by this electronic wizardry: on their computer screens are rotatable, multicolor images of complex molecules whose detailed shapes play essential roles in their chemical efficacy. Let me give a typical example of the role of molecular shape. For many years Western medical practice scorned the notion of acupuncture as a means of relieving pain. Eventually, however, Western doctors learned that the procedure triggered the production of encephalons in the human brain. And a detailed examination of these organic molecules revealed that the shape of the active part of the molecule mirrored the shape of the morphine molecule. Morphine acts as a painkiller because its pattern matches the natural painkillers that the human body can produce under special circumstances. Today, the chemists' ability to explore the role of molecular shape is enormously enhanced by the image-processing capabilities of modern computers.

Similarly, the handling of immense quantities of data electronically is essential to modern particle physics. To explore the realm of massive nuclear particles requires high energies, as Einstein's famous $E = mc^2$ equation indicates. A high-speed head-on collision of a proton and an anti-proton, for example, has a reasonable chance of yielding one of the elusive heavy nucleons such as a W or Z particle. The problem is that for every head-on collision, there are a thousand glancing collisions that are unlikely to yield the sought-for fragments, and a few thousand of these collisions are taking place every second. It takes an almost incomprehensible amount of computing power to sort out the useful data from the flood of irrelevant information.

These brief, essentially anecdotal, notes on the recent role of computing provide the springboard into any projection about the next four decades of physical science. Surely progress in physical science will continue to be closely linked with the growth of computing capability. While it is foolhardy to predict specific new discoveries or breakthroughs in theoretical structures, we can see that the vast expansion of the physical sciences in the last few decades has been tightly linked to technological developments, and of these, computing power has been one of the strongest driving forces. Probably the safest prediction I can make regarding the future of physical science is that enhanced computing power will be the key to many of the advances in astronomy, chemistry, and physics, as well as in geology, meteorology, and oceanography.

*   *   *

More specifically, what are the leading unsolved problems that we can hope to illuminate in the coming decades? Just to cast the question in this form gives us pause for a further digression. One of the questions might well be: Is there intelligent life on other worlds? Suppose that we have answered that affirmatively and are in touch with another civilization. Now we on earth have had meaningful possibilities of interstellar radio communication for fifty years at the most, and the chances of encountering another civilization in exactly the same infant state of cosmic communication would be exceedingly improbable. Therefore we can assume that this alien civilization would be far more advanced than we, and presumably able to provide answers to some of our unsolved problems. However, it's also improbable that such an alien civilization would be close at hand, and so communications traveling at the speed of light would take at the very least two centuries for the round trip. It is highly likely that the solutions to any scientific problems that we can articulate clearly will be solved here on earth long before the answer comes back from outer space.

Any leading unsolved scientific problems that we can frame will probably be well on their way to solution in the next four decades, and the ideas that will characterize the scientific scene in the year 2026 will undoubtedly concern concepts that we can't even pose as questions in the twentieth century.

Nevertheless, let us pick a few key problems whose solution might be imminent. Astronomers would dearly like to know the value of the Hubble constant, that is, the rate of expansion of the universe with respect to distance. When the concept of the expanding universe was first observationally established in the late 1920s, the proposed rate erred by an order of magnitude, primarily because the distances to the galaxies were poorly known. In the 1980s, the number was known within a factor of 2. Data to be obtained with the Hubble Space Telescope should narrow the uncertainty to under 10 percent by establishing the distances with greater certainty. Because the reciprocal of the Hubble constant has the dimension of time, this parameter is related to the age of the universe. Once the Hubble constant is pinned down, astronomers will be in a better position to judge the temporal meaning of the parameter, and can decide with more certainty whether the age of the universe bears a simple or more complex relationship to it. If the Hubble constant turns out to be large, the age will be short, that is, 10 billion years or less. Since some globular clusters seem to be a few billion years older than this, such a discrepancy will force the cosmologists into states of deep meditation.

Astronomers would also like to know more about the early stages of the universe, say the first billion years or two, when the extremely smooth and homogeneous cosmic gas went over into the highly structured, inhomogeneous patterns of galaxies. Over the past several years the popular press has puffed up a discussion about the possible demise of the "big bang" theory of the expanding universe, and the unsolved problem of galaxy formation has been cited as evidence that the present cosmological scenario was in trouble. Actually, there is rather little connection between this evolutionary puzzle and the overall cosmological framework of the expanding universe. Likewise, when the scientists who had been exploring the microwave background with the COBE satellite announced they had finally detected a low level of inhomogeneities in background radiation, a great hurrah went up that the big bang cosmology had been saved. Both the threatened demise and its rescue tell us more about the rhetoric of science than about the status of the big bang cosmology. In any event, the question of how galaxies formed, and how they aggregated into large-scale structures, awaits a solution, but an acceptable explanation is likely to be found closer to 1993 than to 2026.

Are there planets around other stars? That is a critical aspect of investigating whether intelligent life exists elsewhere in the universe. It is a question for which the present technology can begin to address the problem, but a major observational effort is still wanting. There is now only one convincing case of planets beyond the solar system, but within three decades the list should be longer than the average astronomy textbook would care to tabulate.

Do gravitational waves exist? According to Einstein's general theory of relativity, the presence of a mass produces a warp or distortion in space-time. If a large mass moves—the massive infall in the collapse of a supernova core or the revolution of two neutron stars around each other—a ripple in space should propagate outward with the speed of light and should in principle be detectable. There seems little doubt that gravitational waves exist—they are key to the interpretation of the changing period of the double pulsar PSR 1913 + 16—but the question really is, can they be detected on earth? It is surely within our technical capabilities to find them in the next few decades.

Do black holes really exist? The general theory of relativity has never been verified under such severe conditions, so their existence remains problematic. By their physical nature, they can never be seen, but at least evidence for the presence of highly collapsed massive objects should be unambiguous. Given four more decades of study, the list of candidates should be lengthy, and the answer should be far more obvious than today.

And does dark matter exist? We turn now into the borderland between astronomy and particle physics. By "dark matter" I do not mean black interstellar dust or giant molecular clouds, essentially the domain of astronomy (though the chemists might claim a share since they, too, are intrigued by such things as the "buckyball" carbon molecules). The dark matter in question is something far more mysterious, and it's linked with another puzzle: can any empirical evidence be brought to confirm or disprove the so-called inflationary epoch scenario?

Let me put these paired questions into context. Most astronomers accept the idea of the expanding universe and believe that our present observed cosmos arose from a compact, super-dense state; they assume that these concepts will easily survive the next forty years. There are some curious questions, however, such as why the space in the universe is so nearly flat, that is, why does Euclidean geometry prevail in the large? General relativity says that the mass in the universe can curve the space, so why does it come out flat? You might say, as most astronomers would have said until comparatively recently, "So what? What's the big deal? Why shouldn't space be Euclidean?" It turns out, however, that any departure from flatness in the original primordial nucleus of the cosmos gets rapidly magnified in the expansion, and to have the present flatness requires that the original material be flat to one part in 10^{59}. Such a staggering precision could scarcely be accidental—surely some specific feature of the universe must have made it so.[11] Secondly, there is the "horizon problem." We can calculate back to the time when the entire observable universe was the size of a baseball—that's about one gigagigasecond (10^{-18} second) after the expansion began—and light, swift as it is, could scarcely begin to cross the baseball-sized universe that quickly.

The more we squeeze the universe down as we go back in time, the more difficult it is for the universe to be in communication with itself and the worse the problem becomes. The problem, that is, of how one side "knows" when the other side is ready to start expanding.

And this is where cosmic inflation comes to the rescue. At some point very close to the initial big bang, perhaps 10^{-26} second after time zero, a phase change took place where some of the fundamental forces separated, and for a brief moment, faster than any presently known physical process, gravity worked repulsively and the universe expanded billions of billions of billions of times—perhaps a lot more—stretching space out flat. Points that had indeed been in communication with each other would be exploded out to the boundaries of observable space. Both the flatness problem and the horizon problem are solved in a stroke; but another difficulty looms. For the universe to be so nearly flat, a certain average density is required by the general theory of relativity, and all the observations fall short in finding enough mass. It's worse than that. It's not just that atoms are hiding somewhere. Other very consistent observations put an upper limit on the amount of mass in the universe in the form of atoms. So, *if the inflationary scenario is correct, about 90 percent of the universe is some presently unknown form of dark matter,* not *atoms.*

The physics behind the moment of inflation depends on massive, short-lived particles known as Higgs bosons. Unlike electrons, neutrons, protons, or photons, these particles have little everyday significance, apart from the fact that several Nobel prizes have hinged on the prediction and experimental confirmation of two of them, the W and Z particles. Theory predicts yet another, known as the Higgs particle. It has a charge of zero and a spin of zero, and that's as far as theory goes. Perhaps there are more than one, "a whole raft of partners for super symmetry," and perhaps super symmetry will give rise to massive, longer-lasting but highly elusive matter that could, in fact, constitute the bulk of the universe. Thus, the more fundamental challenge is not whether dark matter exists, nor whether the inflationary scenario will hold, but to find out more about the Higgs particle (or particles), if indeed it or they exist. Quite possibly, the invisible dark matter might turn out to be only a figment of some theorists' imaginations.

Meanwhile, the experimental particle physicists are locked into intense competition to see who will find the massive top quark, the final particle required to complete the current elegant pattern of leptons and quarks (which make up the neutron, proton, and the bosons). (Because quarks are never found in isolation, the accelerator and collider mavens are looking for "toponium," a fleeting pairing of a top quark and a top anti-quark.) But in the words of one Nobel Laureate with whom I've consulted, finding the top quark will be such a straightforward experimental problem that "it scarcely counts as a serious prediction for the future of physics." But the Higgs particle—that's another matter (to make a bad pun!), and it's of course here that physicists find the prospect of the Superconducting Super Collider so exciting. We're at a fork in the road. Only some experimental input can show the theorists whether we're on the threshold of greater complexity or at the edge of a great particle desert.

In comparison, the task of making practical controlled thermonuclear fusion seems like a lesser challenge. Nevertheless, it heads the roster of key problems in physics formulated by the distinguished Russian Academician V. L. Ginzburg.[12] It has been on the list of every science seer since the 1950s, yet the problem remains stubbornly unsolved. We may not get the greatest insight into the workings of the universe by tackling this problem, but it just might become one of the most rewarding solutions with respect to the future well-being of the human race.

Within the world of physics, there are whole other areas with tantalizing unsolved problems, though predicting the shape of the solutions is risky. We don't need to look back a century to find humbling examples of the hazards of projecting science into the future. Just last December an editorial entitled "A Lesson in Humility" appeared in *Physics Today*.[13] The author, Professor Daniel Kleppner of MIT, recounted how he had been placed on one of those National Academy panels to survey physics for the coming decade. To prepare for the task, he looked at the previous survey in his own field of atomic physics. Apparently nobody had noticed that the laser was about to revolutionize atomic physics and optics, and lots of other advances were also missed. Who were the clods who did his field such injustice? He looked up the list of members of the previous atomic physics panel, and smack in the middle was his own name!

The atomic physicists ask, how can we explain superconductivity, especially at higher temperatures? Perhaps answers are already close at hand in this extraordinarily active area of research, but so far even a satisfactory theory is lacking and the solution is not yet in sight. What other unexpected properties can arise in almost—but not quite—pure crystals? The surface properties of thin films—a study still in its infancy—hold high promise for building compact electronic circuitry and for storing vast amounts of data in an incredibly small space. And, now that recent work has demonstrated how individual atoms can be trapped and studied, experimentalists ask what unsuspected transitions might be lurking, as yet unnoticed, at the atomic level?

The strange architecture of quantum structures, the submicroscopic world, builds into the macroscopic world, where atomic and solid state physicists must cope with the problem of complexity. How can the substances in the world around us be realistically described from a knowledge of individual atoms or arrays of atoms? Physicists, engineers, and chemists must join forces to work with tera-flop computing machinery, that is, enormously powerful computers that can handle a trillion operations per second. Surely a future trend will be the blurring of disciplinary boundaries as scientists strive to understand how materials behave in the everyday world.

These questions bring us close to chemistry. Back in 1950, Linus Pauling played the role of chemical forecaster for *Scientific American*.[14] One of the most inventive and perceptive chemists of our century, Pauling gazed into the crystal ball and came up with some specific predictions. It's interesting to see how well he hit the general areas and how badly he missed the specifics. Pauling guessed that the chemist of the year 2000, with a penetrating knowledge of forces between atoms and molecules, would be able to predict the rate of any chemical reaction with reasonable reliability. This remains an important desideratum, but up to now it's been a far more elusive goal than Pauling imagined. Even with substantial computing power, chemists can now scarcely cope with more than a score electrons. Considering that each carbon atom has six electrons, you don't get very far into organic chemistry when you can't calculate accurately for as many as four of them. Chemists, like the physicists, will need the tera-flop computers.

Pauling next suggested that new chemical reactions would be found at high temperatures and pressures. Indeed, chemists have

found a fascinating world of new reactions at unusual temperatures and pressures—but very low ones, cold atoms essentially in
isolation, and this is an area that now offers some of the greatest
promise and excitement for the next forty years.

Pauling proposed that progress with large inorganic molecules
might become significant. If he hadn't gone on to mention vana-
dium, molybdenum, and tantalum, his prediction would have
been right on the mark; I assume he has been as surprised as
anyone else to learn that a very common element, carbon, comes
in many more pure molecular forms than the long-known graph-
ite and diamond. Besides the C_{60} and C_{70} soccer-ball forms, the
so-called buckyballs or fullerenes named after the gadfly-architect
Buckminster Fuller, there are elongated nets and even tubes of
carbon atoms—an active area of research that should be well elu-
cidated in the coming decades.

Finally, Pauling correctly envisioned that structure of physio-
logically active substances would be an important problem in the
second half of the twentieth century, and in particular, the development of a theoretical understanding of how the physiological
activity worked. Today, we know that the shape of molecules plays
a key role in their activity, regardless of whether they are anti-
bodies, digestive enzymes, or painkillers. We know, for example,
that only left-handed ibuprofen, and not its mirror-image twin,
has any painkilling efficacy. Or, we know that lysozyme, a 1,600-
atom enzyme (approximately), contains a critical cleft into which
a carbohydrate can nestle—a carbohydrate from which energy
can be extracted for cell functions as the lysozyme dismantles it.
Surely one of the principal unsolved problems facing chemists
today is to find more precisely how the forms and configurations
of complex molecules determine their enzymatic or physiological
efficacy; and in turn, learning how to synthesize molecules with
very specific shapes will be *the* major challenge facing chemists
and biochemists in the next several decades. By 2026, "computed-
to-order" molecular shapes should be commonplace. And such
skills could lead not only to new medicines but, for example, to
non-random polymers stronger than steel.

Like chemists, meteorologists today live in a world unimaginable without high-speed computing. Only a few of them can now
remember the days before computer-assisted forecasting, which
met its first great success in the 1950s. Today, computer modeling

and data collecting from space hold the promise that long-term trends can be more accurately predicted. In the coming decades we can expect teamwork between atmospheric scientists and oceanographers to uncover the connections between the jet stream and ocean currents, to make climate predictions reliable some years in advance.

One of the key problems of the 1990s concerns global warming, an issue of great concern. There is no question that the world's climate has over the past century become warmer. What is at stake are the causes, and the extent to which we have control over them. The eruption of Mt. Pinatubo has for the moment reversed the warming trend. At the same time, the accumulation of methane (one of the most effective greenhouse gases) has mysteriously slowed. An understanding of the complex interplay between methane, carbon dioxide, and the sulfurous emissions from volcanoes is high on the agenda of unsolved problems for the atmospheric scientists, but within a decade or two we should have effective answers. We can only hope that the answers will not come too late to avert the consequences of a runaway increase in global temperatures.

Meanwhile, the rather separate problem of ozone depletion in the polar zones of our planet poses a frightening prospect; we must hope that in the coming decades meteorologists, working with chemists and physicists, will learn how to reverse this ominous trend.

The public is keenly interested in accurate weather forecasting, especially with respect to natural disasters such as hurricanes, but in some regions of the world the inhabitants would also welcome more precise warnings concerning volcanic eruptions and major earthquakes. Our knowledge of the great geological forces shaping the earth has increased dramatically with the unifying theme of plate tectonics. Vulcanism and seismic activity are both linked to the great continental movements, but a general understanding of these movements does not translate into immediate local predictive cogency. It is a purely speculative glance into the crystal ball to suggest that within four decades earthquake prediction will reach high levels of confidence, but if this worthy goal fails, it will not be for lack of trying.

At the same time, geologists should have much clearer ideas of the inaccessible interior of the earth. The interpretation will come through greatly refined seismological records combined with experimental work on solids under high pressures, for example, the type of work being carried out with hand-sized diamond anvils at places like the Carnegie Institution of Washington. And before four decades are out, we would hope that renewed exploration of the moon will help us to understand the relation of our satellite to the earth's own structure, and that a solution to the presently unsolved problem of the moon's origin—quite possibly involving a collision between a Mars-sized planet and the earth—will have achieved a consensus.

So much for a brief and hazardous survey of some of the principal problems in physical science that might find solution in the next several decades. However, any predictions about the future of physical science must be seen in social context. Many of the riddles begging for solution will require major funding for experimental facilities, and the next twenty years will see ferocious competition for resources and heavy public debate over priorities. The U.S. 1990 Fiscal Year budget included twice as much funding for NASA astrophysics and National Science Foundation astronomy as the combined total for the National Endowment for the Arts and the National Endowment for the Humanities. Let's face it—science funding has traditionally been associated with national prestige combined with defense interests. The strong German chemical industry contributed so much to Teutonic strength in World War I that America quickly recognized the efficacy of scientific research. And the Manhattan Project of World War II catapulted nuclear physicists into the role of national heroes. The National Science Foundation was created soon thereafter, and science funding has never been the same since.

Is it fair for the scientists to have so much and those in the arts and humanities relatively little? Perhaps not, though the traditional argument is that a strong science establishment contributes to invention and technology, which in turn fuels industrial growth, thereby benefiting the entire economy including the arts and humanities. A strong scientific establishment also contributes indispensably to health and medicine. When the economy is booming, few will look critically at the difference between research on AIDS, the search for extraterrestrial intelligence, or the quest for the Higgs particle. But as the national deficit grows and the economy slackens, everything is under scrutiny and available for political ridicule or pork barreling.

The annual budget for the Superconducting Super Collider in Texas is about half a billion dollars—a colossal sum that was in the summer of 1992 canceled by the full House of Representatives, though it was only 0.1 percent of the projected budget deficit. With an improved economy and in the short term, Congress will probably resume the project. But what can we afford in the long term? The gravitational waves experiment? A space station, which most scientists think will support too little scientific research to be cost-effective? A base on the far side of the moon in a zone protected from terrestrial radio emissions? An expedition to Mars?

All of this will be played out against some very ominous forces that most politicians choose to ignore, and which the rest of us wish would simply go away. One indisputable characteristic of the way forward will be an increasing world population and smaller per capita energy supplies. What we call the doomsday equation was first published in 1960. It is a simple mathematical expression that represents all the then-known data concerning population growth on earth. The striking feature, the one that gave its name to the equation, was its prediction that in the year 2026 the earth's population would become infinite.[15] Since the equation was first published, humankind has marched halfway to that deadline and the equation has proved eerily accurate. Today, there are more people alive than the combined total of all prior centuries. In 1900, there were sixteen cities with more than 1 million population; today, there are four hundred.

But of one thing we can be sure: the doomsday equation has got to be wrong. There is no way the human population can reach infinity in just thirty-three more years. Something has got to change. Indeed, the next thirty years are going to witness dramatic changes in people's expectations. Either the birthrate per couple is going to drop radically, or life expectancy must fall drastically.

The innate drive for species survival has guaranteed rampant breeding. In days past it could hardly be expected that children would survive to maturity. I think of the artist Albrecht Dürer's siblings—only two of his eighteen brothers and sisters grew to adulthood. Now, it's easy enough to criticize the Pope as being irresponsible when he goes into Latin America and preaches against contraception, but sociologists tell us that what really makes high birthrates is not so much religious teaching as inadequate social security, when a society has no alternate provision for support in old age. Nor can one lay the blame for the population time bomb on the doorsteps of the right-to-lifers. Still, when approximately half of all human conceptions abort spontaneously,[16] it's difficult to identify fertilized cells in their early stages with meaningful life and at the same time to believe in a Creator as beneficent who regularly allows a substantial fraction of all meaningful lives to be obliterated at the outset.

But if the world population is not to go infinite, either the birthrate must decelerate or the death rate must rise to insufferable proportions. How can that be? For years we have lived with the sword of Damocles of nuclear warfare hanging over our heads. The human race seemed in serious, even immediate peril. Of late it has been with enormous relief that we have seen the collapse of the Soviet threat. The *Bulletin of the Atomic Scientists* has moved back the hands of its own doomsday clock, now not so close to midnight. But genocide continues apace in our troubled world, though not yet of a magnitude to stem the population tide.

What else can increase the death rate? Starvation, perhaps? In the spring of 1992, *Time* magazine carried a remarkable story about the mysterious demise of the Anasazi Indians from Chaco Canyon nine hundred years ago. A careful analysis of contemporary rats' nests has shown that the Indians simply cut down too many pine trees, creating erosion in their fields and a shortage of food. Perhaps they moved, or maybe they just died out. Today, over 1 million people in Somalia are on the brink of starvation, and probably over a hundred thousand have perished. Is this the future of our race? Or will it be disease? A monster AIDS epidemic threatens to halve the population of Africa before the decade is out. Such agony and suffering in Africa would set back its explosive population growth by only twenty-five years. But perhaps there will be worldwide epidemics even more devastating.

I know this sounds like Malthusian gloom of a bygone age. Such disasters of overpopulation have all been threatened before, whereas more efficient agricultural methods have continuously opened the world to ever larger numbers. But we have anesthetized ourselves into thinking that resources are unlimited.

Fossil fuels now supply 88 percent of the world's purchased energy. At current usage, the oil reserves will last about sixty years. Very conservatively, the doubling time of the world population is under thirty years, and of course the doomsday equation now runs it much faster than that. With the current use, and in the absence of intense conservation and development of alternative sources, the oil reserves will be nearly gone in thirty years. Nations owning the last reservoirs can hold the rest of the world hostage unless they have been bombed into submission. And to say "with the current use" means that less developed countries will never have a chance to share the opulence of the West.

In a sense, scientists are in a race against time to discover the secrets of nature; for example, to find new energy sources—perhaps thermonuclear fusion—that will give abundance on a worldwide basis, and will help provide an alternative old-age security other than depending on one's offspring. There is a race to find a vaccine for AIDS, and a race to understand global warming before it is too late. Our science and our critical scientific understanding can play a vital role in a world where catastrophe is near at hand. I am convinced that scientific understanding of the universe is critical to finding a place in it for so many of God's children.

What happens in Africa or Asia or to the hungry in our own lands happens to our sisters and brothers, and becomes part of our concern. Perhaps salvation is not such an abstract, heavenly concept after all. When Jesus speaks of salvation through servantship to others, he may just be telling us about the deep meanings of human relationships in a world marked by such rampant selfishness that it threatens death to us all.

As scientist-theologian, the seventeenth-century astronomer Johannes Kepler said, "I consider it a right, yes, a duty, to search in a cautious manner for the number, sizes and weights, the norms of everything He has created. . . . For these secrets are not of the kind whose research should be forbidden; rather, they are set before our eyes like a mirror so that by examining them we observe to some extent the goodness and wisdom of the Creator."[17] I can only register my optimism and my hope that creative scientific investigations will mirror the goodness and wisdom of the Creator, and that they will be done in time as we grope for the way forward.

REFERENCES

1. ARNOLD B. BARACH and the KIPLINGER WASHINGTON editors. *1975 and the Changes to Come* (New York: Harper & Brothers, 1962).
2. FOREIGN POLICY ASSOCIATION. *Toward the Year 2018* (New York: Cowles Education Corp., 1968).
3. J. B. S. HALDANE. *Daedalus or Science and the Future* (New York: E. P. Dutton & Co., 1924), p. 3.
4. ARTHUR EDDINGTON. "The Internal Constitution of Stars." *Nature*, 106 (1920), 14–20.
5. C. C. FURNAS. *The Next Hundred Years, The Unfinished Business of Science* (New York: Reynal & Hitchcock, 1936), p. 275.
6. Ibid., pp. 194–95.
7. GEORGE THOMSON. *The Foreseeable Future* (Cambridge: Cambridge University Press, 1955), pp. 87–88.
8. AUGUST COMTE. *The Positive Philosophy,* translated by Harriet Martineau (London: Trübner & Co., 1875), p. 115.
9. A. A. MICHELSON. "Some of the Objects and Methods of Physical Science." *University of Chicago Quarterly Calendar,* 3 (August 1894), 15. Cited by Lawrence Badash, "The Completeness of Nineteenth-Century Science." *Isis,* 63 (1972), 48–58, esp. p. 52.
10. SIMON NEWCOMB. "The Outlook for the Flying Machine." Reprinted in *Side-lights on Astronomy and Kindred Fields of Popular Science* (New York: Harper & Brothers, 1906), pp. 330–45.
11. See ALAN LIGHTMAN and OWEN GINGERICH. "When Do Anomalies Begin?" *Science,* 255, February 7, 1992, pp. 690–95.
12. V. L. GINZBURG. *Physics and Astrophysics: A Selection of Key Problems,* translated by O. Glebov and G. Ter Haar (Oxford & New York: Pergamon, 1985).
13. DANIEL KLEPPNER. "A Lesson in Humility." *Physics Today* (December 1991), 9, 11.
14. LINUS PAULING. "Chemistry." *Scientific American* (September 1950), 60–63.
15. The doomsday equation was first published in *Science,* 132 (1960), 1291; there is an interesting follow-up letter in *Science,* 237 (September 25, 1987), 1555–56.
16. LUIGI MASTROIANNI, JR. "Reproductive Technologies," in *Encyclopedia of Bioethics,* edited by Warren Reich (New York: Free Press, 1978), p. 1450.
17. JOHANNES KEPLER. *Epitome astronomiae Copernicanae,* reprinted in *Johannes Kepler Gesammelte Werke,* vol. 7, p. 208, quoted in Max Caspar, *Kepler* (New York: Abelard-Schuman, 1959), p. 381.

4

GEOPOLITICS

by Orrin G. Hatch

Senator Orrin G. Hatch has represented the state of Utah in the United States Senate since 1977. He has served as a member of the Senate Select Committee on Intelligence and the Senate Foreign Relations Committees.

CONVENTIONAL WISDOM in 1992 argued that the end of the Cold War had ushered in the end of history, that free markets and democracy were now universally recognized as the best economic and political systems, and that global peace and prosperity would be the natural result of their adoption worldwide in the decades ahead. That view, based on projecting immediate trends indefinitely into the future, was wrong. Looking back on the world of 1992 thirty years later will reveal that the world will have been totally transformed. Yet, instead of "one world" of free markets and democracy, what is likely to emerge is three worlds—one advancing rapidly through market economics, democracy, and scientific discovery; one lagging behind due to the legacies of its Communist past; and one regressing as a result of economic failures and demographic crises. Instead of a more prosperous and peaceful world, we will live in a more divided and turbulent one.

Continuity seldom surpasses change as the more powerful theme in the evolution of world history. If we look back at the twentieth century in thirty-year intervals, it is clear that history is characterized not by gradual evolution but by radical change:

- In 1902, the era of empire was in full swing. European powers, mostly governed by monarchical or authoritarian systems, had divided the world. Britain, France, and Russia were the dominant powers, but Germany and the United States were on the rise. The great powers focused their geopolitical competition on the colonial world. Economic growth and social optimism abounded in the West. Totalitarian ideologies, such as fascism and communism, were the preoccupation of small debating societies, not major political movements.
- In 1932, the era of ideology and nationalism had begun. Communists ruled the Soviet Union. Fascists ruled Italy. Militarists ruled Japan. Nazism was on the rise in Germany. Democratic governments were weak and drifting. Nationalism became a major force in the wake of World War I, with the disintegration of the Ottoman and Austro-Hungarian empires. Britain and France squabbled over the Middle East, while the new nations of Central Europe, such as Poland and Czechoslovakia, struggled for stability. At the same time, the Great Depression ravaged the West.
- In 1962, the nuclear era and the post-colonial era had transformed the world. Not only had two nuclear superpowers emerged and formed rival geopolitical blocs based on rival political ideologies, but in that year they came as close as they would come to general nuclear war in the Cuban missile crisis. Other major powers—Britain, France, Germany, and Japan—had been demoted to secondary status. Meanwhile, the superpowers engaged in global competition to see whose influence would prevail among the newly independent countries formed after the disintegration of the British and French empires.
- In 1992, the post-totalitarian era began. Discredited in Eastern Europe in 1989, communism collapsed in the Soviet Union in 1991 and triggered the implosion of the Russian-dominated Soviet Empire. Thus, instead of sweeping capitalism into the dustbin of history—as envisioned by Trotsky—the final act of the Soviet Union was to usher in that very same fate for communism.

In light of that record of revolutionary change, we should expect change of a similar magnitude during the next thirty years.

This essay will try to foresee some of the dynamic changes that will occur in the international community as the world of 2022. It will engage in an exercise of "future history"—that is, an attempt to write a possible history of the next thirty years as it might appear in textbooks in the year 2023. It will then describe the geopolitical shape of that new and different world, and analyze the issues that will face the United States and the international community in each region.

In 2022, new history textbooks looked with amusement on the predictions in the early 1990s that the great revolutions of 1989 and 1991 would unify the world under the banners of free markets and democracy. In their view, instead of producing geopolitical fusion, these events triggered geopolitical fission. A Cold War world divided into two rigid ideological blocs was further fragmented by nationalisms, state rivalries, demographic explosions, uneven economic development, and other factors. Some areas of the world prospered tremendously, while others degenerated into zones of political instability and economic poverty. How this came about will be explained by future histories that could well run along the following lines:

The democratic revolution in the former Soviet Union foundered as a result of national rivalries, failed economic reforms, and a resurgent imperial Russian nationalism. Within three years of the anti-Communist revolution in 1991, the Commonwealth of Independent States dissolved because of tensions between Russia and Ukraine over control of the former Soviet Union's military, the rights of ethnic Russians, and the future of the Crimea. Since all other smaller republics feared Russian domination in a commonwealth minus the Ukraine, fifteen independent and often quarrelsome states succeeded the Soviet Union.

In the final years of the Gorbachev period, economic reforms in half-measures doomed the former Soviet Union to an economic free fall. In 1990, it had entered a period of economic contraction more severe than the Great Depression of the 1930s in the West, with gross national product of the former Soviet Union ultimately shrinking by more than 40 percent in three years. The bold market-oriented reforms initiated after the democratic revolution of 1991 by President Boris Yeltsin, the first democratically elected

leader of Russia in history, failed to reverse the decline. The capability of the democratic political system—weak and divided—was
simply overloaded by the attempt simultaneously to free controlled
prices, privatize state enterprises, decollectivize agriculture, create
new independent banks, make the ruble convertible, and undertake a host of other changes. Reactionary elements of the old regime entrenched in Russia's bureaucracy did their best to sabotage
the reforms, as well as to capitalize on their positions through fla-
grant corruption. In the first years of Yeltsin's experiment, the
Russian people reaped the pains of transition—particularly mass
unemployment—while enjoying few tangible gains from the free
market system.

Major Western powers gave Yeltsin much rhetorical but little
material support. While they granted Russia membership in the
International Monetary Fund and other Western financial institutions, they did not make the success of Russia's new democracy
a priority even after their economies began to recover from the
1991–92 recession. Less than one tenth of the amount in real
terms made available through the Marshall Plan to help Western
Europe recover after World War II was given to the new democratic government in Moscow, and almost all of this aid was provided through uncoordinated and duplicative aid programs.
Japan, which had modest foreign policies during the Cold War,
undertook the most ambitious aid program of the major industrial powers after Yeltsin's government returned four islands
seized by Stalin in 1945.

While an energetic aid program could have given Yeltsin's government breathing room, the West's reluctance to help emboldened the forces of reaction in Russia. Yeltsin, necessarily
preoccupied with implementing his economic reforms, failed to
execute a top-to-bottom purge of the bureaucracy, thus leaving
his new government dangerously vulnerable to the holdovers
from the old regime. In the early 1990s, those elements—and
particularly those in the armed forces and the internal security
apparatus—began to form links with neo-Fascist political figures,
such as Vladimir Zhirinovsky of the Liberal Party, who called for
the reimposition of the dictatorial "strong hand" and a restoration
of Russia's "historical borders." Sympathetic figures within the
government distributed arms and munitions covertly to the neo-

Fascists, as well as to extremists within ethnic Russian minority populations in adjoining republics.

The focal point of the struggle for power became parliamentary elections and the presidential election in the late 1990s. While the reactionaries never attracted majority support, democratic forces were weakened by internal divisions and the failure of Yeltsin's economic reforms. In Russia's parliamentary elections, democratic parties won 60 percent of the seats and reactionaries 40 percent. When the democrats failed to unite behind a single leader, however, the reactionaries made their move. Irregular neo-Fascist forces seized localities where they had strong support. Yeltsin ordered Russia's security forces to intervene, but they refused. After two weeks of political paralysis in Moscow, reactionary officials in the military and former KGB executed a coup d'état that removed Yeltsin from power. Democratic demonstrations were put down in bloody clashes with military units composed of troops indoctrinated with the neo-Fascist line.

The new Russian despotism soon initiated a new Russian imperialism. In the late 1990s, ideal conditions existed for reigniting Russia's expansionist tradition. Extremist nationalists ruled from the Kremlin. All the other republics of the former Soviet Union remained economically weak, politically unstable, and militarily vulnerable. In addition, many were increasingly ethnically divided, with the ethnic Russians living within their borders angered by discriminatory policies and laws. As a result, the Russian despotism had the motive, means, and opportunity to engage in its age-old expansionist tactics: using the Russian minority to create instability and then intervening militarily to "protect" the ethnic Russians. Soon, guerrilla wars had broken out in Ukraine, Byelorus, the Baltic states, and Kazakhstan.

The attempt forcibly to reestablish the former Soviet Union failed, however. Although neo-Fascist Russian forces overran Latvia, Estonia, and parts of Lithuania and Ukraine, the Kremlin lacked sufficient numbers of ideologically motivated troops to overcome fierce Ukrainian resistance or to mount a significant threat to Kazakhstan or Byelorus. Moscow found that each upheaval—the Gorbachev reforms, the Yeltsin revolution, and the reactionary restoration—had progressively weakened the state's instruments of power, leaving the Kremlin with only a few ideologically reliable and effective armored divisions. This was enough to seize and retain power in Russia but not enough to rebuild the former Soviet Union. At the same time, Western economic sanctions squeezed Moscow's hard currency liquidity, forcing it to suspend its payments on international debt and curtailing its ability to pay for essential imports. By 1999, the Russian government declared that it was limiting its objectives to carving out territories heavily populated by ethnic Russians from neighboring non-Russian republics.

Despite this political reversion and descent into civil war, the democratic revolution in the former Soviet Union had a profound effect on China. In 1993 and 1994, Deng Xiaoping accelerated economic reform and began the final process of the eclipse of communism in China. Fearing that the post–Tiananmen Square leadership would reverse his reforms once he departed from the scene, he not only put his personal imprimatur on a new round of market reforms but also backed personnel changes in the Politburo and Central Committee that favored the reformist faction in the Communist Party. By the late 1990s, the state sector in the Chinese economy produced less than 20 percent of total output, despite massive subsidies from the central government. This, in turn, increased the clout of the forces within the Communist Party that were associated with the private sector. By the time Deng died at the age of ninety in 1996, the hardliners were no longer dominant even within the party, with the political heirs of Hu Yaobang and Zhao Ziyang openly speaking of the need for political as well as economic reform.

In the aftermath of the disintegration of the Soviet Union, revolutionary changes also swept through Central Asia, South Asia, and the Middle East. Vast areas gradually became stateless territories, beyond the control of any government, and ruled only by tribal or ethnic groups or by armed bands of secessionist insurgents or drug traffickers. In the 1980s and 1990s, that had already happened in the drug-producing regions of South America. This growing phenomenon—which in the West became known as "expanding stateless zones"—subsumed much of the territory of the Central Asian republics of the former Soviet Union, Afghanistan, and parts of Pakistan and India. Despite a U.N. settlement of the war in Afghanistan in 1992–93, the new government formed after flawed elections failed to achieve national unity, with the country splitting along Pushtun-Tadjik ethnic lines. As central authority collapsed, all these stateless territories became a cockpit of geopolitical competition between Pakistan, Iran, Turkey, and Saudi Arabia.

Pakistan and India, both of which sought to exploit this new instability in the mid- and late 1990s, became victims of its two-edged sword. Islamabad stepped up its covert arming of Kashmiri separatists and also began to supply Sikh and other ethnic insurgents inside India. New Delhi, in turn, escalated its covert aid to Sindhi guerrillas, as well as extending support to Baluch separatists. In 1997, the conflict in Kashmir became so acute that war broke out between India and Pakistan, both of which had by this time developed significant tactical nuclear arsenals. When both India and Pakistan proved impotent in quelling their internal uprisings through force, the insurgents were emboldened, with several of the non-Hindu provinces on India's periphery breaking away and with most of Pakistan's province of Baluchistan and its tribal territories becoming stateless zones.

The brittle regimes of the Middle East fared little better. Iraq, strangled by U.N.-backed sanctions and undermined by Western covert action operations in support of Kurdish and Shia guerrillas, split three ways in the mid-1990s. Although weakened by a fundamentalist purge in 1995, Iran became the dominant power in the Persian Gulf, forcing Saudi Arabia and the Gulf states to seek defense arrangements with the West. Syria, beset by economic crises, descended into civil strife between factions backing and opposing the governing Alawite minority. As a result of the U.S.-led peace process, Israel worked out a tenuous, interim autonomy agreement with the West Bank Palestinians in the mid-1990s. Several years later, after Jordan's President Hussein departed the scene, radical Palestinian elements took over the government in Amman, an event that led Israel to announce that in light of security considerations current autonomy arrangements were the most Jerusalem could safely offer in terms of Palestinian self-rule in the Occupied Territories. A fragile peace, based on Israeli military superiority, lasted out the decade, despite repeated low-level terrorist and counterterrorist clashes.

In the 1990s, the United States did not fully succumb to isolationism but clearly reduced its international activism. The mid-1990s were a period of economic stagnation, with creeping worldwide protectionism, rampant federal overregulation, and expanding government spending as a proportion of gross national product stifling the prospects of technology- and trade-driven growth. In the 1996 presidential election, however, the American people elected an administration committed to fighting against excessive spending on Capitol Hill and stripping away regulations inhibiting growth. As domestic economic growth picked up, the temptations of isolationism abated. This ensured that the United States maintained its security ties with Western Europe and with Japan. But as a result of its initial timidity in responding to the situation in the former Soviet Union, it had lost the chance to cultivate a democratic and non-imperial government in Moscow.

As the twenty-first century began, the phrase "the end of history" from the early 1990s joined the Great Depression–era prediction that "recovery is just around the corner" and the Vietnam-era vision of "light at the end of the tunnel" as another classic example of shortsighted American overoptimism. After the Cold War, the world had become not simpler but more complicated.

The first two decades of the new century witnessed both negative and positive developments. On the negative side, the expanding stateless zones soon covered large tracts of Africa. Liberia, Somalia, and much of Sudan and Mozambique had already been subsumed in the 1990s. But after the year 2000, many of the national borders drawn by the European empires began to unravel. Tentative steps toward pluralistic political reforms in the 1990s died quiet deaths. Explosive demographic growth compounded with anti-growth economic policies and rampant corruption triggered civil strife in half a dozen multi-ethnic sub-Saharan African states. Before long, civil strife that made the Yugoslav civil war of 1991–92 seem tame by comparison was raging across the continent. Political scientists began to refer to this phenomenon as the "Somalia model" of political disintegration.

Within a few years, a substantial portion of the underdeveloped world's territory—including areas in Central Asia, South Asia, sub-Saharan Africa, and Andean South America—essentially had no functioning government. Enclaves in these regions came under the control of drug-producing cartels and terrorist organizations, with dozens of such groups carving out fiefdoms from which they challenged Western interests with impunity. At the same time, no Western power dared to try to intervene in these lawless quagmires.

A new danger arose as the stateless zones began to erode the territories of countries with nuclear weapons. A band of new nuclear club states—not only India and Pakistan but also Iran, Iraq, and Algeria—lay astride the unstable regions in Asia and Africa. In the cases of India, Pakistan, and Iraq, the stateless zones had already subsumed part of their territories. As a result, the West found itself burdened with the unenviable task of trying to maintain stability in unstable regions for fear that nuclear weapons could find their way into the hands of anti-Western forces.

On the positive side, the resistance of the non-Russian republics and the sanctions of the West thwarted the imperial aspirations of the neo-Fascist regime in Moscow. Its leaders were forced not only to renew the pursuit of Yeltsin's market-oriented reforms but also to disgorge much of the territory conquered by its armies. Russia entered a period of state capitalism, with a Pinochet-like regime imposing the discipline of the market on the economy despite the hardships involved. Although Kremlin leaders did so in order to restore Russia's standing as a great power, their policies had the unintended consequence during the first two decades of the twenty-first century of creating a new middle class. This group, upon which Moscow depended for economic progress, made gradually stronger demands for a political voice, until Russia's authoritarian leaders ultimately conceded the need for free elections in 2017, exactly one hundred years after the Bolshevik Revolution.

In 2001, the Chinese Communist Party held a special party conference on the issue of political reform. Pro-reform forces, having achieved ascendancy over the hardliners in internal struggles, passed a new party program that called for separation of the functions of the state and the party, and for the initiation of a dialogue between the party and the people about the political future. At the same time, the program balanced this with statements asserting that under no circumstances would the state permit a deterioration of "social order," which was described as the "indispensable foundation" of economic growth. Western analysts, though initially skeptical about the scope of change, soon proclaimed that China had entered what they called the "Taiwan phase" of its political development, combining progressively more relaxed authoritarian politics with free market economics. Taipei, having held fully free elections in the 1990s, resented the comparison at first, though it welcomed its role as a trailblazer when Beijing held its first partially free elections in the year 2020.

Several countries previously viewed as part of the Third World joined the developed world. Taiwan and Singapore led the ranks. Korea, whose development was temporarily slowed after the post–Kim Il-song unification of the south and north in 2003, trailed slightly behind them. Thailand and latecomer Indonesia were not far off the pace. In South America, where statist economic policies bedeviled would-be entrepreneurs, only Chile maintained the consistent free market, trade-oriented policies needed to escape the ranks of less developed countries. Mexico, despite rapid population growth, capitalized on the North American Free Trade Agreement of 1993 to enter the lower ranks of the industrial powers by 2020 after almost three decades of steady export-based growth.

None of the major industrial powers—the United States, Western Europe, and Japan—achieved economic primacy. National economic success increasingly was determined by how well a state controlled its spending on social entitlements, how well it made use of its savings, and how well it enhanced its labor force through immigration. The European Community, which achieved economic but not political union and which brought not only the European Free Trade Area states but also Poland, Hungary, the Czech Republic, and Slovakia into its ranks as full members by 2002, faltered on all three counts. Japan, instead of becoming the dominant economic power of the century, lost some of its edge as its younger generation adopted materialist values and as its workforce steadily became the oldest among major industrial powers. Meanwhile, other Asian countries matched Japan's capacity to produce high-value-added products, such as electronics and automobiles.

After the reversion to authoritarianism in Russia, global political leadership devolved upon the Group of Seven, the world's major industrialized democracies. Because of the new antagonism with Moscow, the United Nations Security Council was again paralyzed by the Kremlin's veto. NATO, surviving its victory in the Cold War, played an important but no longer a central role in Western security policy because the withdrawal of the former

Soviet Union's forces from Central Europe in the mid-1990s reduced the West's vulnerability to conventional attack. Coupled with America's partial withdrawal into isolationism, Western countries exercised joint global leadership only when common interests compelled a coordinated response, though individual groups of countries combined forces on specific issues. The forum for this ad hoc cooperation became the annual G-7 summit meetings, which soon focused as much on strategic and political issues as on economic ones.

Those analysts who in 1992 foresaw a tranquil era in international relations made one fundamental error: they believed that a major multinational empire could implode virtually overnight without destabilizing vast portions of the globe. Never before had such an event transpired without triggering turbulence on a massive scale. The collapse of the Ottoman Empire produced the modern-day Middle East. The demise of the Austro-Hungarian Empire created tinder for World War II. The passing of the British Empire left in its wake the Indo-Pakistani conflict and opportunities for Communist insurgencies. The legacies of the French Empire were not only the conflicts in Indochina but also instability in Africa. The fall of the Portuguese Empire produced the wars in Angola and Mozambique. In light of this record, it was folly to believe that the collapse of the Soviet Union would lead to unprecedented stability instead of instability.

This is not to say that the demise of Soviet communism was a negative development. The world was clearly better off with the cloud of potential nuclear war lifted. The Soviet peoples benefited even more as a result of the end of the Kremlin's totalitarian controls, even if authoritarian rule returned in some of its new republics. What this does mean is that we would make a fatal error if we assume that over the next thirty years the best possible course of events—the universal triumph of free markets and democracy—is not only the most likely but also virtually inevitable.

The particular course of history depicted above is in no way preordained. It is one of many possible scenarios, but it attempts to predict the level of conflict and cooperation the world could experience. As long as no overarching power exists to settle the differences of competitive states, the age-old logic of geopolitics will reassert itself: states have conflicting interests. In a competitive environment, these interests breed conflicts. To prevail in these conflicts, states can—and sometimes will—resort to coercion.

Looking back on 1992 with the benefit of hindsight in 2022, the truth of one maxim will be clear: Revolutionary upheavals may change the way the world looks, but they seldom change the way the world works.

Instead of the "One World" that Wendell Willkie foresaw in his famous book by that title, international trends and events will create three worlds by the year 2022. This new world will be stratified into three tiers in terms of national income and influence on the international system. The highly developed world, the post-Communist world, and the undeveloped world will differ profoundly not only in the quality of life of their populations but also in the kinds of geopolitical competition that will preoccupy the states within them.

The trends and processes that will produce this fractured world are already to some extent evident:

• Economic growth rates vary tremendously from state to state. The newly industrializing countries of East Asia lead the way with average annual per capita income growth rates in recent years as high as 5 percent, while many countries in sub-Saharan Africa and Latin America have actually regressed economically in the last decade. Even the developed world's middle-range growth rates will be sufficient to maintain their present positions in the global economic hierarchy. Over the course of three decades, these disparate growth rates will produce distinct international economic classes.

• The wide variations in economic opportunity inherent in the trend above will channel the international "brain drain" toward the highly developed countries. Former Communist states and the undeveloped world will lose a significant portion of their talent pools through emigration. This will result in a self-reinforcing process that steadily increases the economic and technological advantage of the developed world.

• Differences in internal political stability will further accentuate the economic stratification of the world. The cohesive political systems of the developed world will allow them to focus on eco-

nomic issues and to leave the rest of world in the dust economically. For the countries of the post-Communist world, the
problems of institution building and the brokering of long-
suppressed ethnic and national conflicts will consume the attention of political leaders. In much of the underdeveloped world,
political instability will be not the exception but the rule, with
power struggles among rival elites often transpiring amid an over-
lay of inter-ethnic violence.

• Internal instability in many cases will be compounded by external threats. In the territories of the former Soviet Union, for
example, the intermingling of national groups—Russians living in
Ukraine, Armenians in Azerbaijan, Uzbeks in Kyrgystan, and so
forth—and the existence of centuries-old territorial disputes will
create dozens of opportunities for subversion and potential flash-
points for conventional war. The need to devote excessive portions of their GNPs to military spending will further retard the
development of such countries.

• Disparate economic growth rates and levels of political stability ultimately will create inequalities in terms of military power.
Only the countries of the developed world will be in a position to
exploit breakthroughs in directed-energy technologies, composite
materials, ballistic missile defenses, and other areas. These high-
tech capabilities will give them superiority over all countries in the
post-Communist and undeveloped worlds in terms of conventional warfare. The United States, building on its present advantages, will hold an unquestioned military lead over all potential
rivals. While many of its advanced military technologies will have
filtered into the rest of the world, its integrated land, sea, air, and
space capabilities will be unchallenged.

The significant gaps in economic and political development
among the nations of the world in 1992 will become great chasms
by 2022. The above-noted trends, as well as others, will create
three separate zones, each with very different issues and challenges for the United States and the international community.

Developed world

In 2022, this zone will encompass not only the major industrial
powers of 1992 but also rapidly developing states in East Asia,

Latin America, and Eastern Europe. With a per capita income equal to that of the United States in the 1940s, even China will be on the threshold of entering the ranks of developed states. In fact, the top two countries ranked by GNP will be the United States and China, followed by Japan, Germany, and Russia. Provided that the major powers and particularly the United States manage their relations responsibly, the competition within the developed world will be transformed from geopolitics into "geo-economics."

At the broadest level, states engaged in this modern-day mercantilism will be competing to maximize their gains from the flows of international trade and investment. Which countries will generate the most investment capital? Which will attract the foreign and domestic investment sufficient to build an advantage in the most productive sectors of modern economies? Which will dominate the industries that will bring the highest wage jobs? Which will most profit from the international flows of dividend and interest payments? These and similar questions will become the primary focus of the pull-and-tug of international relations within the developed world.

To a large extent, this competition will be based on misperceptions about the nature of the global economy. Contrary to popular perceptions, international trade and investment are not zero-sum games in which one side makes gains only at the expense of another, a fact which economists have repeatedly demonstrated. In coming decades, the very idea of an exclusively American, German, or Japanese company or product will be dubious. Stock ownership in major transnational companies will be diffused around the world. Global sourcing of components and transplant assembly facilities will render virtually meaningless present conceptions of "national content" of major products such as automobiles, though disputes about such issues will continue to play a large role in domestic politics.

Nevertheless, this geo-economic competition will lead states to develop new and more subtle tactics to dominate international markets. Japan will perfect the use of the *kieretsu*, its vertically and horizontally integrated corporate structures that collude against market entry by non-member firms. Western Europe will exclude foreign goods by tailoring the technical standards for products sold in its unified market to the strengths of its industries, as well as relying on direct industrial subsidies. The United States will relax its anti-trust laws in order to promote economies of scale and enable companies to pool their research-and-development resources. In markets outside of the developing world, all will find ways to dump high-value-added goods in order to win a market share that will subsequently ensure a continuing export stream through sales of parts and brand loyalty.

The relatively open postwar international trade system depended upon U.S. political and economic leadership. Free trade will not survive in the future if the United States ceases to be its strong advocate. To stem the protectionist trade, the United States must improve its competitive edge, which requires action on two fronts. Domestically, the United States needs an administration and Congress that will lead a renewal of America, repealing the creeping statist policies of the last thirty years and freeing financial resources that will enable individuals and private enterprise to develop the country's human and productive capital. Internationally, the United States must engage in export promotion. Additional resources must go to the U.S. Foreign Commercial Service, which has been chronically understaffed and given short shrift at our embassies abroad. The United States should also provide public funds to create a U.S. organization that parallels some of the functions of Japan's MITI. The key capability is MITI's collection and dissemination of relevant trade information through its export arm, known as the Japanese External Trade Organization (JETRO), which informs Japanese firms on overseas economic trends and marketing opportunities and facilitates business contacts. The idea is not to supplant private enterprise but find ways to strengthen the ability of U.S. firms to compete in the world market.

Post-Communist world

The key to the geopolitical future of this region is what happens in Russia. If Yeltsin's reforms succeed, the United States and the West could focus resources on consolidating a new, democratic, and non-imperial Russian state. If the reforms fail, and if a new authoritarian regime takes power, the West's geopolitical priority must shift to integrating Poland, the Czech Republic, Slovakia, and Hungary into NATO, and to building up the non-Russian republics of the former Soviet Union in order to balance the power of Russia.

In either case, however, we will need to develop a much more comprehensive approach to the economic rehabilitation of the post-Communist world.

First, we will have to organize ourselves for the massive undertaking we face. The post–Cold War transition in the East will be far more difficult than post–World War II reconstruction in the West. We must begin by creating a single organization that will undertake a comprehensive assessment of the needs of the post-Communist states and will delegate responses to those needs to international, bilateral, and private agencies. It would, for example, target and coordinate the activities of the International Monetary Fund, the World Bank, the European Bank for Reconstruction and Development, and others to avoid duplication. Without such an agency, our response will be destined to be both inefficient and ad hoc.

Second, once a state has adopted the "shock therapy" of the Polish model—freeing prices, controlling the money supply, balancing the state budget, and making the currency internationally convertible—the West must provide the funds needed to help create macroeconomic stability. Since this was necessary in postwar Western Europe, it will be even more critical in post–Communist Europe. Even the best economic reforms will fail unless we provide the indispensable backstops, such as currency stabilization funds through the International Monetary Fund.

Third, we must move beyond simply opening up our markets to the goods of the post-Communist world. If we want free market reforms to succeed, we should provide preferential market-access arrangements on a temporary basis. In order to accelerate Japan's postwar recovery and to secure its contribution to containment of Moscow, the United States permitted Tokyo to impose protectionist tariffs while enjoying free access to the U.S. market. Without some protection, Western competition will destroy fledgling firms in post-Communist Europe, which, in turn, will lead to a retrenchment in reform. If we allow limited preferential trade arrangements—which, of course, would be phased out over time—the private sectors of these countries will take hold much more quickly.

Fourth, we must provide technical assistance on a massive scale at the enterprise level. Western firms should send managers and experts, whose expenses would be partly covered by Western governments, to assist individual enterprises make the transition to operating in the free market and to help cultivate a new post-Communist management class.

Fifth, we must temper desires for reckless privatization programs that could become formulas for mass unemployment. Rapid privatization is possible for small enterprises. But to throw state-operated industries into the market overnight would cause massive bankruptcies. The better model is to open up each industry to private competitors and allow the natural growth of the private sector to eclipse the state-owned sector, as happened in the case of China.

More generally, the West needs to develop new instruments of power to operate effectively in the post-Communist world. During the Cold War, the issues we faced emphasized the instruments of state-to-state relations, such as alliances, bilateral aid programs, diplomatic mediation, and others. In the post-Communist world, more emphasis will be placed on influencing the political and economic evolution of societies. This is not a question of the old-style "nation building" of the 1960s. Instead, we will need the capability to engage in "institution building," transplanting and adapting the political and economic institutions that work in the West to the soil of the post-Communist world. It is not just a matter of teaching free market economics but also of providing information about how to transform judicial systems based on rule by the party to ones founded on rule of law.

Primacy in this post-Communist zone will go to the states that first master the capability to influence the sinews of these developing political and economic structures. We have experimented with such instruments with the National Endowment for Democracy in the United States and the Westminster Foundation in Great Britain. Proposals exist for a new "enterprise corps" that would send U.S. managers abroad on exchange programs. Innovative international broadcasting programs—such as the proposal to create a Radio Free Asia patterned on the successful Radio Free Europe—should also be adopted. Though only a beginning, these kinds of instruments will be the key to advancing Western interests and values in the countries of the post-Communist world.

Undeveloped world

During the Cold War, the Third World was a principal battle-ground between the United States and the Soviet Union. The two sides clashed in Iran, Korea, Vietnam, Cambodia, Laos, Malaysia, the Philippines, the Congo, the Horn of Africa, Angola, Cuba, Nicaragua, El Salvador, Afghanistan, and other developing countries, as well as dueling in the more enduring Arab-Israeli and Indo-Pakistani conflicts. After the end of the Cold War, the West will have only peripheral security interests in much of the undeveloped world.

In 2022, U.S. geopolitical strategy for this zone will be generally characterized by limited engagement, both militarily and economically. The United States will avoid ideological crusades—such as trying to export democracy universally—because such messianic policies will neither prove feasible nor win broad domestic support. Americans will recognize that the United States cannot remake the world in its image. In addition, the United States will avoid the role of global policeman, involving ourselves in particular conflicts between undeveloped countries only if we have a clear economic or security interest at stake. Finally, the White House and Congress will provide economic assistance only to states that have adopted the lessons of free market, export-oriented development that characterized the economic miracles in Korea, Taiwan, Singapore, and other new industrial states.

Although we will on the whole keep the travails of the undeveloped world at arm's length, there will be three exceptions that require a more direct Western role.

The first is the security of the Persian Gulf. Oil will remain the lifeblood of industrial economies. The Gulf states will have the largest reserves and will be the cheapest producers of oil. Historically low oil prices will discourage development of alternative energies, particularly nuclear power. As a result, the Gulf states will be the "swing producers" in the global energy market, virtually monopolizing the capability to add production on the margin to meet growing demand. That, in turn, will mean that the West's industrial economies will develop a growing dependence on imports from the Persian Gulf, and that we cannot afford to have that region dominated by a hostile power. Although the United States imported only a small portion of its energy from the Persian Gulf in 1992, that share will steadily grow over the next thirty years.

In 2022, the United States will still be the only power capable of guaranteeing the security of the Persian Gulf against what will then be a principally Iranian threat. Japan, though playing a wider international role than today, will be a secondary military power. Europe, united economically, will not have integrated armed forces or significant power-projection capabilities. The main potential challenge to Western interests will come from Iran, both in terms of a conventional threat and of a subversive threat exploiting the dissatisfaction of Shi'a minorities in the Gulf states. The linchpin for the U.S. position will be Saudi Arabia, whose gradual evolution toward a more modernist Islamic society will enhance its political stability. The arena of competition in coming decades will be Iraq, where the West will seek to build up a post-Saddam regional counterweight to Iran while Tehran will seek to infiltrate and subvert the Shi'a regions in the south.

The second critical issue in the undeveloped world will be the danger that a rogue state will acquire nuclear weapons and long-range delivery capabilities. By 2022, there will probably be at least a half dozen more nuclear weapons states. Some—potentially including Iran—might not only be virulently anti-Western but might also be involved with supporting international terrorists, thereby posing a nuclear threat against which traditional deterrence strategies might not work. At the same time, intelligence projections foresee at least twenty states acquiring ballistic missile capabilities in coming decades, with some perhaps even achieving intercontinental ranges that would enable them to target the United States.

The third critical issue will be problems arising from the world's stateless zones. Lebanon in the 1980s—its terrorists, ethnic strife, guerrilla forces, and so forth—will typify the possible dangers. Despite their distance from the United States, the stateless territories will affect us through drug production and trafficking, with areas in Andean South America specializing in cocaine and others in Central Asia focusing on heroin. Moreover, this drug money will potentially support terrorist groups that find safe haven in these areas beyond the reach of the laws of civilized governments. The general instability in these regions could propel the number of the world's refugees—which totaled 24 million in 1992—even higher, creating a humanitarian crisis that will tend to draw in the United States and other Western countries.

These three issues pose a unique challenge to the United States and its Western allies. Indeed, the diversity of these security threats will require closer coordination than ever among political leaders and the intelligence services of the United States, the European Community countries, and Japan. It should be noted, however, that the United States will be the sole country in the world by 2022 with the military capability, force structure, and resources available to counter these emerging threats to Western interests.

While U.S. forces cannot be expected to handle the burden of Western security alone, there is little doubt that de facto leadership in the international community will continue to be placed squarely on the shoulders of the United States. On occasion, the mantle of international leadership will require Washington to send forces overseas to protect Western security interests during a crisis. The deployment of American troops would demonstrate the political resolve of the United States to counter legitimate threats to Western security. It would also serve as a catalyst for allied participation.

In light of these security considerations, the United States and the West will have to possess and maintain robust military forces by the year 2022, and to develop five new capabilities to defend Western interests:

• Rapid deployment force: In Operation Desert Storm, the United States and its coalition partners had six months to send and prepare forces for combat. Because we cannot count on having the luxury of time in the future, the United States must put priority on enhancing the air- and sea-lift capabilities of the Central Command.

• Space-based strategic defense: Because of the future danger that megalomaniacs such as Saddam Hussein will likely have intercontinental ballistic missiles armed with nuclear warheads, we must develop and deploy a space-based strategic defense system that will protect the United States and its allies from a limited attack by a secondary nuclear power.

• Technology export controls: In order to slow the proliferation of nuclear weapons and missile technology, the West must adopt a stringent technology control regime.

• Intelligence penetration capability: While the United States will still need a global intelligence capability, its methods will have to focus more on clandestine human collection than on technical collection. In the future, the United States will need to operate not in European but in Asian, African, and Latin American cultures, particularly if American policy makers hope to cope with the challenges presented by the unstable areas of the undeveloped world.

• Internal security assistance: In the past, our security aid has focused on conventional and counterinsurgency capabilities. In the future, more emphasis will be on helping train governments of countries on the periphery of stateless zones in intelligence and internal security.

During the next thirty years, all three zones—the developed world, post-Communist world, and undeveloped world—will present novel problems. In the Cold War, the West developed capabilities and strategies that ultimately defeated the Soviet threat. Today, the West faces the question of whether it has the creativity and determination to overcome the challenges of geopolitics in the twenty-first century.

To a large extent, the shape of the world of 2022 depends on what kind of geopolitical strategy the United States pursues before 2022. Its traditional strategy of preventing the domination of the Eurasian landmass by a hostile power should be the centerpiece. But the growing importance of other regions and the potential threats that could arise in them will force the United States to adopt a strategy of flexible, selective, and limited engagement around the world.

In thirty years, America will need such a strategy on two levels. The first will be its direct military security, which concerns alliances, foreign base rights, mutual defense cooperation, and other policies. The second will be its stake in seeing the broader political evolution of the world channeled in directions favorable to Western interests and values. The West might not be directly imperiled if conditions in various regions deteriorated into armed conflict or lawlessness, but it would certainly be better off if they did not.

The central geopolitical objective of the United States has always been to prevent the domination of the Eurasian landmass by a hostile power or coalition. Given its isolation between two oceans and the continental scope of its territory, the security of the United States can only be challenged if the massive human, economic, and natural resources of Eurasia were controlled by hostile forces. And it is astonishing to see how consistently U.S. strategy worked to prevent that outcome. In the nineteenth century, the limits of military technology and Britain's role as the balancer in the European balance-of-power system enabled the United States to opt out of the geopolitical struggle and to avoid the "entangling alliances" about which George Washington warned in his Farewell Address. In World War I, the United States intervened to prevent Germany, which had defeated Russia and had France and Britain on the ropes, from dominating Europe. In World War II, the United States sought to block the Axis powers from controlling Eurasia as a whole. In the Cold War, it formed alliances with, and deployed substantial military forces in, Europe and East Asia to keep Moscow from dominating by force or intimidation the industrial power not only of its European allies but also of our former enemies in Germany and Japan.

Avoiding the domination of Eurasia will remain the enduring geopolitical baseline of U.S. security. The task will be much easier and cheaper than during the Cold War, requiring far fewer forward-deployed forces and far lower levels of defense spending. With the former Soviet Union's 380,000 troops withdrawn from Central Europe, the cutting-edge issue will not be the defense of the Fulda Gap but rather will involve finding ways to insulate Central Europe—particularly Germany—from the effects of geopolitical instability in the former Soviet Union. This will require the West to invite the new democracies of Central Europe into NATO, thereby creating a buffer for Germany and preventing the need for Berlin to rearm to a level that would breed insecurity across the continent. In addition, it will require a flexible engagement in the former Soviet Union to create balances of power between a potentially resurgent Russia and the non-Russian republics, particularly Ukraine and Byelorus.

On the far eastern periphery of Eurasia, U.S. strategy will focus on acting as a broker between Russia, China, and Japan in order to keep their traditional national rivalries—which produced five wars in the twentieth century—from triggering military competition. National rivalries—such as those between the Greeks and the Turks, the Russians and the Ukrainians, the Chinese and the Japanese, and the Germans and the Russians—will reemerge in the post–Cold War world, in some cases in a much more virulent form. In East Asia, where the West has had vital political and economic interests at stake, the United States is the only country that has the power and credibility with all players to keep such rivalries in check. And the countries of the region—with the odd exceptions of North Korea and Vietnam—want the United States to play that role.

How large a military presence will this strategy require from the United States? It will need to maintain approximately half of the forces of our worldwide deployments during the Cold War, though reconfigured for the threats posed in the new era. Because the West has vital interests around the world, the United States cannot afford to withdraw from Eurasia militarily. And if the United States wants to be a geopolitical player—particularly in the Gulf region—it must maintain a military presence in Europe, Asia, and the Middle East.

Moreover, the international community should not underestimate how much the U.S. presence stabilizes these regions. If the United States were to break camp and withdraw into isolation, Germany and Japan would have to rearm and would almost certainly acquire nuclear weapons. Alarm bells would, in turn, sound in the capitals of their neighbors, leading to arms races and destabilizing international competition. While the United States cannot be the world's policeman—no state will have sufficient power to play that role—no one would want to live in a world without any policemen. In 2022, the central focus of U.S. geopolitical strategy should be to act as a bulwark of stability in those three regions—Western and Central Europe, East Asia, and the Persian Gulf—that affect Western vital interests.

Because the West will have lesser interests at stake in the rest of the world, its engagement there should be flexible, limited, and selective. The West will not seek to right every wrong that occurs and certainly will not automatically deploy military forces to do so. It will have some democratic allies—such as Israel—for whose survival and security it will spare no means. In general, however, the United States and the West will adopt a twenty-first-century version of the Nixon doctrine: a policy of providing friendly states with the training and arms that they need to defend themselves against their rivals, but without committing ourselves to a direct engagement. In the event that a regional hegemon hostile to Western interests begins to emerge, the West might adopt a more active policy of building up economic and military counterweights among its neighbors. But the era in which Western leaders proclaimed a willingness to "bear any burden" and "fight any foe" in the defense of freedom will be over.

Will the American people be willing to shoulder the cost of even this more limited geopolitical strategy? I believe that they will. As we enter the next century, the American people will come to understand how much their own well-being depends on what happens in the world at large. Trade will account for an ever-growing share of American GNP. The possible acquisition of nuclear weapons and intercontinental ballistic missiles by rogue states will refute arguments about security through isolation. The danger of the world's oil reserves falling under the control of a hostile power will require a formidable military establishment.

By the year 2022, the American people will come to understand as never before that the United States has essential international goals and that it can achieve these more easily with allies and friends than alone. America will not fall prey to the hubris of believing that it can right every wrong in the world. But it will understand that as a great power, the United States should address those wrongs that threaten important Western interests and that lie within the West's power to set right.

5

THE ECONOMY

by John Marks Templeton

I. THE PAST—PROBLEMS CREATE OPPORTUNITIES

This is an exciting time to be alive and to experience the vast changes now taking place—changes that will enhance the freedom and future prosperity of hundreds of millions of people. But, to try to foresee the future, we should first understand the past. So, let me recall a few of the changes that have occurred just in my lifetime.

When I was born, 1912, in Tennessee, the world was more prosperous than ever before, but there were no calculators, no computers, no transcontinental telephones, no holographic images, no talking pictures, no airlines, and no photocopiers. There was no genetic engineering, no nuclear energy, and no man-made satellite in space. Now we have entered a remarkable period of progress. Who back then could have even imagined the variety of new developments that would come in one lifetime? And who now can imagine the even greater new blessings that may be in store for our children?

It is true that new developments are often accompanied by problems—problems such as depressions, wars, bear markets, and inflation. My observation is that people focus too little on the opportunities that problems present. To concentrate on short-term difficulties obscures the big picture. There is an unfortunate aspect in human nature that makes us dwell on bad news, on catastrophes, on problems. If one looks carefully, one will see that we are living in a world that is blessed by the most remarkable achievements—ten blessings for every problem. And, recently, the pace at which the world's problems are being solved has escalated.

I have seen remarkable strides on the economic, social, political, cultural, and spiritual fronts. I see fewer problems today than there were in almost any one of the fifty-one years since I became an investment counsellor. Many of these problems have diminished because generous and enterprising people seized and acted on the opportunities that the problems presented.

We live in a time of spiraling progress. People are better educated, better fed, and better housed than at any time in the history of the world. One of the greatest secrets of progress is to understand this good fortune and be thankful—to understand our blessings and use them in accordance with God's purposes for His children.

A landmark for economic and political freedom was the publication in 1776 of Adam Smith's great work entitled *Inquiry into the Nature and Causes of the Wealth of Nations*. At the time Smith was writing, 85 percent of the population had to work in agriculture just to produce enough food. Now fewer than 4 percent of the people work on farms in North America, yet they produce great surpluses of goods—so great that economists now worry about food surpluses, not food shortages. Smith believed that the economic system was self-regulating—the less interference by government, the better. He argued that free competition was the basis for an efficient economy and the proper allocation of our scarce resources. Smith saw that problems would be conquered by the "invisible hand" of opportunity and development as long as the free market forces were allowed to operate unfettered. Recent developments that are reducing the pervasive role of government and increasing the spirit of free enterprise are moving the global society closer to Adam Smith's vision of how the world should properly function.

Not only is the standard of living increasing as never before, but the quality of life is increasing and its rate is accelerating. I have been fortunate to live during this era's explosion of knowledge, technology, and prosperity.

The conditions in the world today and throughout history show that many nations and their people remain impoverished because they neglect the principles of wealth accumulation—or because of the flight of capital into safer places. There are many examples of great poverty in otherwise rich lands, poverty arising because government alone owns almost all the wealth and neglects to stimulate entrepreneurship. I have observed that encouraging individuals to accumulate wealth brings both prosperity to nations and happiness to workers. That, I believe, is the major lesson in economics of the past.

II. THE PRESENT—WHERE HAVE WE BEEN?

The past decade has been one of the most dramatic in history, with the two main worries of the world—the imminent threat of global nuclear war and the related Cold War conflict between superpowers—all but disappearing. In addition, massive information and technological, educational, and spiritual advances have changed the world dramatically.

On the political side, the stage has indeed been set for the future. Over the past forty years, one of our most serious collective concerns was the possibility of nuclear war. Now, the erosion of communism and the end of the Cold War has greatly reduced the threat. It appears that the threat of eventual domination by communism has been broken. From 1919 on, the Communists devoted enormous resources in their effort to dominate the world. Until recently, some twenty-three nations were under their control—and no nation captured by communism had ever regained its freedom until 1989. Today, governments and individuals alike are coming to recognize that the forces of free enterprise are far superior in producing economic well-being.

In a period of just under twenty-four months, the course of world history was favorably altered. In 1989, the world witnessed the fall of the Berlin Wall and the overthrow of Communist governments in East Germany, Poland, Czechoslovakia, Hungary, Romania, and Bulgaria. And, in 1991, the Soviet Union collapsed. This second Russian Revolution—born in the ashes of a failed coup by hard-line Communist reactionaries—reversed seventy-four years of history. The feared KGB has been essentially dismantled, the Communist Party outlawed, and the gradual introduction of free elections and democratic governments is poised to inextricably impact the fabric and quality of life in Russia and its adjoining republics. With hope and prayer, the new countries of the former Soviet Union will peacefully transit to a market-based system with minimal social disruption.

The momentous events in Eastern Europe have permanently changed the nature of the world's economies and capital markets. The short term may in fact be quite painful in these countries, but the benefits will be real. In the former East Germany, for example, unemployment is expected to reach 25 percent of the labor force. The country's infrastructure is badly outmoded and considerable rebuilding is necessary. Roads are in truly poor shape; there are not enough telephones; more electric power is needed. The country will require massive injections of capital and technology. The people that see this as an opportunity rather than a problem are the ones who will lead the way. Those who remember the United States' generous Marshall Plan and the subsequent reconstruction of post–World War II Western Europe know that the reflowering of Eastern Europe is not only possible but very likely.

The Soviet people were blacked out for seventy years from concepts that are taken for granted in many countries. Very few at this stage understand competition, accounting, costs, markets, and marketing. It will take some time before these countries become prosperous. To a lesser extent, that's true in the former satellite countries, too. There are great problems to overcome. These newly liberated states are likely to pass from one crisis to another, but each crisis has in it the seeds of opportunity. A trainable and disciplined labor force will rebuild these countries; over the longer term, I expect a more rapid increase in world prosperity because of the developments in East Germany and other formerly Communist nations. The stabilization of the Eastern European economies will require the introduction and proliferation of corporations and markets, a new legal system, and rules designed to safeguard private property. Accompanying this will be a massive reduction of government intervention.

Following those developments, Western European, Japanese, and American companies will begin operating in Eastern Europe, and we will see a sustained increase in East European standards of living, as we have in the newly emerging countries in Asia. Indeed, an axiom of economics might proclaim "where free trade expands, accelerated growth follows."

Markets are the cornerstone of capitalism and prosperity. An efficient market functions to allocate capital and resources in an equitable manner for the best interests of society. Already a number of Eastern European countries have begun the development of primary and secondary capital markets, laying the foundation for an eventual transition to the free enterprise economic systems. The Budapest Stock Exchange was reopened forty-two years after it was closed under Communist rule. The exchange, which originally opened in 1864 and was a relatively flourishing trading place at the turn of the century, became redundant in 1948 when free enterprise was essentially abolished in Hungary. Governments in other Eastern bloc countries, such as Poland and Czechoslovakia, have also announced their intentions to establish central trading markets for the securities of newly privatized companies. The Moscow Commodities Exchange and the Moscow Banking Union (a consortium of new commercial banks) have signed a letter of intent to create a stock exchange. Markets are even developing in the People's Republic of China, which has announced plans to open what should be the first futures market in a Communist country. We have already seen special "B" shares for foreign investors introduced to the recently opened Shanghai Exchange.

I believe that our children and grandchildren will view the period 1989–91 as one of the great turning points in world history, a fulcrum toward greater freedom and prosperity and increased spirituality. Thanks to the events of those years, we are poised to enter a new historic era, an era that will offer substantial opportunities to investors. More generally, the benefits are not merely for investors—there are benefits in terms of greater freedom, greater commerce, more communications, more travel, and the spread of religion in previously atheistic nations.

One reason why I am so optimistic about the future is the steady improvement I have noticed on the business educational front. Young people are receiving more and better education than ever before. They are sharpening their management skills and developing new business tools. When I was born, there were only two graduate schools of business in the world. Today, there are over six hundred in North America and about eight hundred world-wide. The number of business graduates is steadily rising and MBA programs continue to grow at an accelerating rate. New and important disciplines such as business ethics and entrepreneurship are appearing more frequently in business school curriculums. That's a very encouraging sign. It means better management skills, which imply lower costs, higher quality, a greater quantity of goods, and a greater variety of goods and services. In the long run, this will translate into higher profits, higher share prices, and higher dividends, just as it has in the past.

The same degree of development is occurring on the business technology front. Since I became an investment counsellor in 1940, the number of people enjoying the benefits of share ownership has increased more than tenfold. The dollars invested in American mutual funds has increased a thousandfold in only fifty-five years. Part of this is caused by the explosion of information and technology, which has had truly profound effects on our investment world. Consider just a few recent technological developments.

As a result of remarkable advances in both computer hardware and software, trading problems associated with the human factor are disappearing as many of the world's stock exchanges see opportunities with the new electronic technology. Fully electronic market auctions are in place now on some exchanges, such as the Australian Associated Stock Exchange, in which all trading is conducted on the electronic SEATS (stock exchange automated trading) system. The Toronto Stock Exchange, the Paris Bourse, the Frankfurt Bourse, the Rio de Janeiro Exchange, and the Madrid Stock Exchange have introduced rules to require that all trading be subject to an electronic book, which provides instantaneous access to terminals. Buy and sell orders for all stocks are now shown on computer screens. Stockholm's 127-year-old trading floor was replaced in 1991 by the Stockholm Automated Exchange, which is linked with a satellite providing information from other Nordic exchanges. The computer age has struck the exchanges with a vengeance.

Traders can now buy and sell massive blocks of stocks—possibly to replicate a market index—in a single transaction. Electronic crossing networks have been introduced. These are trading systems in which institutional orders are matched electronically in cases where immediate and floor-based trading execution isn't necessary. Hand-held computers are used by traders on the floor of the Chicago Mercantile Exchange for entering orders. There is now a wide avenue of trading opportunities to pursue. Stock traders can trade on a stock exchange with a broker as agent; they can trade directly with a broker as a principal; they can trade in crossing or upstairs markets. And trades can be accomplished through shares, American Depositary Receipts, convertibles, warrants, or other derivative products.

We now have computerized exchanges, electronic crossing systems program trading, instantaneous information flows, linked stock markets, derivative products, and new and complex securities—all occurring against changing views of how markets should be priced. New theories and models are appearing in the economics and finance journals at a rapid pace. In 1990, three American researchers—Harry Markowitz, William Sharpe, and Merton Miller—shared the Nobel Prize for their achievements in advancing our knowledge of the investment and valuation process.

III. THE FUTURE—WHERE ARE WE GOING?

Will the trends of the past few years continue? How will future problems be dealt with? And finally, what is the future for investors? Turning to the last question first, let's examine some of the powerful trends that are already under way. First, let's consider the trends I anticipate in the future investment community.

Important events will include a steady improvement in the global standard of living, the persistence of inflation and, particularly in emerging nations, the continued movement toward global interdependence and global investing, reconstruction of markets and exchanges, and increased savings available to buy shares.

The past fifty years have been marked by dramatic worldwide economic growth. And the world is likely to see a rise in the standard of living over the next fifty years greater than in any previous half century. There are a number of underlying factors at work that suggest that the future will be even more prosperous than the past.

Just consider some of the following data. The number of people employed in America grew from 63 million in 1960 to over 115 million in 1990. In the next thirty years I am told to expect a further increase of about 60 percent in American jobs. The amount of scientific research being done all over the world is staggering. Over U.S. $2 billion each business day is now being allocated to scientific development and this, in turn, will lead to a higher quality of goods and services, bringing a higher standard of living. Today, for the first time in history, there is almost total peace on earth between nations. But prosperity often has a relentless companion: inflation.

Inflation has been one of the severe realities for sixty years and, unfortunately, it is likely to be the reality of the future. As long as governments continue to create liabilities, to borrow heavily, we will have inflation. The problem I see with national government debt is not deflation, but inflation. Given the nature of democratically elected political systems, world debtor countries—including the United States and the United Kingdom—will most likely continue their current profligate government spending behavior, and this will inevitably lead to more inflation. The irresponsible attitude toward spending at the government or macro level has filtered down, in my opinion, to the micro or personal level.

In North America, many people are no longer thrifty. People are not willing to save, to wait for the future. Likewise, governments show no willingness to exercise enough restraint. The U.S. debt is now so enormous that it will soon be greater than the aggregate debt of all other countries. Because I do not anticipate major shifts in these personal and government attitudes toward spending, I think that inflation will remain a serious economic phenomenon of our times and a key factor in the investment environment. During the next thirty years, government and personal spending may remain at recklessly high levels and we may expect inflation in North America to average about 6 percent per annum—a rate corresponding to a doubling in the cost of living about every twelve years. There will be some discouraging years when inflation could be as high as 10 to 15 percent, and some more favorable years when it will be down to 1 or 2 percent. I do not expect either individuals or governments to significantly alter their behavior; so, looking ahead to more than another generation, I doubt there will be even one year in which the cost of living drops (the last deflation year was 1949).

I believe that there is no currency on earth which will have higher buying power in ten years than it does now. I project that the currency of every nation is likely to be devalued in the next thirty years in relation to the cost of living. But some currencies will be stronger than others, especially for those nations that continue to value honesty, thrift, and diligence. Fluctuations in foreign exchange rates are likely to continue to be frequent and wide from year to year. My projections suggest that the U.S. currency may remain one of the world's strongest and is likely to appreciate against most currencies, except possibly the Japanese yen. The yen is projected to remain strong because of support by the savings ethic and spending discipline of the Japanese people.

With a dramatic increase in the cost of living on a global basis, this means clearly that investors cannot play safe by holding on to cash. Cash will continue to lose its purchasing power. Therefore, investors are advised to avoid cash and to put a good portion of their wealth into vehicles that protect against inflation. These include real assets and shares of good, solid businesses whose sales and earnings will rise as much as or more than the rate of future inflation. Numerous studies have shown that investing in shares in North America over the long term has always provided the highest total return—higher than bonds, higher than Treasury bills, and higher than the increase of the cost of living. The studies— carried out by such well-known statisticians as Roger Ibbotson and others—are consistent in their results. Common stocks, over the past fifty years, have earned higher rates of return than all other investment forms, and this will probably be the case in the future. In each decade from the 1920s to the 1980s common stocks have outperformed short-term instruments. This was even the case in those decades, such as the 1970s, that experienced two recessions.

Corresponding to the persistence of inflation, I foresee an unstoppable climb in the global standard of living. The most dramatic growth may occur in a number of the poor nations where the standard of living is doubling about every nine years. For example, in countries like China, Mexico, South Korea, Thailand, and Turkey, the standard of living is rising two to three times as fast as it is in the United States.

Peaks and valleys, bull and bear markets, are inevitable in a free market capitalist economic system. There have been nine business recessions since the end of World War II; yet in every recession year, the nominal U.S. gross national product has ended up higher at the end than at the start. Looking ahead, I fully expect that there will be occasional business slowdowns, possibly one every five to seven years or so, although I've never been able to find any person or organization who could correctly predict the turning points of either bear markets or business recessions. I do know that recessions normally last about twelve to eighteen months and are typically followed by renewed waves of economic prosperity that results in new record levels of economic activity. The effects of a business slowdown are painful in the short term, but recessions do create opportunities. They provide opportunities for healthy companies to capture greater market share and for investors to increase their stock holdings, sometimes at bargain prices. Furthermore, recessions do not always cause bear markets. Since 1946 there have been three bear markets without a corresponding recession and two recessions without a bear market. I cannot predict bear markets except that history suggests we may expect an average of two bear markets every ten years.

Forty years from now, I expect that our standard of living will have quadrupled while prices will have increased by a factor of 900 percent. As a result, nominal U.S. GNP may be forty times greater than it is now. If this is so, there may be proportionate increases in corporate sales, earnings, dividends, and share prices. Thus, when investors look forward, they should be able to see remarkable nominal and real returns—if their investments are diversified and they hold the shares of established well-managed companies.

The world continues to progress toward economic and political interdependence. The astute managers of the larger companies recognize this and have adjusted their long-term strategies accordingly. Recently, the development and expansion of international market and information links have come under close scrutiny.

Critics claim that—with instant telecommunication information flows, a large number of international investors, increased mobility of capital, interlisted stocks, and formal exchange and information link-ups—markets are likely to move together in a domino-type effect, such as that witnessed in October 1987. Because Japanese capital is a major fueling agent for world markets, these critics believe that a world market crash could well emanate from Japan. However, it didn't happen in 1990, when Japan suffered its own unique crash with share prices down 48 percent in only ten months, and I do not believe it is likely to happen in the future. Although the markets are interrelated, the events unique to each country or region will still dominate. Any plunge in overvalued Japanese land prices may have a tangential impact on European bourses or North American stock exchanges, but it is unlikely by itself to cause more than a temporary cycle in worldwide share and commodity prices.

Increasingly, investors continue to be attracted to the features of cross-border or global investing. I am watching the major banks, insurance companies, and investment firms globalize their activities. Those financial institutions with blinders that stubbornly maintain a high degree of domestic concentration will increasingly find that they are facing severe international competition. Business barriers began to crumble long before the collapse of the Iron Curtain. For example, less than twenty major foreign investments were expropriated in the 1980s as compared to over four hundred documented cases in the 1970s. There are still many impediments to international investing—disparate accounting principles employed in overseas countries, diverse government regulations, different methods of valuing stocks, to name a few. But we see the transition from domestic portfolio concentration to global investing as relentless. Already, we see a movement toward common settlement rules, elimination of physical settlement, and a focus toward reducing trading costs. The computer will eliminate most, though not all, of these frictions. A primarily paperless settlement system, where all trading is conducted through matched electronic transactions, will undoubtedly prevail. But there will still be many differences among countries' reporting practices and exchanges—and hence opportunities.

I have long believed in the virtues of global investing. This has been a guiding principle from my early days as a fund manager. Research shows that a globally diversified portfolio will in the long run yield higher returns at a lower level of volatility than a simple, diversified, single-nation portfolio. Given barriers to entry, difficulties in obtaining information, varied market trading systems and accounting methods, the easiest and most efficient way to hold a global portfolio is through mutual funds managed by investment counsellors with worldwide experience.

Recently, the globalization process has accelerated. Numerous markets have been liberalized and deregulated; global strategies have been developed. There is a trend toward allowing foreigners to invest—typically on a limited basis—in previously restricted markets, such as Mexico, Korea, India, and Brazil. Links between markets have been developed and commentators have started talking—if a bit prematurely—about the twenty-four-hour global marketplace.

Thirty or forty years from now I expect that securities markets will have entirely different complexions. It is possible that our current set of manual trading and semi-automated systems will be unable to compete effectively and will be replaced with a high-technology, high-efficiency, twenty-four-hour international market with a set of relatively uniform rules and regulations. Security analysts will evaluate a company's shares more on the basis of international standards than those of the country where it is domiciled or listed. Trading rules will evolve as well.

Because of the increasing shortage of American shares, common stocks may represent now more than ever the best potential for growth. In 1984, for almost the first time in any major nation, there was a significant shrinkage in the number of American shares available. In that year in the United States, the normal increase from new underwritings was overwhelmed by hundreds of corporations buying back their own shares and by corporate mergers and acquisitions to the extent of about $80 billion. Very large shrinkage occurred in 1985, 1986, 1987, and 1990, and even more in 1988 and 1989. About one fifth of all American shares were eliminated.

This increasing shortage of American shares may not create higher prices unless there is also a surplus of cash available to buy shares. But, in fact, there is now more cash available to buy stocks than ever before in history. Analysts estimate that less than one fifth of the assets of North American families are held in common stock, whereas in the past, families have often held as much as 50 percent in common stocks. Corporation and government pension funds are also rapidly growing—so much so that these pension funds alone already have assets almost as great as the total supply of all stocks in North America.

The increased appetite for quality investments in corporate and individual pension and tax-sheltered retirement plans suggests an unprecedented degree of buying power, arising at a time when the supply of American shares has been shrinking. That imbalance could create a shortage which could considerably bid up the price of stocks.

IV. THE FUTURE—INVESTMENT OPPORTUNITIES

What countries, markets, industries, and areas will benefit most from these new trends? Many businesses and investment managers continue to devote their efforts to the markets in North America, Western Europe, and Japan, which account for over 50 percent of the world's output, but less than 15 percent of its population. This, of course, overlooks many large and promising nations.

As a general principle, investors are wise to buy shares in industries that are temporarily out of favor. Popular industries should be viewed with caution because, where rapid growth is obvious, it is already reflected in high prices for the shares. Bargains are found in shares that are neglected or unpopular, and therefore low-priced.

One exciting area I see for the future is in the markets of emerging nations. These countries are defined by the World Bank as all nations with low and middle income per capita. The most dramatic growth may occur in certain of these lesser-developed nations where the standard of living is rising at a rate of about 8 percent per annum. In the aggregate, the stocks of emerging markets constitute less than 10 percent of the world's U.S. $10 trillion supply of shares. The smallest of the emerging nations, such as Nigeria, Zimbabwe, and Peru, are below U.S. $1 billion in capitalization, while the larger ones, such as Korea and Taiwan, are over U.S. $130 billion.

It is projected that by 1995, developing nations will account for only 28 percent of the world's GNP. Yet these countries will account for more than 80 percent of the world's population. This implies outstanding growth potential for the capital markets of the emerging countries. Research suggests that, over the next thirty years, the emerging market sector may well be one of the strongest performing segments in the world.

Indonesia, for example, is a sleeping giant—a country that wasn't really a marketplace at all until the late 1980s. The market of the world's fifth most populous country could well become one of the largest in Asia. India is the second-largest country in the world. The middle class of India alone is almost as large as the entire U.S. population, and is growing at a rate of almost 20 percent per year. The government has recently begun lowering its subsidies and loosening the regulations on its over-protected industries. Mexico's government has sold off, given away, or shut down two thirds of its state-owned industries over the past seven years. Only a handful of major industries, such as railroads and electricity, remain closed to foreign investors. Mexico now finds U.S., European, and Japanese multinational businesses rushing to invest. Not surprisingly, the Mexico Stock Exchange has been one of the top-performing equity markets over the past seven years.

Hong Kong is an interesting situation. Often, shares trade at bargain prices in the Hong Kong market because of the perception that the People's Republic of China will cause changes in 1997. But perhaps prices of stocks in that marketplace have already discounted the worst that may occur. There are several other important factors of which not all investors may be aware. The Sino-British Joint Declaration gives Hong Kong many rights up until the year 2047 or fifty years after this colony becomes part of China. Under the Declaration, Hong Kong can maintain its capitalist system until 2047. This includes electing a government, maintaining the legal system, and negotiating international accords on its own, including shipping and air transport agreements. Hong Kong will still have the right to employ civil servants and will have complete autonomy in economic, financial, and monetary areas. It is likely that Hong Kong will in fact perform a similar function for Mainland China to the one that New York does for the United States. Hong Kong has many important attributes that have not gone unnoticed in China and in the rest of the world. It is one of the world's leading financial centers, and in the recent past, about two thirds of direct investment made in China has come from Hong Kong. The real question may in fact turn out to be, Will Hong Kong take over China rather than China taking over Hong Kong? Not politically, but maybe commercially and financially.

The potential for China is also remarkable, although opportunities are yet off in the future. The 1 billion citizens certainly understand thrift—they actually save about one third of their income, in contrast to the 4 percent savings rate that has characterized U.S. citizens recently.

As discussed earlier, the liberated Eastern European countries offer interesting possibilities. Although the fall of communism and corresponding rebuilding programs are not without their problems, often the best bargain opportunities are found when circumstances look their worst. We include many of the countries of Eastern Europe, including the former East Germany, in our definition of emerging countries. The benefits of the Eastern European renaissance will not be immediately evident, but will probably be spread gradually over the next ten to fifteen years, spanning the birth of the twenty-first century. Reconstruction of the former Eastern bloc, coupled with the changes that will affect Europe and free trade in 1992 and upgrades to the infrastructures (as much as fifty years out of date), will create strong opportunities for companies in construction and manufacturing. Pollution problems are so significant that forward-looking companies concerned with the environment will also prosper. The education and vocational training of East Germans, coupled with the thrifty habits developed under thirty years of Communist rule, plus substantial blocks of inexpensive real estate, provide for some fascinating future opportunities—but these opportunities are for the patient, because it may take many years for the events to unfold properly. East Germany, Hungary, and Czechoslovakia in the aggregate have a greater GNP than China, as well as well-trained and low-paid workers. More importantly, their exports enjoy easy access to the world's biggest and richest market, the European Community. Many companies in the previous Soviet satellite countries represent attractive joint venture candidates for astute managers of Western companies. The opening up of Eastern Europe may have beneficial spill-over effects on Western Europe. It is possible that the rebuilding process could add as much as .75 percent and 1 percent GNP growth per annum to Western and Southern Europe, respectively. Increased trade throughout all parts of Europe and Eastern Asia will require better roads, bridges, telephone systems, and power plants.

Let me share with you an investment principle which will be useful in capitalizing on these opportunities. I believe that there is no investment selection method that is more lasting than the idea of buying "value"—buying shares available at the lowest price in relation to the true value of the corporation. I have developed yardsticks of value—and using them is not always simple to do. It takes a well-trained person to evaluate a corporation. And, even if one can do this, the information is not useful until thousands of other corporations have been studied. Only then can an investor know which share is most attractive related to its valuation. Evaluating thousands of companies in a search for undervalued companies is a difficult task. Therefore, the accumulated wisdom approach to value investing will continue to be one of the best methods one can use for selecting investments. Although there are short-term aberrations—such as the emphasis on takeover targets in the 1980s—value eventually rises to the top. In fact, it is those aberrations or anomalies that create bargains for the astute investor. And current research indicates that chances are better than ever that investment performance in the next thirty years may be even more favorable than the results of the past thirty years.

My best piece of advice for investors? Don't try to outguess the market. Investors who sold their shares or funds in the panic of the investment-point market drop of September and October 1987 missed one of the great buying periods in history when the market was setting all-time records within three years. Don't move in and out often. The longer you hold shares, the better. And don't follow the crowd. Buy whatever stocks are unpopular. Look for those that are most depressed in price.

My second piece of advice is not to use borrowed money. People should buy with their savings. If you don't borrow money, you can live through any kind of catastrophe or any market cycle. Your portfolio should be mainly in those things that give you inflation protection. Cash gives you no inflation protection, but well-selected common stocks and well-managed corporations are among the best. And they are available today at modest prices. The rewards will be there.

My third and most important rule is that of share diversification. You would be unwise to select the share markets of certain nations today and never consider future changes. Each year, the world's best investment opportunities are available in different nations. Rarely does one country's market remain at the top for more than a single year. Sometimes the market with the highest rate of return in the world one year suffers the largest losses in the next. Of course, it is not possible, in my opinion, to accurately predict which market will perform best. But if you hold a globally diversified portfolio of shares, you should avoid the danger of selecting the wrong countries by owning shares in well-managed companies in a variety of industries and nations.

V. THE FUTURE—FEWER PROBLEMS AND MORE PROGRESS

We live in a most exciting period. There has been more progress than ever before in virtually every field of endeavor. In my lifetime alone, real consumption per person worldwide—that is, the standard of living in real goods—has more than quadrupled.

The future is bright. Discovery and invention have not stopped or even slowed down. Who can imagine what will be discovered if research continues to accelerate? And each new discovery reveals new mysteries. The more we learn, the more we realize how ignorant we were in the past, and how much there is still to discover. The halting progress of past ages is over; the centuries of human enterprise are now bursting into flower.

So, as we look into the future, each of us should be overwhelmingly grateful for the multitudes of blessings which surround us—and for the prospect of even more wonderful blessings for our children and grandchildren. We should be overwhelmingly grateful to be living in the most glorious period of God's ongoing and accelerating creative process.

6

HEALTH AND MEDICINE

by Denton A. Cooley, M.D.

Dr Denton A. Cooley is surgeon-in-chief at the Texas Heart Institute, Houston, Texas. A pioneer in heart transplants, he implanted the first artificial heart in 1969. He has received numerous awards and other honors, and has written several books and more than 1,000 scientific articles.

As we near the end of the 1990s and prepare to enter not only a new century but also a new millennium, we sense the approach of a major boundary. It is hard to escape the fancy that, on January 1, 2000, we will wake up to a radically different world. Indeed, the term "twenty-first century" has a highly futuristic ring. What changes and challenges will the new century bring to us? Equally important, what attitudes and attainments will we take to it?

No field of human endeavor holds greater promise than medicine. Before attempting to characterize the next few decades in health care, let us gain a sense of perspective by examining the evolution of my own specialty, cardiac surgery, during the past forty years. We will then briefly evaluate the current medical scene.

THE EVOLUTION OF CARDIAC SURGERY

In the first half of the twentieth century, direct cardiac operations were undertaken only as desperate attempts to treat perforating injuries. During World War II, however, battle wounds provided a major stimulus to the development of modern cardiac surgery. Since that time, no specialty has witnessed greater miracles. With the advent of the heart-lung machine in 1953, surgeons were finally able to stop the heart, open it, and repair intricate congenital defects. At the same time, new diagnostic breakthroughs enhanced physicians' ability to detect specific diseases. By the mid-1950s, those of us involved in cardiac surgery found ourselves in the role of pioneers. It was as if we had suddenly found the key to a previously inaccessible realm: progress abruptly accelerated and infinite possibilities beckoned. No sooner did acquired valvular heart disease become amenable to surgical correction than the introduction of cardiac pacemakers brought rhythm disturbances under control. About the same time, surgeons began to bypass atherosclerotic blockages in the coronary arteries.

The culmination of these endeavors was reached when Dr. Christiaan Barnard, in Cape Town, South Africa, performed the first human heart transplant on December 3, 1967. Shortly thereafter, I and my colleagues at the Texas Heart Institute implanted the first artificial heart in a human being. Despite initial enthusiasm, neither of these advances began to fulfill their promise until more than a decade later. Meanwhile, the introduction of balloon angioplasty in the late 1970s provided a non-surgical means of treating arterial blockages and heralded a new, minimally invasive approach to surgery in general. By the mid-1980s, new methods of treating tissue rejection had allowed cardiac transplantation to become a widely accepted option for patients with end-stage heart disease.

THE PRESENT HEALTH CARE SCENE

For the past fifteen or twenty years, the American health care system has been undergoing a major transition. Probably the greatest change has involved the transfer of power and authority from physicians to patients and third parties. Until the 1970s, there were few restraints on health care decision making and spending; doctors' dictates and motives went unquestioned, either by patients or supervisory agencies. Not only did physicians enjoy virtual autonomy within their own practices, but they also tended to be glorified by the public at large. This attitude was reinforced during the late 1960s by the advent of "high-tech" procedures such as heart transplantation and devices such as the artificial heart. Many persons believed that it would be only a matter of time before medical science conquered mankind's major diseases.

As we entered the 1970s, however, this optimistic attitude waned. The failure of heart transplantation to fulfill its initial promise symbolized a more general, widespread disillusionment. In the face of nationwide economic difficulties, physicians began to be held increasingly accountable to insurers, regulators, lawyers, consultants, and risk managers. Moreover, public confidence was eroded by a growing number of medical mishaps and malpractice suits. Physicians began to see their long-cherished autonomy, income, and status fading away.

Today's health care scene is characterized by aggressive intervention and an aversion to the concept of natural death. Heavy usage of diagnostic tests is promoted by a fear of litigation, as well as an emphasis on high-tech methods in current training programs. At the same time, health care has become a consumer issue. Numerous medical decisions are now in the hands of third parties. In an attempt to control expenditures, government and private insurance companies decide in advance how much certain treatments should cost and refuse to pay more than the specified amount.

To survive in an increasingly competitive environment already oversupplied with physicians, many solo practitioners have been forced to join new health delivery systems such as independent practice associations (IPAs), health maintenance organizations (HMOs), and preferred provider organizations (PPOs), all of which operate according to the concept of prepaid group practice (i.e., the patient pays the organization a flat annual fee in exchange for care by one of its member doctors). Under this arrangement, doctors become employees of the organization and must account to it for their decisions. Physician services are being increasingly controlled by the business community, and many of America's largest hospitals have come under corporate ownership.

One of the most serious criticisms leveled against modern medicine is its alleged lack of humanism, that is, its emphasis on treating diseases rather than human beings. Indeed, this attitude is fostered by many factors, including the overwhelming predominance of science in the medical school curriculum, the fragmentation of medicine into numerous specialties, the "coldness" of high technology, the threat of malpractice litigation, and the business ethic that pervades the health care industry. Traditionally, physicians have been taught to be formal, detached, and somewhat aloof, not visibly displaying any emotion. When carried to the extreme, this attitude can cause doctors to resemble skilled mechanics rather than compassionate healers. In a recent address to the American College of Surgeons, the president of that prestigious organization acknowledged that much of medicine's current dilemma is due not to a lack of science but to "a perceived lack of humanism." He further stated that "more science, per se, will not solve the problem."[1]

Despite these forces of change, including the erosion of doctor-patient relationships, American patients have high expectations of medical treatment. They no longer want to be patronized, depersonalized, or kept in the dark. They are better informed about health issues than ever before and want to assume an active role in their own treatment. Medical solutions are being applied to a constantly expanding range of conditions such as baldness, obesity, and sagging chinlines, which were previously considered a normal part of being human. This "medicalization" of society tends to heighten our distress at these conditions, as well as our expectation of what medicine can do to relieve them. As Dr. Arthur J. Barsky states in his book *Worried Sick,* "We have redefined the notion of 'patient' to include not just the sick person, but the potentially sick person as well."[2] Indeed, it seems that almost every aspect of our daily lives—from our choice of breakfast cereal to our use of common electrical appliances—is fraught with medical implications. The following ten predictions explore some of these issues further.

TEN PREDICTIONS FOR THE EARLY TWENTY-FIRST CENTURY

In a world as complex as ours, not even the most accomplished seer can predict the future with absolute assurance. Moreover, a major war or natural catastrophe could impose an entirely un-foreseen pattern upon our lives. As a result of the collapse of Soviet communism, however, and the promise of a Mideast peace, we can hope that the prospects for war have receded. Unfortunately, the threat of nuclear weapons has not yet been eliminated.

On the basis of recent progress and current trends in health care, I have formulated ten predictions for the twenty-first century. Although my expertise is in cardiovascular surgery, I have tried to include a broad range of health care topics, including some that are highly controversial. Let me make it clear that by forecasting a specific trend, I do not necessarily wish to imply that I advocate that trend or agree with the philosophy behind it.

(1) *Health care facilities will be strained by a vast increase in the number of elderly patients.*

Of the ten predictions included here, this one is probably the most certain. Because of a constantly increasing life expectancy, Americans are now older longer. In 1900, only 4 percent of our ancestors were age sixty-five or older; since that time, the percentage of elderly persons has almost tripled. Because medical care can more easily delay dying than it can postpone the ravages of aging, the proportion of our days spent in ill health has increased. Some chronic diseases such as senile dementia have actually become more prevalent. Moreover, as the average lifespan continues to be lengthened, old age is perceived as beginning earlier.

The 78 million Americans who comprise the postwar "baby-boom" generation have been alluded to as a human tidal wave. Indeed, they comprise fully a third of our country's present population. For the past forty-five years, this group has had a major impact on our culture. By the year 2000, its oldest members will be halfway through their fifth decade. By 2030, our country will have almost twice as many senior citizens as it has today. Because women have always had a longer life expectancy than men, about 70 percent of this multitude will consist of elderly women. In describing the imminent aging of the population, *Newsweek* magazine has stated that "perhaps no other change in the 21st century will have a more profound effect on how American society looks, feels, thinks and behaves."[3] The real squeeze will begin in about twenty years, when the vast tide of new retirees begins to draw Social Security benefits. From that time on, the segment of the population in the prime of life (i.e., the taxpayers) will increasingly dwindle until, by 2030, there will be only 100 middle-aged persons for every 250 senior citizens.

Unfortunately, we cannot be sure that government-funded programs such as Social Security, Medicare, and Medicaid will still be in existence, much less be adequate to meet the challenge. Even now, many government and private programs either refuse to cover extended care or cover it only after the patient's own resources have been depleted. Even if this policy were changed, however, today's nursing homes are not equipped to handle the quadrupling of the eighty-five-and-older population that is expected within the next forty years.

In light of these considerations, our increased life expectancy may prove a mixed blessing. Although the expected "graying" of the population poses immense difficulties for health care planners, perhaps we can hope that the presence of so many senior citizens, most of them women, will have a gentling effect on our culture.

(2) *Restructuring of America's health care financing system may leave us with an arrangement similar to that currently seen in Canada or the United Kingdom.*

Health care financing is one of the most difficult immediate challenges faced by our society. Developments in this field are hard to predict because they are so dependent on political variables. The difficulty is not so much a scarcity of resources as a lack of workable methods for underwriting and delivering them.

In 1989, health care accounted for 11.1 percent of our gross national product, or about 12¢ out of every dollar. This unprecedented expenditure reflects not only the effects of inflation and an aging population but also an expanded use of medical services, particularly sophisticated diagnostic and surgical techniques. It also reflects the omnipresent threat of litigation. According to some critics, as much as 25 percent of this expenditure is wasted because it either does not buy needed care or does not provide a better quality of care.

Although these figures confirm that health care is the most highly valued of human services, access to such care is shockingly uneven. About half of all medical services are received by 5 percent of the population, and 35 million uninsured Americans are barred from any health care at all. Many of these unfortunate individuals lost their medical coverage because they lost their jobs; others are either self-employed or the victims of a growing cutback in employee health benefits. (Indeed, if the present rate of inflation continues, employers may soon be unable to provide health coverage.) Children account for a large number of the uninsured. Ironically, South Africa is the only other Western industrialized nation that does not provide national health insurance for its citizens. Taking the current inequities into account, debates about possible health care rationing are beside the point. Medical services are already being rationed, whether we use that term or not.

Currently, the cost of health care is rising at more than twice the rate of inflation. According to Richard D. Lamm, former governor of Colorado, "The miracles of medicine have outpaced the ability of even wealthy societies to pay for them."[4] Many Americans would agree with Lamm's contention that our country already spends too much on health care and that reformers should concentrate on diverting funds away from the system's many excesses in order to cover its desperate inadequacies.

Because of the twin dilemmas posed by uncontrolled inflation and the plight of the uninsured, the need for health care reform has galvanized public attention to such an extent that the issue loomed over the 1992 presidential campaign. Many Americans are uncomfortable with the idea of national health insurance. We are equally uncomfortable, however, with the idea that patients should be denied necessary treatment because of financial considerations. There is no simple solution. In a world of perpetual trade-offs, we must acknowledge the economic impossibility of making every available beneficial treatment equally accessible to everyone.

Although the need for a governmental response to the health care dilemma is obvious, it is not yet clear what form that response will take. We may well end up with a system like the current Canadian or British one. Under such a system, every American would be entitled to a basic level of government-funded medical care; more elaborate or specialized treatments would be financed by the patient or a private insurer.

In addition to restructuring our health care financing system, we must reexamine our national priorities. In 1990, the following special projects were funded by the National Science Foundation and the National Institute of Mental Health: $2,500 to study the cause of rudeness, cheating, and lying on tennis courts; $46,000 to investigate how long it takes to cook eggs; and $500,000 to build a facsimile of the Great Pyramid of Cheops. Because there is such a desperate need for funding on the part of other mental health programs, such as those involving Alzheimer's disease, it is hard to comprehend how our priorities can have become so schizophrenic.

(3) *As minimally invasive outpatient procedures continue to gain ground, traditional surgery will be deemphasized.*

Within the past few years, we have witnessed one of the most astounding revolutions in surgical history: the widespread use of minimally invasive techniques that eliminate the need for major operative incisions. These techniques involve the practice of endoscopy—insertion of a thin tube into the patient's body, through a natural opening or a small puncture-type incision, so that the internal organs can be inspected and treated. (When used for abdominal procedures, such tubes are called laparoscopes.)

Although already familiar to gynecologists, this "keyhole" approach was not used for other purposes until 1987, when Philippe Mouret, of Lyons, France, removed a patient's diseased gallbladder during laparoscopic gynecologic surgery. As the idea caught on, conservative practitioners were shocked and scornful, but the results soon proved so satisfactory that a tidal wave of enthusiasm was unleashed. By 1990, laparoscopic cholecystectomy was the leading topic at the prestigious annual clinical congress of the American College of Surgeons.

The excitement is readily understood when one realizes that, with many traditional operations—especially those involving the abdominal organs—the necessity for a major incision generally causes more trauma than does treatment or removal of the diseased organ. For example, after undergoing a traditional cholecystectomy, patients are usually disabled for about six weeks. In contrast, laparoscopic gallbladder removal is an outpatient procedure, involving minimal pain and recuperation. Once general anesthesia has been induced, the surgeon inserts the laparoscope through a half-inch umbilical incision; two other punctures are necessary for the introduction of additional instruments. The operative field is magnified and projected onto a television monitor, so that the surgeon can see better. After the gallbladder has been dissected away from the liver bed, the organ is deflated and removed through the laparoscope. The entire procedure takes about thirty minutes. Most patients remain hospitalized overnight, but some return home the same day. Pain and scarring are minimal, and normal activity can be resumed within five days.

By early 1991, laparoscopy was being used for a wide range of other procedures, including appendectomy, selective vagotomy, bowel resection, treatment of perforated ulcers, and hernia repair. The abolition of a major incision is expected to help reduce wound infections, as well as the risk of adhesions and incisional hernias. The laparoscopic approach is particularly useful in obese patients, since it keeps the surgeon from having to slice through dense layers of fat. Furthermore, because the operation is performed within a closed physiologic environment, it greatly decreases the surgical team's risk of exposure to the patient's blood.

The laparoscopic revolution is undeniably the wave of the future. Rarely has medicine seen such a beneficial advance gain ground so rapidly. In fact, one can safely predict that the advent of minimal-access procedures spells the demise of classic surgery as we have known it. Although traditional "open" techniques will never be totally abandoned, we can expect that within the next decade they will cease to dominate surgical practice.

(4) *Hospitals will be used only for the acutely ill or for those whose conditions are otherwise unstable.*

Because of advances in outpatient treatment options, including minimally invasive surgical techniques, many patients are already able to avoid hospital admission. Within the next few decades, the hospital population can be expected to dwindle to about half its current size, despite the increased numbers of elderly. At the same time, the typical hospital patient will be sicker than before, because less seriously ill patients will be treated faster and cheaper outside the hospital setting.

Already, American hospitals are in severe financial straits, their potential clientele being lured away by outpatient surgery centers, minor emergency clinics, home health care agencies, and hospices for the dying. In many instances, these alternative facilities can provide treatment for less than half of what a hospital would charge. As a result of diminishing usage, more than half of America's hospitals failed to cover their expenses in 1989. Hardest hit are the nation's public and non-profit institutions, which treat most of the uninsured. Although federal and state governments are responsible for half of the hospital industry's income, government payments increased by only 13 percent from 1983 to 1989, whereas hospital costs rose by 28 percent during that same period.

With the rise of for-profit hospital chains—dominated by Hospital Corporation of America, Humana, American Medical International, and National Medical Enterprises—non-profit and even public hospitals were drawn into competition and forced to become "economic entities." In an attempt to win over consumers, hospitals began to diversify their services and to rely heavily on advertising and marketing. Nevertheless, the American Hospital Association has estimated that, by the mid-1990s, at least a thousand hospitals will be shut down or converted into psychiatric, drug-abuse, or other specialty centers. Small community institutions will be the first to go. At many of these facilities, Medicare patients currently account for the bulk of admissions. As of January 1, 1992, the Health Care Financing Administration implemented new rules for paying Medicare claims, based on the resource-based relative value system (RBRVS). According to the new rules, each medical service is assigned a relative weight composed of three geographically adjusted values for work, practice costs, and malpractice premiums. These weights are multiplied by a monetary conversion factor to turn them into Medicare dollars and to determine the RBRVS payment rate. The new rates will decrease the Medicare reimbursement for many services. Thus, as the federal resource-based relative value system comes into play this year, many hospitals that are dependent on Medicare payments will be forced either to close altogether or to stop performing sophisticated procedures. Such procedures will be reserved for specialized medical centers, which, in turn, will relegate more routine operations (appendectomies, etc.) to the smaller hospitals. Although this arrangement may further the demise of struggling institutions, it should prove advantageous in the long run by eliminating the duplication of expensive facilities and by channeling the sickest patients into the most experienced centers.

Experts predict that tomorrow's hospitals will be defined not by their number of beds but by the kinds of services they offer, the most important of these being diagnosis, outpatient surgery, birthing facilities, and outpatient rehabilitation.

(5) *Emphasis will move away from heroic, technology-intensive intervention toward public health measures that can prevent disease in a large population.*

Until now, medical science has been almost exclusively treatment-oriented. Past a certain point, however, personal medical care has little effect on overall mortality. After being subjected to the life-saving application of ultra-sophisticated techniques, many patients soon die anyway, of other complications or illnesses. Critics of modern medicine have their doubts about the wisdom of using extraordinary measures to prolong life indefinitely, particularly in patients who have no further hope of enjoying a meaningful existence. Many experts believe that the funds devoted to these efforts would be better used to provide basic health care for a broader segment of the population. According to Dr. Christiaan Barnard, the first surgeon to perform a human heart transplant, "Where once we sought to improve the quality of living for all, much effort is now spent on increasing the quantity of life for a few."[5]

The dilemma is a difficult one, because it seems to demand that human life be assessed in terms of monetary value. If the cost of performing a liver transplant in a small child equals the annual cost of running an inner-city clinic involving thirty thousand office visits per year, who is to say which expenditure is better justified? As a pioneer of heart transplantation and artificial heart implantation, two sophisticated, expensive techniques that have only recently begun to fulfill their early promise, I cannot agree with critics who denounce high-tech medicine per se. We must continue to search for cures to the diseases that afflict us and for methods to bring quality to the lives of those who cannot be cured. I do agree, however, that in order to have more equitable health care, we—as a society—may be forced to modify our idea of what constitutes "necessary treatment," particularly in the face of impending "natural" death.

Most experts agree that, in reducing overall mortality, prevention is not only the simplest, most effective, and least expensive approach but also the one that benefits the largest number of persons. Nevertheless, Senator Daniel Inouye (D-Hawaii) estimates that, in 1990, the United States spent less than 50¢ per capita on preventive medicine versus about $1,440 per capita on curative and palliative care. What seems ironic is that so little emphasis is placed on education and prevention when today's most common causes of death (cancer, cardiovascular disease, substance abuse, automobile accidents, homicide, and suicide) may be directly related to destructive behaviors and lifestyles. Moreover, attacking poverty and malnutrition would do more to lower the mortality rate than the most sophisticated medical treatment. Indeed, many of the breakthroughs that have had the greatest effect on public well-being did not originate from the medical field. Such advances include modern sanitation and plumbing, as well as improved nutrition and public housing. As Dr. Dennis Burkitt recently stated in a major surgical journal: "If people are falling over the edge of a cliff and sustaining injuries, the problem could be dealt with by stationing ambulances at the bottom or erecting a fence at the top. Unfortunately, we put far too much effort into the provision of ambulances and far too little into the simple approach of erecting fences."[6] As soaring medical expenses continue to threaten us with bankruptcy, we can expect to see a trend toward cost-efficient public health measures based on prevention rather than heroic intervention.

(6) *A permanent artificial heart will become available.*

The foregoing prediction notwithstanding, one high-tech dream that promises to come true within the next few decades is the development of an artificial heart that can permanently replace the disabled natural heart. Although permanent cardiac replacement is already possible through transplantation, the number of patients who could benefit from a new heart far exceeds the number of available donor organs, approximately two thousand per year.

Research involving mechanical cardiac systems has centered on two main goals: (1) development of ventricular assist devices that can keep patients alive until their own hearts recover or transplantation can be performed; and (2) creation of a total artificial heart that can be used for either temporary assistance or permanent cardiac replacement. The Committee to Evaluate the Artificial Heart Program estimates that in the year 2010, 70,000 Americans could be candidates for mechanical support of the heart.[7] Between 10,000 and 20,000 of these Americans will need an artificial heart. During its twenty-nine-year history, the Texas Heart Institute has been closely involved with both ventricular assist devices and artificial hearts.

In early 1969, the enthusiasm for heart transplants provided the incentive for me and my associate Dr. Domingo Liotta to perform the first clinical implantation of an artificial heart. The mechanical organ, which resembled the human heart in size and configuration, had been tested in various calf experiments. The artificial heart kept a forty-seven-year-old man alive for sixty-four hours, until cardiac transplantation could be performed. Unfortunately, he succumbed to pneumonia thirty-two hours later. The artificial heart had performed well, though, and the experience proved that such a pump could serve as a bridge to transplantation, thereby allowing two-staged replacement of the human heart. Although critics claimed that the device had been used prematurely, there was much less public outcry than at the time of the first human heart transplant.

The next implantation of a total artificial heart did not occur until July 1981, when our Texas Heart Institute team made a desperate bid to save a thirty-six-year-old man who had suffered heart failure after undergoing coronary artery surgery. Once implanted, the artificial organ sustained the patient's circulation for thirty-nine hours before a donor heart was obtained and transplantation performed. The patient survived for seven and a half days, but then died of infection and multiple organ failure.

In December 1982, the total artificial heart gained renewed publicity when William DeVries and associates implanted a Jarvik-7 heart into Dr. Barney Clark at the University of Utah. The device, which was intended to be a permanent replacement,

supported Dr. Clark for 112 days before he died of other complications. Between late 1984 and early 1985, DeVries performed
three additional Jarvik-7 implants at the Humana Hospital in Lou-
isville, Kentucky. One patient, William Schroeder, became a medical celebrity by surviving for a record-breaking 620 days; the
other two patients survived for 10 and 488 days, respectively. In
April 1985, a fifth Jarvik-7 heart was implanted by a surgical team
in Stockholm, but the patient lived for only 229 days afterward.
Since that time, surgeons have made no further attempts to im-
plant an artificial heart on a permanent basis. As of 1989, however, artificial hearts had been used as bridges to transplantation
in some seventy instances worldwide.

Before permanent implantation is again justified, the total artificial heart must undergo several important modifications. Despite its life-saving promise, the device can cause potentially lethal
complications such as hemorrhage, thromboembolism, infection,
and stroke. Moreover, the ideal energy source has not yet been
defined. Having abandoned experiments with nuclear-fueled systems, investigators are now concentrating on other options, such
as heat, biologic systems, and electrical power. Although these
problems will take some time to overcome, we can expect to see a
permanent, totally implantable artificial heart become available
within the relatively near future.

At the Texas Heart Institute, we have recently implanted the
first battery-driven ventricular assist device, the Thermocardio-
systems HeartMate. Because it is powered by a small battery pack,
the HeartMate is the first device that will allow patients whose
hearts need permanent assistance to return to normal lives. Currently, the HeartMate has been approved by the Food and Drug
Administration only as a bridge to transplantation. Based on its
early success, however, the device should soon be made available
to patients who need long-term cardiac assistance.

(7) *AIDS will become a treatable, if not a preventable, disease.*

In November 1991, Americans were stunned when basketball
superstar Magic Johnson announced that he had tested positive
for the human immunodeficiency virus (HIV), the agent responsible for AIDS. According to health officials, it would be hard to
find a better spokesman for promoting AIDS awareness. As a

nationally admired athletic hero, a non-drug user, and a "nice guy" who recently married his high school sweetheart, Johnson transcends most of the public's stereotypes about AIDS victims. In becoming a spokesman for AIDS awareness, he is uniquely qualified to influence young people—particularly blacks and Hispanics, who are twice as vulnerable to the disease as other races but are hardest for health educators to reach. Now that Johnson has proved that no one is immune, AIDS activists hope to see increased private donations to AIDS research, as well as increased public pressure on government agencies.

The AIDS epidemic presents one of the greatest medical and humanitarian challenges known to us. In November 1991, the World Health Organization estimated that 8 to 10 million adults worldwide carry the human immunodeficiency virus. As many as five thousand new cases are contracted each day; in 75 percent of these cases, the disease is transmitted through heterosexual sex. This means of transmission is the most common one in Third World countries, which are among the hardest hit by the disease. Although homosexual men and intravenous drug users are still the primary victims in Western countries, heterosexual transmission is also on the rise in the United States and Europe. Already, the incidence of heterosexually transmitted AIDS in the United States is twelve times higher than it was five years ago. Experts predict that, by the year 2000, this form of transmission will predominate everywhere.

No longer only a medical problem, AIDS reflects many of the world's major ills: ignorance, poverty, prejudice, drug abuse, sexual promiscuity, and poor public health. The populations at greatest risk tend to be those with the least access to medical care. In the United States, about 40 percent of AIDS victims end up on Medicaid; many receive no care until they are totally disabled. In our country alone, AIDS research and treatment has accounted for $1.6 billion in federal subsidies during the past nine years.

While investigators continue the search for a means of halting the virus, treatment is being aimed at the opportunistic infections and cancers that are usually responsible for AIDS-related deaths. Scientists are also testing drugs that could bolster patients' immune systems. Some experts believe that a preventive vaccine may become available within the next decade. Unfortunately, however, the virus is not an isolated, well-identifiable target; it comprises dozens of different strains, not all of which would be susceptible to a particular vaccine. It seems safer to predict that, within the next decade, AIDS will be turned into a long-term, treatable condition like hypertension or diabetes. In mid-1990, U.S. scientists alone were working on twenty-one different drugs designed to interfere with HIV's reproduction cycle. Such drugs would prevent the more debilitating stages of the disease and allow victims to function normally, under life-long medical supervision.

(8) *Genetic engineering techniques will lead to cures at the molecular level.*

The advent of DNA recombinant technology provides a means of treating disease at the molecular level, either by removing harmful genes or by introducing therapeutic ones. So far, geneticists have identified more than 440 human illnesses associated with single-gene defects. Before the end of this century, we can expect to see gene therapy being used to repair some of these defects.

Genetic engineering may prove useful in the quest for an AIDS vaccine. Moreover, spin-offs from AIDS research should provide new insights into many common viral disorders. A long-time enemy of mankind, viruses are extremely simple entities, consisting of a core of genetic material (a DNA or RNA molecule), surrounded by one or two protein coats. Their only means of replication is to appropriate the genetic material of their host cells. In this manner, they produce many familiar diseases, including herpes, influenza, the common cold, and about 25 percent of human cancers. Viruses have even been implicated in rheumatoid arthritis and insulin-dependent diabetes. There is growing evidence that all viral diseases involve some type of immune deficiency. In the near future, physicians should be able to control many of these disorders by means of recombinant DNA technology. According to Lewis Thomas, author of *The Medusa and the Snail*, this technology is the twentieth century's single most profound breakthrough in biological science.

Already, genetic engineering is allowing laboratory workers to produce, in quantity, natural proteins such as human insulin, growth hormone, and interferon, which have important therapeutic value but are not produced in large amounts within the human body.

In a related field called molecular epidemiology, researchers are using genes and biologic markers to determine why certain individuals are vulnerable to cancer and heart disease. In the battle against lung cancer, scientists have long wondered why some smokers get the disease and others do not. Recently, investigators have identified an enzyme that is responsible for converting the chemicals in cigarette smoke into deadly carcinogens. This enzyme is borne by a gene that is present in approximately 10 percent of Caucasians—about the percentage of smokers who get lung cancer. By screening smokers for the gene in question, physicians should be able to tell which individuals are at greatest risk for lung cancer; they should then be able to prevent the disease before it develops. On another front, scientists have identified a gene defect that renders about 25 percent of the population vulnerable to a premature heart attack. By means of a simple blood test, soon these persons could be identified and treated before their heart disease has a chance to develop.

Within the next few decades, DNA recombinant techniques will no doubt prove invaluable in helping to control cancer and heart disease, the two greatest killers of mankind.

(9) *Physicians may be forced to broaden their concept of what constitutes appropriate therapy.*

In a reaction against the perceived dehumanization of so-called hard medicine, with its emphasis on drugs and surgery, an increasing number of Americans are turning to a wide range of alternative therapies. Many of these remedies are based on ancient Asian healing traditions that view the body as the outward manifestation of the mind. Most susceptible to unorthodox approaches are patients whose conditions are least amenable to conventional treatment—those with chronic pain and so-called incurable diseases. Alternative medicine is now a $27 billion-a-year industry that represents an entire subculture, the chief adherents of which tend to be middle-aged members of the baby-boom generation. A few therapies such as acupuncture and biofeedback have become respected enough to be covered by many insurance companies. Other techniques such as guided imagery for pain relief have been accepted by a few traditional practitioners. However bizarre some alternative therapies appear, almost all of them emphasize treating the patient as a whole person—body, mind, and soul. This approach contrasts dramatically with the orthodox viewpoint, which sees the mind and body as completely separate entities.

Critics of orthodox medicine charge that, in light of the conceptual revolution effected by modern physics, the strict biomedical approach, with its reductionistic and dualist logic, is anachronistic. In continuing to view the human body essentially as a machine, which is the physician's task to repair, practitioners have failed to transcend the seventeenth-century presuppositions upon which modern medicine was founded. By relying almost exclusively on a physical approach to disease, critics claim, orthodox medicine has achieved brilliant technologic successes but has remained otherwise tragically shortsighted.

During the past ten years, adherents of "mind-body" medicine have gained increasing credibility because of new evidence that the brain and the immune system are linked via direct neurologic pathways. Investigators have concluded that the two entities affect each other by means of a complex "feedback loop." This type of research has created a new discipline called psychoneuroimmunology (PNI), which may eventually influence our view of physiology. Some devotees of PNI even claim that the mind-body movement represents a "third revolution" in Western medicine, equivalent to the advent of surgery and the discovery of penicillin. They predict that physicians may eventually be able to program the immune system to prevent illness and repair wounded tissue.

So far, the medical establishment remains skeptical of mind-body medicine. Nevertheless, future practitioners may be forced to broaden their concept of what constitutes appropriate treatment, and to become more open to methods that enlist a patient's mental and emotional forces against illness.

(10) *Health will be increasingly viewed as a state of balance, not merely as a function of physical well-being.*

The all-pervading belief that health is a function of physical well-being, which can be defined in strictly clinical terms, has taken a toll on our society. Despite this century's brilliant medical advances, a feeling of genuine well-being continues to elude many Americans. According to A. J. Barsky in *Worried Sick:* "[E]ven if we do happen to feel fine today, that is no guarantee that tomorrow will not bring the first sign of some dreaded disease. Rather than living exuberantly, we are timid and apprehensive, afraid of getting sick, easily thrown off track by minor infirmities, dismayed by the specter of advancing age."[8] Lewis Thomas reiterates this idea in *The Medusa and the Snail:* "The new consensus is that we are badly designed, intrinsically fallible, vulnerable to a host of hostile influences inside and around us, and only precariously alive. We live in danger of falling apart at any moment, and are therefore always in need of surveillance and propping up. Without the professional attention of a health care system, we would fall in our tracks."[9]

Members of the current generation have been characterized as narcissistic and egocentric, without faith in anything beyond their personal selves. In many ways, cultivation of the physical body has become a substitute for the traditional religious concept of salvation. Good health, defined as physical well-being, has become an end in itself—a sort of supervalue without which one cannot have happiness, fulfillment, or a successful life. Ironically, this viewpoint tends to heighten our anxiety. As Barsky states:

> A health-conscious culture focuses our attention on our bodies, engenders a mood of alarm about health matters, creates an atmosphere of disease omnipresence, and furnishes the suggestion that minor symptoms are caused by serious diseases. . . . Thus, beyond a certain point, a heightened health consciousness may engender more bodily discomfort and unease by supplying a context, a belief system, an attentional focus, and an apprehensive mood, which all magnify health concerns and bodily symptoms.[10]

I do not wish to imply that health consciousness is undesirable or that bodily discomfort should be ignored. At some point, however, we must stop our frantic quest for personal longevity and redefine our concept of health, as well as our attitude toward life and death.

In more traditional cultures, health is viewed as a state of balance that depends on an interplay among many factors, including human beings, the environment, and the cosmos. Such cultures are noted for their patience, reverence, and humility—qualities that our society often lacks. They see death as part of the natural order, not an enemy to be thwarted at any cost. According to traditional philosophies, healing is a matter of wholeness, not mere physical betterment; moreover, the important factor is not one's length of life but the fullness with which one lives each moment. Most of these philosophies are based on the belief that life transcends and survives the physical form.

Because of our great confidence in scientific progress, we tend to forget that, if all known diseases were cured tomorrow, mankind would still have a 100 percent mortality rate. Moreover, the ability to cure today's major maladies would not prevent the development of new, and perhaps more devastating, ailments. Therefore, medical science will never be able to give us immortality. At some point, we must reevaluate the insatiable need that impels us, in Barsky's words, "to survive at all costs, to live a day longer, to sculpt a flawless appearance, to be perfectly fit,"[11] and must come to terms with our bodily vulnerability and impermanence. Only then will we be free to sense a more profound strength and vitality that does not depend on physical well-being.

CONCLUSION

In a strictly literal sense, what we will experience at midnight on December 31, 1999, will be not the passage from one millennium to another but merely the ordinary transition from one second of time to the next. Unlike ordinary new years, however, the occasion will offer us an unprecedented chance to evaluate our progress and enjoy a sense of renewal. Whatever the twenty-first century brings, we can be sure that health care will continue to be the arena for many exciting challenges and discoveries.

REFERENCES

1. F. C. SPENCER. "The Vital Role in Medicine of Commitment to the Patient" (presidential address). *American College of Surgeons Bulletin* (November 1990), 12.
2. A. J. BARSKY. *Worried Sick: Our Troubled Quest for Wellness* (Boston: Little, Brown, 1988), p. 109.

3. "THE GEEZER BOOM." *Newsweek* (Special edition: The 21st Century Family) (Winter–Spring 1990), p. 62.
4. R. D. LAMM. "The U.S. Doesn't Have Resources to Give Citizens Equal Health Care." *Houston Post,* October 7, 1991, p. A-13.
5. C. BARNARD. "Medicine and World Health Negated," in *Medical Science and the Advancement of World Health,* edited by R. Lanza (New York: Praeger, 1985), p. 211.
6. D. BURKITT. "An Approach to the Reduction of the Most Common Western Cancers: The Failure of Therapy to Reduce Disease." *Archives of Surgery,* vol. 126, 1991, 347.
7. COMMITTEE TO EVALUATE THE ARTIFICIAL HEART PROGRAM OF THE NATIONAL HEART, LUNG, AND BLOOD INSTITUTE. *The Artificial Heart. Prototypes, Policies, and Patients* (Institute of Medicine, Washington, D.C.: National Academy Press, 1991).
8. BARSKY, op. cit, p. 157.
9. L. THOMAS. *The Medusa and the Snail* (New York: Bantam Books, 1979), p. 38.
10. BARSKY, op. cit, pp. 35–36.
11. Ibid., p. 237.

(I would like to acknowledge Marianne Mallia, Manager of Scientific Publications at the Texas Heart Institute, for her assistance in the researching and writing of this manuscript.)

7

THE FAMILY

by Armand M. Nicholi, Jr., M.D.

Dr. Armand M. Nicholi, Jr., is Associate Clinical Professor of Psychiatry at Harvard Medical School and a member of the staff of Massachusetts General Hospital.

In 1979, at a conference of futurists from Stanford University, NASA, the National Science Foundation, and several other organizations, I presented a paper entitled "The Family and the Future." The conference focused on what the decade of the 1980s held in store for those of us living during the latter half of the twentieth century. In that paper, I predicted what would happen during the next decade if current trends affecting the family continued. I made five predictions:

1. "Family life will continue to deteriorate, producing a society with a higher incidence of mental illness than ever before. . . . The nature of this illness will be characterized primarily by a lack of impulse control." I pointed out that this lack of impulse control would be expressed primarily in unprecedented expression of sexual and aggressive impulses.
2. "All crimes of violence will increase . . . making our streets and even our homes less and less safe."
3. "Violence will increase even within the family." Because battered children—if they survive—tend to become parents who in

turn abuse their children, the amount of violence within the family will increase exponentially.

4. "Aggression turned inward will also increase and the suicide rate will continue to soar."

5. "As sexuality becomes more unlimited and more separated from family and emotional commitment, the deadening effect will cause more bizarre experimenting and more widespread sexual perversion."

These predictions, needless to say, have come true more quickly and more intensely than even I expected. To understand what changes will take place within the family over the next forty years, one must have a clear understanding of the trends that have led to the state we currently experience.

For the past twenty-five years or more, my research interests have focused on the impact of absent parents on the emotional development of children. To speak of the family today often means you represent the ultra-conservative right, which embraces traditional family values, or, more recently, the ultra-liberal left, which attempts to redefine the family to include all people who live together—regardless of sex, marriage, and so forth.

I have no political views on the family and am about as non-political as one can be. Although I have become known among some of my colleagues as a strong child advocate and a proponent for family values, I did not begin that way. I began, as I now think back on it, with a rather radical view of the family. Not only was I not a child advocate, I questioned the whole idea of having children. I stated often that children tied one down, interfered with one's career, usurped one's energy and time and resources that could be directed to doing something important for society. As a medical student, I recall asking people why they had children and could never get a satisfactory answer. If they mentioned that children were necessary for continuing the human race, I would reply we already had problems with overpopulation. As for a wife, I wanted someone with at least a Ph.D. and a full-time exciting and demanding career. I thought nothing would be more depressing than coming home at night and trying to communicate with someone who had spent the day changing diapers and reading children's books to toddlers.

But I changed—slowly, reluctantly, and with no little resistance. Many factors contributed.

When I finished my medical training, I was offered a position as psychiatrist to the students and faculty at Harvard. At that time about 60 to 70 percent of the student body came from private schools—just the opposite of the way it is now. In my clinical work, I began to see students from privileged backgrounds who presented a specific cluster of symptoms:

- Low self-esteem and feelings of worthlessness;
- Inability to establish close, trusting relationships;
- Difficulty with authority;
- Inability to get their work done and feeling out of sorts with themselves and with the world generally;
- Anger bordering on rage close to the surface and directed often toward the parents.

What these students had in common was that their care as infants and young children had been relegated to nurses and nannies. They had relatively little physical or emotional contact with their parents. Most of them had been sent to boarding school at an early age.

During these years I also worked some evenings in a clinic for the poor from the inner city. And, much to my surprise, I noticed that same cluster of symptoms. And I also observed that like the wealthy Harvard students, these patients from poor families also had very little contact with their parents. The father was usually not present and the mother was out working long hours in order to survive. Infant care was relegated to a grandmother, a neighbor, or whomever was available.

Although these two groups shared a common background of inaccessible parents and the same symptoms as adults, I observed one marked difference: those from wealthy backgrounds tended to turn their anger inward, becoming depressed and expressing their anger in self-destructive behavior—heavy drinking, psychoactive drugs, sexual acting-out, and so on. Those from poor backgrounds turned their rage outward, into violent crime and other antisocial behavior.

At that time I attributed no importance to the observation that both of these two groups had in common inaccessible or absent parents.

What causes families—even relatively affluent families with all the advantages that money and education can offer—to fall apart? What makes them fail? How do we explain the feelings of emptiness, low self-esteem, and depression among the spouses, and the anger, rebelliousness, and incapacitating emotional conflicts among the children within these families? Conversely, what about families that succeed—that not only stay together, but develop strong, stable, supportive relationships, and thriving, caring, emotionally healthy offspring? Do these successful families have common denominators? Can we apply this knowledge to our own families?

Why talk about the family? We all make mistakes in this area and the talk only makes us uncomfortable. The answer is simple. Our family experience is the most profoundly meaningful experience of our lives. Regardless of differences in cultural, social, educational, and religious backgrounds, we all share the experience of being a child and spending our days of childhood in the context of the family. Here the seed is sown for what we become as adults. Early family experience determines our adult character structure, the inner picture we harbor of ourselves, how we feel about ourselves, how we perceive and feel about others, our concept of right and wrong—that is, the fundamental rules of human conduct that we call morality or ethics—our capacity to establish the close, warm, sustained relationships we desire, as well as the intimate sexual relationships necessary to have a family of our own, our attitude toward authority and how we resolve our ambivalence toward it, especially toward the Ultimate Authority in our lives, and finally, our attempt to make sense of our existence on this planet. No human interaction has greater impact on our lives than our family experience.

And, on the negative side, the breakdown of the family contributes significantly to the major problems confronting our society today. Research data make unmistakably clear a strong relationship between broken or disordered families and the drug epidemic, the increase in out-of-wedlock pregnancies, the rise in violent crime, and the unprecedented epidemic of suicide among children and adolescents.

Is there danger, as scientists have warned, that the American family as we know it today will cease to exist? I don't think so. We do have, however, serious cause for concern, concern not that the family will disappear, but that certain trends or patterns prevalent today will incapacitate the family, destroy its integrity, and cause its members to suffer such crippling emotional disorder that they will become an intolerable burden to society.

Can we make any general statement from our knowledge of human development and from the medical literature concerning the relationship between presence or absence of parents and the emotional health of their children? If any one factor influences the character development and emotional stability of an individual, it is the quality of the relationship that person experiences as a child with his or her parents. The difficulties encountered in homes today can be attributed in large measure to a lack of time with the family and thus to a lack of emotional accessibility. We fail to meet one another's emotional needs because we are essentially absent from one another—from our wives and husbands, and especially from our children. We use the cliché, "It's the quality, not the quantity, of time that counts." But time and emotional accessibility are like the oxygen we breathe. Although the quality of the oxygen is important, the quantity determines whether we live or die.

A parent's inaccessibility, either physically, emotionally, or both, can exert a profound influence on the child's emotional health. A vast body of research during the past five decades led the World Health Organization to make this statement: "What is believed to be essential for mental health is that the infant and young child should experience a warm, intimate, and continuous relationship with his mother. . . ." In the years following that statement, research throughout the world has demonstrated that a separation from the mother, even for brief periods of time, and the quality of the mother's relationship with the child, can profoundly affect both the child's physical and emotional development. And more recent research has demonstrated the full emotional impact on the child of the missing or inaccessible father. What has been shown over and over again to contribute most to the emotional development of the child is a close, warm, sustained, and continuous relationship with *both* parents, but especially the mother, during the first three years. Yet certain trends in our society make this accessibility difficult today. Let's look at a few of these trends.

The trend toward quick and easy divorce has a strong bearing on family life in this country. The ever-increasing divorce rate subjects an ever-increasing number of children to physically and emotionally absent parents. Secondly, the increasing number of married women with young children who have joined the labor force and work outside of the home has a profound effect on family life. Two-career families compound the problem of emotional inaccessibility. And single-parent families, where the mother is burdened with providing the children with emotional support as well as economic support, are an overwhelming problem in our society. Thirdly, there is the tendency of many colleges and universities in this country to convey the notion that the role of parent is passé, and that to settle for such a role is to settle for second-class citizenship.

Many young women no longer feel free to stay home with young children. Unless they can pursue a career while raising a family, they consider their lives a failure. My clinical and research experience indicates clearly that no woman with young children can do both *at the same time* without sacrificing one or the other—the quality of work or the quality of child care. Many professionals in my field know this, but few have the courage to say it. And most mothers that I see—though not all—know this instinctively.

Fourthly, the tendency to move frequently imposes great stress on families. Parents often travel long distances as part of their work. Because of such travel, a parent may be absent from home for many days or even weeks at a time. The job also frequently causes the whole family to move. We have only begun to understand the enormous psychological uprooting that a move can have on a family. Fifth, the obtrusion of the television set into the American home has had an effect on the family that we have not yet even begun to fathom. When parents are home physically, television often interferes with interaction between members of the family and poses another of a growing number of reasons for keeping the TV set turned off. These are but a few of many trends in our society that foster parental inaccessibility.

These trends, I believe, exert an extremely negative influence on family life—primarily because they contribute to a change in childrearing that has been taking place in this country during the past few decades. The change is this: in American homes today, child care has shifted from parents to other agencies. A home in which both parents are available to the child emotionally as well as physically has become, in some areas of our society, the exception rather than the rule. And I refer not only to the disadvantaged home where the father is missing and the mother works. I refer to even the most affluent homes. Cross-cultural studies show that American parents spend considerably less time with their children than almost any other population in the world. In most other countries studied, emotional ties between children and parents are stronger and the time spent together considerably greater than in the United States. In some of these countries, fathers have said they would never let a day go by without spending two hours with their sons. A study in Boston of how much time fathers spend with their young sons shows that the average time per day is about thirty-seven seconds.

A child experiences an absent or an emotionally inaccessible parent as rejection, and rejection inevitably breeds resentment, anger, and alienation. Depending on the age of the child, the particular emotional makeup of the child, and the sex of the parent who is missing or inaccessible, the child when he or she becomes an adult may experience various kinds of crippling emotional conflict.

You say, "You've made your point. Perhaps parents are not as accessible today. Most hardworking, successful corporate executives and physicians never have been. (Children of physicians, by the way, have three times the number of psychiatric problems as those from other families.) But what hard evidence do you have that it does harm? You've presented suggestive evidence, but certainly nothing conclusive." My data comes from three sources: (1) my clinical experience; (2) my research; and (3) the research of others reported in the world medical literature.

I began by alluding to some of my clinical experience. Let's consider some of the research. My interest in the impact of parental absence began while conducting research on college students. At that time I noticed a cluster of psychiatric symptoms that occurred among a rather significant number of undergraduate men. The syndrome included the following:

1. Unusual preoccupation with motor vehicles, especially the motorcycle;
2. A history of accident-proneness that extended to early childhood; all had been referred because of serious accidents;
3. Persistent fear of bodily injury;
4. Extreme passivity and inability to compete academically, athletically, or in any other area of life;
5. A defective self-image;
6. Poor impulse control and a propensity for heavy use of drugs and alcohol;
7. Impotence and intense homosexual concerns;
8. A distant, conflict-ridden relationship with the father.

These young men had in common a highly successful father who wasn't around very much. At that time, I wrote in the *American Journal of Psychiatry* that "the young man sees the father as all-powerful, critical and one with whom it is hopeless to compete. Each patient within my sample feared his father and as a young boy learned to avoid him. The fathers of these patients are highly successful in their careers. Several had the unusual quality of being outstanding both as athletes and scholars, making them, of course, more formidable competitors." I often informally referred to these young men as suffering from the "famous father syndrome," where the father has given the child everything but himself. This paper appeared to strike a chord—*Time* magazine and CBS discussed it at some length.

From my clinical experience and from my research with college students, I began to notice (1) that a large number suffered from an incapacitating symptomatic or characterological conflict; (2) that they seemed to have in common a number of traumatic early experiences with a rejecting, inaccessible, or absent parent; and (3) when we looked at their histories carefully, there appeared to be some causal relation between the earlier experiences and the emotional illness they were suffering as an adult. I then began a research project studying several hundred young men who dropped out of Harvard for psychiatric reasons. Two characteristics of the group were: (1) a marked isolation and alienation from their parents, especially their fathers; and (2) an overwhelming apathy and lack of motivation. In addition, among those who had the most serious illness, that is, those hospitalized and diagnosed as schizophrenic, a large number had lost one or both parents through death. When compared with several control groups, this finding proved highly significant statistically. This provided my first clue that there might be an association between a missing parent and emotional illness.

As I became involved in my own research and as I began to gather more experience with patients clinically, I began to realize that absence through death was the most severe kind of absence. There were, however, many other kinds of absences that affected children. Parents could be absent because of emotional illness, because of a time-demanding job, and, more and more often in our society, because of divorce. The more recent research on parental absence focuses on separation from parents as a result of divorce. The divorce rate has risen over 700 percent in this century, most of this rise occurring during the 1970s and 1980s; 13 million U.S. children, over half of all children under eighteen, have one or both parents missing from their homes.

Perhaps the most extensive and well-known study of the effects of divorce on children is Wallerstein and Kelley's five-year study in California of sixty divorced families. Let me mention a few findings:

• The initial reaction of over 90% of the children was "an acute sense of shock, intense fears, and grieving which the children found overwhelming."

• Half of the children feared being abandoned forever by the parent who had left (a realistic fear in light of other studies reported in the *New England Journal of Medicine*, which show that within three years after the divorce decree, 50% of fathers never see their children). One third feared being abandoned by the custodial parent. The children were preoccupied with the fear of waking to find both parents gone.

• Following the divorce, a significant number of children suffered feelings of despondency, rejection, anger, and guilt. The researchers report: "Two-thirds of the children, especially the younger children, yearned for the absent parent . . . with an intensity we found profoundly moving."

• Five years after the divorce, 37% of the children were moderately to severely depressed, were intensely unhappy and dissatisfied with their lives, and their unhappiness was greater at five years than it had been at one and a half years after the divorce.

• Ten years after the divorce, 41% of the children were doing poorly, "entering adulthood as worried, underachieving, self-deprecating and *angry* young men and women." Some children showed no symptoms until they were about to enter a close relationship themselves as young adults. Adolescents appear to be most vulnerable to the effects of divorce. Studies indicate that 80 to 100% of adolescents in inpatient mental hospitals are children of divorce. So much for absence because of divorce.

The early studies on parental absence focused primarily on the absence of the mother and can be summed up as follows:

1. The research showed that when a child is separated from its mother permanently and not provided with adequate substitute care, the infant becomes visibly distressed and is subjected to high risk for both physical and psychological disturbances in development.

2. When a child is separated from its mother unwillingly, even for brief periods of time, the child shows visible distress, and when placed in a strange environment and cared for by a succession of strange people, that distress becomes more intense. The reaction follows a typical sequence. The child at first protests vigorously and tries desperately to recover the mother. Later, the child seems to despair of recovering her, although he/she remains preoccupied with her return. Still later, if she does not return, the child seems to lose interest in her and to become emotionally detached from her.

These early studies have considerable relevance to recent trends in our society, where an increasing number of mothers with young children work outside the home and where the care of the children is relegated to outside agencies.

Other studies focused on the absence of the father. For a representative view of these studies, let's look briefly at a study published in the *Archives of General Psychiatry* on two hundred children seen at a military medical clinic, where the father's absence was due to his military occupation. The children ranged from three to eighteen years of age.

The researchers found that the early reactions to the father's departure resembled the reactions of children who lost a father by death: (1) rageful protest over desertion; (2) denial of the loss and an intense fantasy relationship with the parent; (3) efforts at re-union; (4) irrational guilt and a need for punishment; (5) exaggerated separation anxieties and fears of being abandoned; (6) a decrease in impulse control; and (7) a wide variety of regressive symptoms.

The researchers noted that when the father left home, the child was often allowed to do things not otherwise permitted. This made it difficult for the child to internalize a consistent set of standards for controlling his behavior. In several instances, the father's leaving was followed by disobedience, decline in school performance, and aggressive antisocial behavior. The child seemed unable to control himself, and this loss of control is especially interesting in light of the observation that more adults today come to psychiatrists because of a lack of impulse control.

Several other recent studies bear on the absence or inaccessibility of the father, and all point to the same conclusions: A father absent for long periods contributes to (a) low motivation for achievement; (b) inability to defer immediate gratification for later rewards; (c) low self-esteem; and (d) susceptibility to group influence and to juvenile delinquency. The absent father tends to have passive, dependent sons, lacking in achievement, motivation, and independence.

These are general findings with many exceptions. We fathers have seldom spent sufficient time with the family. Mothers, instead of bringing fathers more into the family, have left the family to join the fathers. This trend has resulted in both parents being less accessible to one another and to their children, and contributes to both the high divorce rate and the pervasive social problems we have outlined.

When we consult the scientific and medical literature, we find an impressive body of data based on carefully controlled experiments that corroborate the impression that a parent's absence, whether through death, divorce, or time-demanding job, can exert a profound influence on a child's emotional health. The magnitude of this research paints an unmistakably clear picture of the adverse effects of parental absence and emotional inaccessibility. Why has our society almost totally ignored this research? Why have even the professionals tended to ignore it? The answer is the same reason society ignored for scores of years sound data on the adverse effects of cigarette smoke. The data are simply unacceptable. We just don't want to hear the facts because they demand a change in our lifestyle.

Because families provide the foundation of our lives as individuals, as well as the vital cells of our society, we can no longer afford to ignore this research on the family.

What do we know about successful, healthy families? What do we know about families that stay together? Once in a while one sees what appears to be an ideal family. The parents have a deep respect and concern for one another, and the kids a healthy sense of who they are and some sense of where they're going. Though by no means free of conflict or adversity, they have resources to draw on that help cope with and resolve that conflict. If you enter that home, you find it a warm, nurturing place, a comfortable place to be, and you understand why the parents as well as the children hurry back to it once they leave. As the children mature, they too have a deep love and respect for one another. And when they marry, they seem to reproduce the same kind of ideal family. What does research reveal about these families? Do they have characteristics in common? Several national and cross-cultural studies of families show that strong, healthy families have a number of common denominators.

1. The parents have a high degree of commitment to the concept of family and a strong commitment to their own family. They give the family the highest priority. The family plays a key role in the way they order their lives.
2. They find time to spend together and know how to spend this time profitably in a way that permits them to be emotionally, as well as physically, accessible to one another.
3. I have observed that in most of these families, one parent—often, but not always, the mother—makes the family their primary responsibility and in essence gives their life to fulfilling that responsibility. Successful families don't just happen.
4. They embrace a philosophy of life that provides a spiritual dimension for the family. Most of these families possess a strong faith, which helps bind them together and provides

resources they can draw on to help cope with crises and adversity.

How does faith contribute to family stability and strength? First, when we look at the Judeo-Christian faith, we find that it gives a new perspective on the family and places it high on our list of priorities. If we turn to the Scriptures—and read these documents objectively, free of the aura of religiosity and piousness so repugnant to most of us—we find more wisdom about how to live this life with meaning, abundance, and fulfillment than all the scientific knowledge acquired by humanity since the beginning of time.

This wisdom is perhaps most succinctly summarized in what these documents refer to as the two great commandments: the first, to love God with all of our soul and heart and mind; the second, to love our neighbor as ourselves. The two great commandments make clear that our lives, if we are to find fulfillment, must focus first and foremost on our relationships. First, our relationship with the Creator; and secondly, our relationship with others. These documents indicate clearly that until we establish this vertical relationship and give it first priority, we will continue to experience some sense of loneliness and emptiness. Once we establish the first relationship, we then have resources to carry out the difficult second commandment, our second priority, of loving our neighbor as ourselves. When the Lord was asked, who is my neighbor, He replied by telling the story of the Good Samaritan—implying that our neighbor is the first person we come across in need. Because we all have needs, our neighbor includes first and foremost our families—those for whom we have primary responsibility. So, a strong faith helps first of all by establishing clearly our priorities.

A second way faith fosters stability and strength in a home is by giving us a new standard for our relationships—referred to as *agape*. *Agape* is a unique kind of love, a love devoid of sentimentality, yet considerably more than kindness. A love based not primarily on feeling, but on the will—though as we carry it out by exertion of the will, it contributes to how we feel and to our sense of fulfillment. *Agape* involves stepping out of our own needs sufficiently to become aware of the needs of others, and then acting to meet those needs, whether we feel like it or not. *Agape,* therefore, involves thought, effort, time, accessibility, and at times self-sacrifice and self-denial. It's a difficult kind of love to practice; but it's the key to all successful relationships, especially those within the family.

Third, faith within a family fosters forgiveness. The capacity to forgive is absolutely essential to all relationships—especially the close, intimate relationships within a family, where the very closeness makes others particularly vulnerable to our selfishness and our other shortcomings. Those families that follow the scriptural admonition to "be kind and compassionate to one another, forgiving each other just as in Christ, God forgave you," have a formula that can contribute significantly to maintaining family stability.

With our knowledge of the vast body of research on the family, of past and current trends contributing to the high family failure rate, and of what contributes to strong, successful families, what can we say about the future? Where will the family be forty years from now?

Our society will choose one of two possible directions. We will allow the current trends of family dissolution to continue, or we will make radical changes in our thinking about the family which will dramatically reduce the number of families that fail and increase those that succeed.

If we allow current trends to continue, the future will bring the following results:

1. An accelerating increase in violent crime so that no street in the nation will be safe at any time. The homicide rate will increase across the nation. A huge percentage of federal, state, and legal financial resources will be directed to law enforcement and to building larger and more numerous prison facilities.

2. The lack of control of aggressive impulses that results from family dissolution will manifest itself in increased riots, occurring in more and more cities and towns across the nation. The death toll from these riots will increase year after year. Because children brought up in homes with one or both parents absent feel devalued, they will value other people's lives no more than they value their own.

3. Because they value their own life so little, the suicide rate will

increase even more rapidly than the rate of homicide. The unprecedented explosive increase of suicide among children and adolescents during the 1970s and 1980s (Deykin, 1986) will continue to increase during the next forty years. This increase will be reflected most among male adolescents.

4. A lack of control of sexual impulses that results from the breakdown of the family will also continue to manifest itself:

    i. Out-of-wedlock pregnancies will continue to increase as they have during the last two decades.

    ii. The AIDS epidemic will explode out of control and cause people to overreact. AIDS patients will be quarantined. The homosexual will be the focus of a backlash of fear and hatred. This climate will force those struggling with homosexuality back into the closet.

    iii. Because absent parents contribute to sexual disorders and gender disturbances (Rekers, 1983; Rekers, et al., 1983), the number of people afflicted with these disorders will increase steadily over the next forty years. People with sexual preference for children (pedophilia), for animals (bestiality), for the same sex (homosexuality), for inanimate objects (fetishism) will also increase steadily—as will exhibitionism, voyeurism, sexual masochism, and sexual sadism. Special clinics for treating these disorders will be as common as fast-food restaurants.

5. The continued breakdown of the family will result eventually in the total breakdown of our society, and will prove the first major step toward the end of our civilization. Some of the changes predicted by George Orwell in his book *1984* that involved the breakdown of the family will begin to take place.

If, however, the pendulum begins to swing back and we take steps to restore the family, our society will begin to enter a new era of progress and prosperity. This will involve going back and recapturing some of what we now call "traditional values." Sometimes going back, however, as when one takes a wrong turn in the road, is the shortest way to moving ahead. As first steps in moving in this direction, I offer the following recommendations:

1. The family is given the highest priority in the functioning of all of our institutions, from the federal government to the

corner grocery store. The working hours of our institutions must be geared to husbands and wives spending part of every twenty-four hours with one another and with their children. (The current disorganized functioning of our Congress, which keeps its members from any sustained contact with their families for days and sometimes weeks on end, is a national disgrace and an abhorrent model for the rest of the country.)

2. Schools and colleges inculcate the research findings alluded to in this paper and other research which indicates that fulfillment and happiness are closely related to family relationships and love within those relationships, that striving for individual status ultimately proves empty and frustrating if gained at the sacrifice of these relationships, that parents must be free to stay home with young children if they have the desire and the opportunity to do so, and that time spent to earn money for a second TV set, a second car, or even a private school can never compensate for time with the child as far as that child's well-being and quality of life are concerned.

3. Our institutions make it possible for parents to work at home as often as possible, abolishing outdated laws that discourage this work. Conferences and conventions stop taking spouses away from the family for days or weeks, but include their families. Employers permit individuals to refuse to be moved to another location so as not to uproot the family, without fearing a demotion. Young mothers who must work are provided facilities for superb care of their children, time to visit them during the day, and flexible hours so as to be home when their children return from school.

4. Divorce will be considered only as a last resort, after every effort is made to resolve the conflicts in the relationship. The myth of divorce, which portrays divorce as merely a change of partners, like a new car or new job, will be totally exposed. Courts of conciliation will be established where lawyers will encourage—in place of the adversary posture—a process of reconciliation, forgiveness, and a new beginning, if for no other reason than the emotional health of the children.

In summary, we need a radical change in our thinking about the family. We need a society where people have the freedom to be whatever they choose; but if they choose to have children, then those children must be given the highest priority. In this way, we will make a most important contribution to the future of our society.

REFERENCES

1. L. BENDER, and H. YARNELL. "An Observation Nursery: A Study of 250 Children on the Psychiatric Division of Bellevue Hospital." *Amer. J. Psychiatry*, 1941, 97:1158–72.
2. J. BOWLBY. "The Influence of Early Environment in the Development of Neurosis and Neurotic Character." *Int. J. Psycho-Anal.*, 1940, 21:154–78.
3. ———. *Maternal Care and Mental Health* (Geneva: WHO; London: HMSO; New York: Columbia University Press, 1951). Abridged version, *Child Care and the Growth of Love* (2nd. edn. Harmondsworth, Middx: Penguin Books, 1965).
4. U. BRONFENBRENNER. "The Origins of Alienation." *Scientific American*, 1974, 231:53–59.
5. D. T. BURLINGHAM, and A. FREUD. *Young Children in War-Time: A Year's Work in a Residential War Nursery* (London: Allen & Unwin, 1942).
6. ———. *Infants Without Families: The Case For and Against Residential Nurseries* (London: Allen & Unwin, 1943).
7. DEYKIN, E. "Adolescent Suicidal Self-Destructive Behavior." *Suicide and Depression among Young Adults*, edited by G. L. Klupman, American Psychiatric Press, Washington, D.C., 1986.
8. W. GOLDFARB. "Infant Rearing and Problem Behavior." *Amer. J. Orthopsychiat.*, 1943, 13:249–65.
9. C. HEINICKE. "Some Effects of Separating Two-Year-Old Children from Their Parents: A Comparative Study." *Human Relations*, 1956, 9:105–76.
10. ———, and I. WESTHEIMER. *Brief Separations* (New York: International Universities Press; London: Longmans, 1966).
11. M. JELLINEK, and L. SLOVIK. "Divorce: Impact on Children." *N. Engl. J. Med.*, 1981:557–59.
12. D. LEVY. "Primary Affect Hunger." *Amer. J. Psychiat.*, 1937, 94:643–52. "Observations of Attitudes and Behavior in the Child Health Center." *Amer. J. Public Health*, 1951, 41:182–90.
13. NATIONAL ACADEMY OF SCIENCES. *Toward a National Policy for Children and Families* (Washington, D.C., 1976), chapters 2 and 6.
14. A. M. NICHOLI, JR. "Harvard Dropouts: Some Psychiatric Findings." *Amer. J. Psychiatry*, 1967, 124:651–58.

15. ———, and N. F. WATT. "Death of a Parent in the Etiology of Schizophrenia," in *Scientific Proceedings of the 129th Annual Meeting of the American Psychiatric Association* (Washington, D.C.: American Psychiatric Association, 1976), pp. 116–17.

16. A. M. NICHOLI, JR. *Children and the Family*. Report of the Massachusetts Governors Advisory Committee, 1980.

17. ———. "American Youth—And the Families That Raise Them," in *Fighting for the Family*, edited by K. Perotta and J. C. Blattner (Pastoral Renewal, Ann Arbor, MI, 1990).

18. ———. "The Impact of Family Dissolution on the Emotional Health of Children and Adolescents," in *When Families Fail*, edited by B. C. Christensen (New York & London: University Press of America, 1991).

19. G. A. REKERS. "Father Absence in Broken Family: The Effects of Children's Development," in *Oversight on the Breakdown of the Traditional Family Unit* (Washington, D.C.: U.S. Government Printing Office, 1983), pp. 131–75.

20. ———, S. L. MEAD, A. C. ROSEN, and S. L. BRIGHAM. "Family Correlates of Male Childhood Gender Disturbance." *J. Genet. Psych.*, 1983, 142:31–42.

21. J. ROBERTSON, and J. BOWLBY. "Responses of Young Children to Separation from Their Mothers." *Courr. Cent. Int. Enf.*, 1952, 2:131–42.

22. G. S. SMALL, and A. M. NICHOLI, JR. "Mass Hysteria Among School Children: Early Loss as a Predisposing Factor." *Arch. Gen. Psychiatry*, 1982, 39:721–24.

23. R. A. SPITZ. "Anaclitic Depression." *Psychoanal. Study Child*, 1946, 2:313–42.

24. T. L. TRUNNELL. "The Absent Father's Children's Emotional Disturbances." *Arch. Gen. Psychiatry*, 1968, 19:180–88.

25. U.S. BUREAU OF THE CENSUS. *Social Indicators, 1976* (Washington, D.C.: U.S. Department of Commerce, 1977).

26. J. WALLERSTEIN. "The Impact of Divorce on Children." *Psychiatric Clin. North Amer.*, 1980, 3:455–68.

27. ———. "Children After Divorce: Wounds That Don't Heal." *The Psychiatric Times* (August 1989), 8–11.

28. I. ZWERLING. "Struggle for Survival," in *The American Family* (Unit 1, Report #4) (Smith, Kline and French Laboratories, 1978), p. 5.

8

EDUCATION

by Theodore M. Hesburgh, C.S.C.

*The Reverend Dr. Theodore M. Hesburgh, an ordained
priest of the Congregation of Holy Cross, is president
emeritus of the University of Notre Dame, which he served as
president from 1952 to 1987. He has also served in many
public posts, received numerous awards and honorary
degrees, and published a substantial number of books and
articles.*

This essay will try to envision the face of education in the next
century, the beginning of the third millennium.

One might begin by observing that there will be at least a billion
or more, probably several billion more people to educate in the
next century than there are today. And today more than a billion
people in the underdeveloped world are still illiterate, despite
enormous efforts in promoting literacy during the past fifty years
or so. It further complicates the picture to observe that more than
90 percent of this increased population to be educated will be
born in precisely that part of the world where education is currently least available and least effective.

Then, add to the negative side of this prospect the fact that
human knowledge is doubling, especially in science and technol-

ogy, about every fifteen years. There will not only be more people to educate where education is poorest, but there will also be an increasing body of knowledge to be transmitted by education, which is much more than simple literacy.

On the plus side of the ledger, there is the modern development of English as a world language, partially due to the influence of the former British Empire, to World War II, to the enormous increase in world trade and tourism, and finally to the simple fact that English has become the common language of modern science and technology, as well as aviation and news broadcasts and popular TV programs worldwide. Three fourths of the data stored in a language in the world's computers is in English. As a common medium of education worldwide, the English language will help simplify the educational process and the publication of educational materials.

One might counter all of these initial observations by simply denying that all future people should be educated, holding to the earlier pattern of an educated elite who will govern and manage the world. I personally believe that the day when that could even be imagined is long gone. The tide today is running to democracy, which of its very nature requires an ever more educated citizenry involved in the goals and governance of each nation or region. The day of victimizing ignorant serfs or slaves is gone, one hopes. In its place there is a vital desire and movement among all peoples for realizing the personal dignity of each human being, a surge of rising expectations for human development and human freedom everywhere in this world. Human rights are the order of the day, and among the most important of modern human rights is educational opportunity, without which human development and human freedom are impossible. These are the motives and dreams that are driving us today toward what has often seemed an impossible dream: global educational opportunity for every human being on earth.

Let me say here that the dream is impossible if education is visualized as it always has existed in recent centuries: a schoolroom with a teacher and students. It could be the little red rural schoolhouse in Iowa at one end of the spectrum, where in the last decade of the nineteenth century my paternal grandfather and namesake, Theodore Hesburgh, taught eight grades at once to a classroom of students at different levels of ability and achievement. His son, my father, was one of his students. I am compelled to say that the elementary education my father received was good. His handwriting was better than mine, his arithmetic quite superior, his spelling, always difficult in English, impeccable, and he always beat me at Scrabble or crossword puzzles. This was a reasonably good education for the end of the nineteenth century, but an impossible model for world education at the beginning of a new millennium.

At the other end of the spectrum from the little red schoolhouse are the great universities of the world: magnificent campuses, great buildings and spacious grounds, libraries with millions of volumes, laboratories with the latest instrumentation, and last but not least, a numerous faculty in all of the arts, sciences, and professions. The scholarly distinction of the faculty is matched by the academic potential of their baccalaureate students, the upper 5 percent of their high school graduating classes, as well as their advanced students, culled from the best of their college graduating classes.

This is the wide spectrum of education as we imagine it in most civilized countries today. I have seen it at its worst and best. I remember a primitive schoolroom in a village on the upper Amazon beyond Manaus. It was a rickety and mainly open room with a leaky thatched roof; crude wooden benches and no desks, no blackboard or pencils or paper or books; but worst of all, *no teacher.* Obviously, there had once been a teacher here in this riverside jungle village, but that was only a memory now. Yet the building, bad as it was, was there. And there was still the yearning that another teacher would come this way and brighten the hopes of all those smiling village children. This picture is the worst I have seen, and I must say that I have seen it often in many primitive parts of the world—in Asia, Africa, and Latin America.

The best? It would be easy to speak about Harvard, where I serve on the Board of Overseers. It was our first university in the United States, founded in Cambridge, Massachusetts, in 1636. Over three thousand other colleges and universities have been established in the United States since then and now serve over 14 million students from the United States and all around the world. At my home university, Notre Dame, in Indiana, we have, among our student body of ten thousand (one-fourth graduate and three-fourths undergraduate students), over six hundred international students from about seventy countries. I believe that there are over 400,000 international students in U.S. universities (up from 25,000 forty years ago), by all odds the greatest concentration of international students in any country in the world.

Harvard and all of the 3,500 universities and colleges that survive and prosper in the United States are matched by other thousands of institutions of higher education all around the world. While these members of the International Association of Universities represent a serious attempt to educate students at the highest level, they touch only a fraction of the potential students in the world. Also, these universities are generally located in the more developed areas of the world; not that there have not been heroic efforts to create great universities in the less developed areas of the world. Let me mention one such attempt.

I speak with some sadness of a university that came into being as the former Belgian Congo achieved independence as the new country of Zaire. I believe that there were absolutely no Congolese college graduates in the Congo at that time, although a few were studying in Belgium. The Belgian government commissioned one of their top nuclear physicists, Monsignor Luc Gillon, to found a university at Kimuenza, on a high plateau not far from Léopoldville, now Kinshasa.

Gillon worked miracles. A superb modern university took shape there above the jungles: student and faculty residences, classrooms and laboratories, a modern library with a fine microfiche collection, a chapel and an Olympic-size swimming pool. There was also a 450-bed modern hospital, a good medical faculty, and even a nuclear research reactor.

All who saw this wondered how Lovvanium, as the new university was called, came to be developed in a few years, despite all the obvious difficulties. Faculty arrived by charter planes from Belgium each year and students came from all over the Congo. Gillon was a veritable genius.

Then independence came. Gillon, the rector and creator, was replaced by a Zairian. The university was nationalized, politics and graft took over, nothing was maintained, nothing was replaced, everything, beginning with the faculty, deteriorated. A great educational dream simply died. The education minister of Zaire, when I last visited there, was a high school dropout. Amid great dreams for educational opportunity everywhere, even in Zaire, this was a great disappointment, but only one of many.

Against this background of good and bad educational developments at the present time, it is evident that any future dream of educational opportunity for all the world cannot depend on the best and certainly not on the worst of what has developed in education thus far in the history of humanity. Bringing in a limited number of international students to the best universities in the developed world has created a small elite often with nowhere to go after graduation. I know of one doctor in biochemistry who returned to Asia, only to find that the only job available to her was washing dishes. Many Third World students just stay in the developed world after graduation. As one famous educator, Sir Eric Ashby, put it: "The drain in brains goes mainly west in planes."

As to the primitive educational endeavors in so much of the underdeveloped world, most of them are not working—hence the growing number of illiterates in the Third World, despite the heroic efforts of UNESCO and other secular and missionary efforts.

The rector of Notre Dame College in Dhaka, a colleague of mine, strove valiantly to teach modern biological science to his students. Other local colleges simply imparted a smattering of taxonomic terms, mainly based on Western flora, which the students never saw. When the time came for the university entrance exams, he wondered at how well these uneducated students did until he found out that their teachers just told them the order in which the specimens to be identified were displayed. My friend went into the examination room before the next exam and changed the positions of all of the specimens. His own students passed the exam with distinction; all the others failed. This obviously is not education. However, education of any kind is so greatly cherished that some professionals in India display on the door of their offices: "B.S.—University of Calcutta—failed."

It should be fairly obvious at this point that we need a completely new plan and vision for worldwide access to education at all levels, if the next century is to see a quantum leap in educational opportunity everywhere. It is well enough to proclaim worldwide education as one of the most basic of human rights, but it will be a meaningless and empty proclamation unless we produce a realistic and workable new plan to achieve it. How to do this is the subject of the rest of this essay.

Obviously, this is a great challenge and no easy task. No revolutionary scheme is without enormous obstacles, mainly because it is completely new and involves a basic change in the old order of procedure. This is guaranteed to face immediate opposition from all those who have a stake in the old order, however bad or ineffectual it is. Then there is the usual resistance to change, especially fundamental change. We are bombarded today with dozens of chiliastic world schemes that the end of the millennium seems to hatch in abundance, together with prophecies regarding the end of the world.

In this climate every suggestion for world change faces considerable opposition, even though the matters involved are of fundamental importance to the human race, such as disarmament in the face of a possible nuclear holocaust, environmental concerns in a world where the basic elements of life—air that we can breathe, water that we can drink, and land on which we can produce food—are increasingly degraded by worldwide pollution. These are physical challenges, in a way easier to handle than the lack of universal access to education, which is more of a spiritual challenge. Education is that which makes all of us more truly human and humane.

Education is central to the human condition, all over the world. It is central to human development, central to civilization, central to the spiritual maturity of humans everywhere. Even religion is something that must be learned before it is practiced. Education is so all-embracing that it is difficult to describe in any comprehensive manner; but one must try.

Education is that which enlarges and perfects our special human power of thinking clearly and logically, of judging justly and even compassionately, of discerning between good and evil, between the humane and inhuman, between the substantial and the superficial. It is education that enables us to appreciate knowledge, beauty and art, even wisdom, in all its forms. It is education that enlarges our power and vision to use science and technology for the purpose of improving the human condition on earth—in health, housing, food, transportation, communication, and the general well-being of humanity, so dismal in so many areas of the world today.

Education also teaches us the true meaning and condition of human freedom, "of governance of the people, by the people and for the people," in Lincoln's wonderful phrase. Education through history teaches us all about the great human successes and failures, of heroism and tyranny. As Santayana said, "We either learn from history or we are condemned to repeat its errors." Education through literature exposes us to vicarious experiences in a wide variety of human lives, of great loves and hates, of great joy and sadness, of triumph and tragedy; in a word, we live a thousand lives that typify the best and the worst, the heights and depths of the human spirit. Who could or would deny the great central value and inspiration that changes our lives because of our access to education in the largest sense of the word? Who would refuse it, if it were at long last accessible to every human being on earth? Only a fool or a dolt.

Those in the environmental movement today are shocked at the loss of species, especially in the destruction of rain forests. Of much greater import to the whole world is the loss of human genius—a relatively rare treasure that exists more or less randomly all over the world in gifted persons of every race. If not perceived and developed through education, each special genius is lost forever, and the whole human race is the loser.

Ivan Mestrovic was an unschooled peasant shepherd boy in Croatia when someone noticed the artful figures he was carving from wood as he watched his sheep. Some thoughtful person had him apprenticed to a local stonemason. Then he was sent to the Academy of Arts in Vienna. At age nineteen, he had his own art exhibition in Paris. Rodin said he was the only authentic genius he had ever known.

Abdus Salam was another peasant boy who early showed great mathematical skills while living in the mountains of Pakistan. Again someone sent him to a decent school, thence to Cambridge University in England. Today he heads the Institute of Theoretical Physics in Trieste, educating Third World scientists. He is also a Nobel Laureate.

What would Mohandas Gandhi have accomplished without the legal education he achieved at a British university and in the Inns of Court in London?

The basic question remains: How to make education in all its forms accessible to every human being who desires it? I believe there is a way to accomplish this, and it is surprisingly simple.

First, what this solution is not. It is not multiplying master teachers by the millions. It is not creating modern classrooms by the millions. It is not building laboratories and libraries by the millions. It is not increasing national educational budgets by billions of unavailable dollars.

All of these methods reflect the old order, which has failed miserably in attempting to make good education available to all the world, all peoples, all nations, all races, rich and poor alike.

What I am proposing is a worldwide educational network which can be accomplished today by launching three geosynchronous satellites that hover above the same location on earth at an altitude of 22,600 miles, equidistant from each other. These three can blanket the whole inhabited earth with their transmissions. Below them are three world educational libraries. Remember that today it is possible to put all of the *Encyclopaedia Britannica*, Shakespeare, the Bible, or the Koran onto a single small recording disk. These automated disk libraries would contain all human knowledge from teaching basic literacy to astrophysics; all literature and arts, all science and technology, all history, social sciences, and religion. All of these could be taught, in all the principal languages of the world, by the best available teacher in each subject. All would be updated as knowledge grows. All would be available to everyone on earth through worldwide television, with the additional advantage of also transmitting needed texts, illustrations, diagrams, formulas, whatever.

How would it work? As to hardware, if usage required more satellites, why not use the extensive network of military surveillance satellites, no longer needed in the absence of the Cold War? We have all the necessary knowledge to create the three identical universal libraries. Still to be accomplished would be the selection and utilization of the master teachers in each of the fields of knowledge and on every level of learning, from elementary to postdoctoral research.

How to access the satellites? We already do it every time we make a transoceanic phone call. But this time we would need at every ground location a new kind of phone directory, indicating the subject matter, the level of learning, the teacher, the language requested—all summed up in an appropriate numbered dial system. Just dial a course, and *voilà*, there it is.

Amazingly, on the ground, wherever there is a television set and a fax machine, here is a schoolroom for one student or many, twenty-four hours a day, every day of the year. Having its own power pack, it might be located in a current classroom, however primitive, but now with the best teacher on earth in this or that subject doing the teaching on call. It might be located in a town hall, a church or theater, a community center in a jungle village, even in a great college or university.

Obviously, it would be helpful, especially in rural areas, to develop local teacher aides who could schedule the classes, youthful and adult, and help with the paperwork and exams. These teaching aides, too, would be learning from the great teachers, the best kind of learning, by simply seeing how the master teacher teaches.

One first thinks of the broad sweep of academic education—from elementary to postgraduate learning in all of the arts and sciences and professions—as being available; there would, of course, be lessons of a practical vocational nature in agriculture, in health, in cooking, in child care, in sanitation.

One of the greatest threats to civilized human living today is the migration from rural areas to the massive slums of exploding cities like Calcutta, Rio de Janeiro, and Mexico City. One reason for this is, I think, the utter dullness of rural life (and rural education as well). With the worldwide educational network in place, rural areas could have access to the very best in culture—the best music, theater, ballet, art, politics, architecture, as well as staged international events, such as world exposition and the Olympics, and landing on the moon, as they are breaking news, all in real time. Just think of what the Public Broadcasting System in America and the BBC in England do today.

I would hope that the greatest use of the network would be educational in the broadest sense, but it could well have this additional value of enriching everyday life where it is now very boring and dull. Anything that can slow down rampant urbanization would be a blessing.

Is this an impossible dream? Only if we are unwilling to take a completely new approach to education worldwide, in all of its beneficial dimensions. The technology is there waiting to be used. The per capita cost would be trivial in comparison with present educational methods. No school buildings, no books, no laboratories, no local teacher teaching everything, often poorly. The times and seasons of learning could be adapted to the local customs and economic necessities, such as planting and harvest times.

There will always of course be people who do not want to learn. That is their loss. But the value of this new access to knowledge to talented and eager youngsters who are now deprived of all schooling is evident. Think also of the greatly neglected education of women, especially in the developing world. Besides formal education on every level, women would benefit from other subjects like health, hygiene, child care, nutrition, and home economics now inaccessible to them. Birth control information could be available to those who desire it. The hours that women, men, and children are now unavailable for learning do not matter. They can pick their own time for learning—morning, noon, or evening; spring, summer, fall, or winter.

It has been said that we are experiencing a knowledge revolution—but often enough not for those who need it most, such as illiterate children and village women. No longer need that be the case. For the first time in history, the basic human right to education can become a reality for all.

It is fair to ask what objections there may be to this blueprint for worldwide educational opportunity. One may ask why this new revolutionary plan now, after three millennia of educational efforts dating back to 1000 B.C. The answer to that one is simple: We never had this technology before.

When I was a youngster, breaking news stories were only known from special editions of the local newspaper. I can remember running down the street with a stack of newspapers, yelling: "Extra, Extra!" People would rush out of their homes to buy a paper and see what had happened. Then came radio, first primitive crystal sets, then better ones with tubes. Television was next to come. It seemed unreal in the summer of 1991 to be in a provincial hotel in Toulouse, France, during the attempted coup in Moscow and actually to see Boris Yeltsin climb on a tank and defy the military. So far have we come in so few years. The implications for education are startling, if we are imaginative enough to see them.

Some of the new technology is due to the space age beginning with Sputnik, some of it is due to computers, some of it is due to fantastic new methods of information storage and high-speed retrieval, some is due to new electronic capacities and new miniaturized power sources. The tiny Voyager is still broadcasting from beyond our solar system. In addition to all of these technical advances, I believe we are today more conscious of human rights worldwide, more sensitive, at long last, to the basic needs of women and children, more democratically oriented to all those who for centuries have been poor, isolated, and deprived of all this educational opportunity. In my judgment, this is a huge plus for the human race in its entirety.

It will be asked at the outset: Who is going to pay for all of this? My response is simple enough: the same people who in the United States, the USSR, and the other developed and underdeveloped countries somehow managed to spend a total of a trillion dollars ($1,000,000,000,000) a year for nuclear and conventional armaments that threatened the lives of all, killed millions, and benefited no one but the arms sellers.

As mentioned already, this new scheme is a monumental bargain if one considers, first, the low *per capita* student cost; second, the quality and versatility of the educational opportunity for everyone in the world; and, third, the comparison with current educational efforts worldwide, which are more costly, less effective, of lower quality, and have left uneducated and illiterate more than a fourth of humanity, particularly in those areas of the world that most need education for sustainable development.

I do not preclude a continuation of the best of current educational efforts in our better elementary, secondary, and university institutions. They will continue to operate for those who want a traditional educational experience. But as the new scenario becomes operative, I suspect that many great teachers will be piped into these schools, too.

Imagine that the chemistry professor drops dead on the first day of class. We'll have to make do with Dr. Glenn Seaborg. I recall him teaching me about transuranium elements. It was the clearest lesson I ever had. After all, he discovered them and won the Nobel Prize in doing so.

If we had inaugurated such a new educational system in the past (admittedly impossible without modern techniques), we would now be able to have Michelangelo teach painting and sculpture,

Beethoven the art of composing symphonies, Einstein relativity theory, Shakespeare dramatic writing, Dickens or Thackeray nov-els, Oppenheimer physics, Galileo and Copernicus the solar system, and on and on and on.

Today, no great teacher, the best ever in his or her subject, or the pioneer in a new subject, need be lost to learning. They can teach, on request, to anyone willing to learn from the master, even long after he or she departs this life.

There is one final objection that must be faced. Who would have the responsibility to implement the scheme and prevent it from becoming an all-powerful means of thought control? First, there would have to be a written educational charter, agreed upon by all the nations of the world. The charter should recognize that while some subjects are in themselves fairly objective, like mathematics, there will be new forms, like Mandelbrot's Chaos theory, that may be controversial at first. Let those who propose new theories teach them and face honest criticism. So does knowledge grow.

In more controversial matters, social and political theories, for example, let the various schools have their say, and again let the attrition of ideas play its role in arriving at truth; let the cream rise above the skim milk.

So also, for example, in the most difficult case: religion. Let the best expositors of each world religion teach its fundamentals and various versions thereof. The Muslims would have to explain Sunni, Shi'ite, and Sufi, and how they differ. Various forms of Protestantism would have to explain themselves. Catholics, too. All would have to be done as honestly and objectively as possible. Each religious group would have to decide who explains them to the world; we are speaking of education, not indoctrination. Controversies would be addressed by the best scholars on either side of a question.

I would hope that all of this could be agreed upon in a *Magna Carta* for worldwide education. No one ever accused the editors of the great encyclopedias of brainwashing. The spirit of this world-wide educational endeavor would be *Lehrfreiheit* and *Lehrnfreiheit:* Freedom to teach and freedom to learn.

I would hope, for example, that the theory of Communism would be as honestly explained as its demise chronicled.

Once a worldwide educational charter is written and universally endorsed, I would assume that UNESCO, or some similar U.N. agency, could spend a few fruitful decades implementing the new educational system worldwide.

Undoubtedly there would be other objections beyond those I have listed, but I would counter one and all by saying: If you have a problem with this general scheme for education worldwide, pray, come up with a scheme of your own. The traditional system of education has not delivered education to those who desperately need it, and is unlikely to do so in the future. The crucial question then remains: Is access to education on all levels of one's capacity, regardless of where one lives or what resources one has, beyond brains and the capacity and desire to learn, is this equal access a basic human right, moreover, an indispensable human right in today's world?

If the right to an education is both basic and indispensable, can we deny this right to anyone if there is a reasonable possibility of providing it, by the method here described or a better one, yet to be proposed? I believe the moral imperative here is to explore, discuss, and begin to implement universal education for everyone, as best we can.

We face a new millennium and a new century with great hope: an opportunity for a new world order made possible by the demise of the Cold War and a great power struggle for armed supremacy. It reminds one of Shakespeare's famous statement, "There is a tide in the affairs of men, which taken at the flood leads on to fortune."

It would be tragic if this new approach to world educational opportunity, with its real promise, were to be neglected because of a lack of nerve, a vacillation of resolve, and truly malignant neglect. This crucial opportunity should not be lost in a welter of other opportunities, especially if we are serious about facing the future with creativity, a sense of priority, and hope.

All of this, of course, does assume a new world order in which justice and peace are espoused and promoted by all nations on earth, especially the most powerful ones. This involves a new kind of political altruism not common in our long history. Are we capable of it? That is like asking, are we capable of human progress and survival? I think we are.

Only future history will prove me right or wrong. As an incurable optimist, I would much rather envision our future in positive terms of total human development, hope for all God's people, and peace with justice. If all of this is not possible as we look ahead, I would just as soon resign from the human race. But I am not quite ready for that yet. I still live in hope.

9

COMMUNICATIONS MEDIA

by David Brown

David Brown has been, successively, a newspaperman, magazine editor, motion picture story editor, book publisher, film company executive, movie and play producer. He has edited anthologies and contributed to others as well as writing books of his own.

Sir WINSTON CHURCHILL said, "It is a mistake to try to look too far ahead. The chain of destiny can only be grasped one link at a time." Could Sir Winston have imagined that Britain's enemies, so thoroughly trounced by 1945, would less than a half century later emerge stronger than the nations that defeated them, including the once all-powerful United States of America?

Oracles at best have a mixed record. Aldous Huxley in *Brave New World* failed to identify atomic energy. J. B. S. Haldane, the brilliant British biologist, predicted in 1927 that a landing on Mars would not take place for 10 million years. He was dead (literally) right, however, when he wrote in 1924, "the world can be destroyed by a too-successful experiment in induced radioactivity." Orwell's *1984* did not anticipate the demise of authoritarian governments, the Soviet Union in particular. Arthur C. Clarke said that technology would give us more leisure time. Wrong. Americans, for example, are working longer and harder. Nobody predicted the cruel recession we were to experience.

Forecasters are optimistic by nature, believing the problems of the present will be overcome instead of, as has too often occurred, exacerbated. Those who make grandiose predictions of scientific, political, and sociological progress ignore the fact that most such progress is forged in the crucible of war, when unlimited resources are available. Credit wars for the development of aviation, radio, television, nuclear energy, miracle drugs, cosmetic surgery, and even art, music, and literature. Now that major war seems obsolete, today's prognosticators too often do not take into account that capital availability may lag behind invention and forestall for years realization of what is technologically feasible. Example: hypersonic aviation. The English Channel Tunnel barely squeaked through—it might never have been undertaken in a recession era.

With full knowledge of the perils of prediction, and the help of experts, I will try to outline what changes and progress may occur in the media in the next four decades. It may be useful or even entertaining for us first to consider what it was like in the *past* forty years.

The year 1952 was a very good one. Dwight D. Eisenhower was elected as the nation's thirty-fourth president, promising "neither [to] compromise, nor tire, nor ever cease" his efforts to preserve peace. Color television began, but sales were tepid. Three years earlier, there were only 6 million black and white sets in use. By 1953, there were 20 million. Today, there are more than 250 million.

Television began covering special events in 1951. Audiences were riveted by the Senate investigation of organized crime, and in 1954 by Senator Joseph McCarthy's inquisition of the United States Army. America's favorite TV family were Ozzie and Harriet Nelson—white, comfortably off, with well-behaved offspring, Ricky and David. Although newspaper reading had been in decline since the Depression of the thirties and the ascendancy of radio, there were still seven or eight daily newspapers in some major cities. Movies were staggering from the onslaught of television, although a few such as *From Here to Eternity* and *Roman Holiday* commanded large audiences. Magazines too suffered from television competition as advertisers deserted weaker general magazines for the larger demographics of national television; but *Life, Time, Reader's Digest* flourished. Curtis Publishing Company, owners of *The Saturday Evening Post* and *Ladies Home Journal,* employed more than seven thousand people in 1952; today it is a corporate shell with no employees or magazines. There were 2,200 drive-in movie theaters 42 years ago and it was thought they would drive out conventional theaters (the reverse occurred). Passenger ships were still crossing the Atlantic—a new superliner, the *United States,* was launched and set a record of three days, ten hours, and forty minutes from New York to Southampton (today, Concorde's record is under three *hours*). Two years later, Boeing launched its new jetliner, which, with successive generations of jet aircraft, would drive passenger ships such as the *United States* from the sealanes, except for cruise voyages. U.S. population was then 150 million (against today's more than 250 million) and Americans averaged a per capita income (counting men, women, and children) of $1,436 a year.

FLASH FORWARD

Let's go to the movies. It is 2032. It won't be all that different. The theatergoing experience will still be favored by the dating generation and those older folks who like to get out of the house. Sound and picture will be clearer and better, and theater screens will be larger, if only to combat superior home entertainment systems featuring large screens and high-definition television. Holographics, giant screens, and other processes will go the way of the 3-D and split-screen processes of the fifties and sixties, but computer images and electronic cameras will make film production less costly, allowing a greater diversity of product. Seeing movies in theaters will survive because most people like responding to entertainment en masse. Legitimate theater will also survive, if only because it will continue to be a novelty to see and hear actors without the intervention of cameras, electronic devices, and state-of-the-art sound systems. Box-office prices will rise further, causing audiences to become even more selective. I will not begin to predict trends in music except to guess that hip-hop and hard metal will be found in the "oldies" section of your compact disc store.

Will pay-for-view provide an overnight bonanza for film companies? Perhaps, but not always for first-run product. Premier-class, exclusive exhibition in theaters will continue to provide a necessary cachet for subsequent and broader play dates, whether

on small or large screen. As for audience preferences, the truth of
the lyric from "As Time Goes By" (*Casablanca*) will obtain: "It's
still the same old story, a tale of love and glory, a case of do or die,
The world will always welcome lovers—as time goes by." Stories
have not basically changed since Greek playwrights wove their
tales and men drew stories on walls of caves. Their plots will be
recycled well into the twenty-first century. As for the technology
of motion picture production, distribution, and exhibition, ah,
there's the revolution. Arthur C. Clarke correctly predicts in his
book *July 20, 2019,* that "cable video will be battling with movies
delivered directly by satellite."

New technology will probably eliminate the need for photo-
graphic film and reduce the cost of production by the use of
computerized lighting. Radically new electronic cameras as well as
computer-generated effects are already making costly sets and
even extras unnecessary. Thousands of movie theaters operating
in different time zones may be fed product by satellite or special
cable, emanating from one master projection center. As for television, Clarke points out that niche broadcasting—channels for
far more special interests than are available now—will still be provided. And, yes, networks will survive. Whoever controls the most
desirable programming will still override technological progress.
Technology is, after all, merely the conveyor. A hit in the live
theater in the category of *Phantom of the Opera, Les Misérables,* and
Cats will pile up huge grosses even though legitimate theaters
seem like artifacts, often uncomfortable ones, of another age.

The French aphorism, the more things change the more they
remain the same, applies as much to television as to movies. Even
though there will be a plethora of dazzling, high-definition, three-
dimensional image technology and hundreds more channels
down to the minutest areas of personal interest to distract audiences, Will Shakespeare's "the play's the thing" will continue to be
as true in the mid-twenty-first century as it was in his time. Interactive television—audience participation—after the first flush of
novelty subsides, will be useful for electronic "town meetings,"
"call-ins," while radio will continue to provide music and fast-
breaking news.

What will change—and radically, I believe—are the economics
of the various media. Just as capital is finite at any given period,
time is finite at *every* given period. There is only so much time to

spend on television, films, newspapers, and magazines. In America, at least, available leisure time has actually diminished in the last ten years, contrary to predictions of a four-day work week and six-hour day. How then will people absorb what Martin Porter reports in *GQ* magazine as the *present* menu of what is available to the owner of a backyard "dish" trained on a satellite—specifically, "more than 1,500 movies monthly, 1,600 baseball games a year, several 24-hour news stations, 10 shopping channels, 75 audio-only services, and 84 subscription services"? *That's today.* Money will be lost competing for the fragmented viewer's time.

By 2008, or, in the case of high-definition television, much earlier, current TV technology will be obsolete; receivers and the equipment of broadcasters will have to be upgraded or replaced. According to a dispatch in *USA Today,* the Federal Communications Commission (FCC) has approved a timetable that would bring high-definition television to homes by 1998—meaning clearer images and sharper sounds. To avoid confusion, the FCC plans to choose a standard system for the technology. There would be a five-year overlap during which existing television stations would get a second channel to broadcast their existing signal and one to start high-definition transmissions.

Thirty years hence, the rapidly growing satellite television industry will have taken its place beside cable systems and conventional on-air broadcasting—the pre-cable variety known as free television. Satellite dishes small enough to fit on city window sills or inconspicuously fitted on roofs of suburban homes are already in final stages of development. Compact disc–quality music will be available in automobiles as satellite radio is picked up by car dishes mounted over the trunk. Cableless programming of television and radio will be provided by Hughes Communications' Direct TV (bounced off satellites into your home or car) as early as 1994—just as it is now available in Europe.

The problems, which will or will not have been sorted out by 2040, are twofold: (1) How will the money be collected to pay for all this programming and technology? Will it be subscription fee-driven or advertiser-driven or both, and will there be enough of it? (2) How much can the viewing public absorb of the galaxy of information, news, special-interest programming, and entertainment? Will the erosion of network viewing be so severe that the networks will become what *Life, The Saturday Evening Post,* and other general magazines became in the fifties, when national television made them dinosaurs because they could no longer deliver enough readers to attract advertising support?

My guess is the networks will make a virtue of their shrinking viewership and offer in-depth, niche programming to compete with cable programmers, much as *Time* and *Newsweek*—their original news franchise obliterated by faster-moving network and cable news services—turned to more intensive feature coverage that broadcasting competitors could or would not equal.

Will there be networks in 2040? Yes. Will there be radio as we know it? Yes. Will there be cable systems? Yes—and delivered by fiber-optic telephone wires or satellites. And there will be direct satellite broadcasting, too.

What there will not be is any more time to absorb it all and probably not enough money to support it.

The scramble for hit shows will continue. Audience tastes, ever fickle, will continue to baffle the experts. Research techniques will fail to indicate what audiences will favor next, but rating systems will still indicate what they favored last. Because of the impossibility of filling the vast spaces of programming time, there will be an even greater boom in nostalgia programming. Movies of the thirties to nineties will enchant (or bore) future generations. The flickering images of Groucho Marx, *Bonanza*, *All in the Family*, "The Tonight Show" starring Johnny Carson, will be seen in homes with solar heating and perhaps even in the first space colonies.

As for new programming, writers will continue to pace up and down waiting for inspiration but settling for perspiration. They'll prosper from all those re-run residuals—but the technology won't help them come up with hits. Divine providence, luck, or propitious timing will, as it always has. Hard-core sex and mindless violence will continue to draw more viewers than they deserve.

In the twenty-first century, report experts gathered at an *Atlanta Constitution* symposium on May 5, 1989, viewers will be able to choose from hundreds of programs from all over the world and to see them in 3-D or theater-size screens or wristwatch-size terminals. These same experts predict that programs will be available for call up by viewers when they are free to see them instead of having to conform to the schedules of broadcasters. As mentioned, viewers will increasingly be able to talk to their TV sets and participate in game or public affairs talk shows. *The Wall Street*

Journal reports (May 21, 1992) that the Interactive Age is dawning, with IBM and Time Warner contemplating a marriage of IBM technology and Time Warner movie and TV resources, to provide a full-service, on-demand, home entertainment center with "talk-back" television capability. Reports the *Journal:*

> The talks, which neither side has publicly confirmed, are likely to accelerate the race toward what is likely to be the next technological revolution. If that revolution comes to pass, it could transform the humble television set into a powerful new medium, through which viewers sitting at home could order videos, pick their own camera angles for TV sports, play games with other viewers, buy and sell products—and train the set to anticipate their needs. They could program the set to pick only the fare they want and air it when they feel like watching, or pull off other slick tricks no one has thought of yet.
>
> Such a scenario could radically alter the nation's media, and maybe even its people. Since the 1960s, television has acted as one of the few central shared experiences for a diverse and fragmented population. Even in an era of dozens of cable channels, a nation of viewers can still tune in together to share a big event, whether it's the Los Angeles riots or Johnny Carson's last stand on "The Tonight Show."
>
> The Interactive Age might change all that, splintering America into a new isolation in which no two homes were watching the same thing at the same time.

Video cassette recorders will be built into future television sets. Cable TV will concentrate on furnishing services to businesses when the wiring of U.S. cities for cable is completed, probably by the year 2000.

AND WHAT ABOUT PRINT?

Print will not die. Pure audio-visual content does not satisfy or possess the stick-to-it-iveness of reading; it goes out of your head after you've seen and heard it, unlike what you've read. There will, however, be radical changes in the way print is conveyed, and in the shape, form, content, and direction of newspapers, magazines, and books in the mid-twenty-first century.

Penny Pugano in the *Washington Journalism Review* writes: "The day may soon arrive when newspaper readers sit down to skim the morning headlines and check stock prices, the weather, classified ads and their horoscopes without getting ink on their fingers. They'll be using a computer or television set linked to a telephone line."

Pugano also reports that a nationwide network of fiber-optic "superhighways" is expected to be completed between 2010 and 2020, making it possible for telephone, television, and computer services all to flow through one or two wires, delivering "libraries of information to American homes." To the world's as well, one might add.

While contemplating the next century, print people would do well to consider the fact, as *Newspapers and Technology* reports, that "families pay several times the cost of a daily newspaper to buy specialized TV presentations via cable." By 2030, the U.S. Census Bureau predicts that "the Spanish-origin population (in the United States) will be four times its present size" (from a report by the Associated Press Managing Editors Association). That adds up to 76 million—or 30 percent of today's total population. Trouble is, states the same report, low newspaper readership is typical among Hispanics, even of high educational and economic status. Similar, although lesser, shifts are taking place in Europe.

If crime doesn't subside, homes increasingly will be the focus of American life in the twenty-first century, the AP managing editors also report. Home reading must compete with TV-driven movies, entertainment, and news programs. Newspapers and magazines are likely to be delivered by electronic means.

"There will always be pages—but not necessarily on paper," according to an article in *The Futurist*. Electronic pages, however versatile and multidimensional, will never replace the portable, permanent "hard copy"—the printed page one can scribble on, ponder, stuff into an envelope or pocket, throw away or recycle.

Omni says the office of the distant future will be at home or on an airliner or the bullet train. True, one will be able to work at home or anywhere, as is possible now by fax and computer, but the human synergy of a workplace will still be necessary and productive. Besides, where else can you strike up a lasting acquaintance with a pretty girl at the watercooler? You can't fax that. The excitement of communicating face to face and generating ideas can never be duplicated.

"All products have life cycles, even newspapers," observes *Survival Guide to the Year 2000*. The *Guide* points out that newspapers have been around more than two hundred years and might be in their end phase. I doubt it. The newspaper, like the magazine, is in its *specialization* phase, the better to compete with a broader-based media. In the United States, suburban and community newspapers are on the rise, as daily metropolitan newspapers are on the decline. Electronic media cannot compete with local print press in depth of coverage, cost, and appeal to a narrowly targeted readership.

First-class newspapers will not only survive but flourish by appealing to an affluent, educated audience, though in smaller numbers, the kind advertisers can never get from television except from the Sunday morning low-rated but high-IQ news discussion programs. As the news commentator John Chancellor says, "Newspapers have many advantages over television. A bigger news role. Op-ed pages. Classified advertising and obituaries. Crosswords. Reviews. Funnies. Coupons. But the biggest advantage print has over broadcasting is in the reporting of fact.

"Reuven Frank, twice president of NBC News and one of television's intellectuals, says that television is best at 'transmission of experience.' Reagan's smile. Nixon's perspiration. The Vietnam Memorial. The shuttle blowing up. I say print is best at the transmission of hard information. The long takeout you can clip and share with friends . . . being more like television won't help."

Agreed. Don't sell the newspaper business short. Fewer and better big papers will be the rule in the next century. Those that do survive are likely to become national newspapers, as *The New York Times*, *The Wall Street Journal*, and USA *Today* are today. There will also be more small, local and special-appeal papers. *The New York Observer* and *Village Voice* are current examples. Magazines, which anticipated the need to target special-interest readers, have reaped the benefits of being non-competitive with television. They will continue to grow in numbers, especially with economic recovery. And if the United States fixes its woeful education system, there will be more readers for all print media.

Computers do aid newspapers in certain areas. A limited program of displaying newspapers on computer terminals attracted a few thousand subscribers in Fort Worth, Texas, a city with hundreds of thousands of home-owned computers. Those subscribers got to read the morning newspaper on their home computer the night before the newspaper went on sale—a foretaste of twenty-first-century early-bird reading.

These are sobering reflections for the print industry, however. According to Anthony N. Casale of the Media and Opinion Research Division at the Gordon S. Black Company, "Over sixty percent of all Americans were not alive the last time newspaper readership was on the upturn nationally." I believe we can attract those Americans with superior, exciting, informative journalism. That is the challenge of the print industry in the next century. On this point, Neil Postman, professor of communications at New York University, believes that "newspapers may have to play a much greater role than they ever dreamed of for the twenty-first century in creating a literate audience." Postman cites Jonathan Kozol's book, *Illiterate America,* as authority for the statement that there are 60 million illiterate people in the United States, "illiterate being someone who cannot read the directions on a medicine bottle." Assuming we don't fix the educational system in this country, Postman postulates, "I think this may be the number-one problem that editors of newspapers and magazines are facing."

One way to promote literacy is to make books, magazines, and newspapers available to five- and six-year-olds. I'm convinced I got a head start on reading by perusing *The New York Times* as a child—relating pictures to words, deciphering the ads, particularly at Christmas. Not hard to decipher Santa Claus and mountains of gifts.

OTHER OPINIONS, OTHER VIEWS

"In the world of magazines," says Everette E. Dennis of the Gannett Center for Media Cities,

> there is continued specialization. Indeed, more than any other medium, the magazine anticipated the age of information and emphasized discrete audience segments that were identified and planned for on the basis of market research. Though they were ahead of the game, magazines now face stiff competition from other media and in many instances, are struggling to survive. Still, magazines have always had somewhat cyclical histories; they are born, they grow up and they die.

Henry Anatole Grunwald, for many years editor-in-chief of
Time, Inc., has given some thought to these questions and writes
to me:

One of the major changes in media communications will be technological. I think print will be with us for a long time, but it will take
new forms. Centralized printing of books and other publications in
locations remote from the reader will fade, along with the cumber-
some distribution systems we now endure. There will be more and
more electronic distribution directly to the home, or other scattered
locations. We can already read books from the computer screen,
and the screen is already on its way to becoming a mere tablet,
rather than an unwieldy box. The result is certainly still "print."

There will be increasing and bewildering choices. I can imagine
an electronic *Reader's Digest* in which people will be able to select
specific articles from a large menu, rather than buying an entire
magazine. Instead of going to the video store, we will call up movies
directly on our TV set. Proliferation of specialized programs has
long been predicted; it will really have to happen.

But all this only raises the question of what the consumer wants
to or can absorb. The common wisdom at the moment is that people
want their information easy, painless and preferably in pictures. I
contend that a continuing harsh climate of economic competition
will make this kind of information-getting untenable. If we really
only want to be entertained, we will (to use my favorite quote from
Beyond the Fringe) "sink giggling into the sea."

But if the public has a duty to make a more serious effort about
being informed (and I think it does), the media have a big obliga-
tion to make information easier to absorb, to explain things more
clearly, to avoid jargon and needless obscurity. Not to pretend that
Aristotle or nuclear physics can be digested in ten sugarcoated bites
(or bytes), but to craft, structure, organize information much more
effectively. It certainly should include the use of the image, but
integrated with the written word, a practice that I find quite rare now
and quite poorly done.

It is a commonplace to say that technological changes bring about
intellectual and political changes—for instance, the printing press
and movable type were indispensable for the Enlightenment and
democracy. Precisely what changes the computer will cause, I am
not brave enough to forecast, but I have a few notions.

One consequence surely is further democratization through the
process of making the dissemination of knowledge almost unlimited. But the next, and much bigger, challenge is how to make sense

of all that knowledge, how to keep the dumb from drowning out the intelligent, the unimportant from drowning out the essential. There already are computer programs to weed out junk mail, etc. This principle could be more generally applied. But this will require standards (just *what* we want to eliminate and why) and thus a much more rigid hierarchy of values than we now possess. This kind of filter is not easily compatible with anything-goes freedom; it points to the need for *responsible* freedom. Can we write the software of responsible freedom, responsible selection? Probably yes, but the *values* must exist first.

One more thought, although it reaches far beyond the thirty-year limit for your project. It is a simple fact of life (or death) that the brains of an Albert Einstein, or a Winston Churchill, or a David Brown (thank you, Henry) disappear when they die, leaving behind only an inadequate written record. I have a hunch that some day we will learn to feed the total contents of the human brain into a computer, thereby allowing it to continue *thinking* long after its owner is gone. Yes, I know this is strictly science fiction, but I couldn't resist it.

As for the future of books, here are some startling possibilities set forth by Tony Rothman in the February 3, 1992, issue of *The New Republic*:

> *War and Peace* in three languages could be put on a CD the size of a fingernail. Even now, there is nothing to prevent Sony from producing portable electronic "books" capable of reading tiny CDs. How much would such a system cost? Apart from the electronic book itself, which might cost several hundred dollars, CDs are cheap to produce—only about 60 cents for a full-sized audio CD. Giving the author $2, the publisher $4, with the same mark-ups for distributor and retailer as before, yields $12.87 for the cover price. Going to mail order yields $6.60 plus postage. Nevertheless, nobody likes to read CD-ROMS. Computer displays are hard on the eye, and no electronic retrieval system yet devised is as convenient as an ordinary book.

Newsletter and book publisher Kenneth Giniger reports in his January 1992 *Publishing World Update*:

> Many books will be replaced by electronic technology to the extent of 25 per cent by the year 2000, according to a Spanish report in the

journal, *Techno Alabrent*. This sees a major effect both on leisure/ entertainment products and large-volume reference material kept in database as well as on scientific books.

One such development, reported by *Publishers Weekly* in the U.S., is a portable electronic book which could be "loaded" from vending machines in libraries and bookstores with any one of an enormous selection of books. No title put into the system would ever become unavailable. Magazines and journals could be published in this fashion.

The U.S. Department of Commerce, forecasting publishing prospects through 1996, points out that the increase in informational materials available in the CD-ROM format may gradually displace reference books.

The threat to books of new technologies is countered by the many advantages these technologies bring to the publishing process for authors, editors, production people and marketers.

Again, from Tony Rothman's *New Republic* article:

A print-on-demand system has numerous advantages. It effectively eliminates distribution costs. It also eliminates book returns. Roughly 40 percent of all books printed are never sold. By abolishing both returns and distribution costs, the $20 book could be sold for about $10.50. At the same time the retailer's rent goes down since shelf space is saved and the concept of "out of print" disappears; any book on a publisher's master disk is always in print. Books can also be printed from libraries. All this scheme requires is a letter-quality printer that can print and bind a book in about a minute—so as not to wear out the customer's patience—at 1.5 cents a page. Such machines are almost available. . . . I find print on demand an aesthetically pleasing idea, but the next step is even more delightful: eliminate publishers altogether. Books could be printed on demand directly from authors' home computers.

The Japanese have already created video "banks" at museums that enable visitors to see parts of collections that cannot be displayed, as well as printing color catalogues and picture books.

Media baron Rupert Murdoch was kind enough to make available to me an appraisal of the future by John Evans, president of *News Electronic Data,* set up by Mr. Murdoch's News Corporation, Ltd. specifically to explore the new technologies. Here is John Evans's prediction:

Over the past several years we have seen, as proof of the Information Age and its new media, the coming together of several previously disparate industries. Four of these industries can now be seen to be converging to the point where there is considerable overlap. These are the media industries of print and television and other electronic entertainment, the computer industries who are themselves overlapping the consumer electronic industries and finally the telecommunications industries.

It is clear that some time in the future an economic and appealing way will be devised to deliver analog information currently residing in newspapers and magazines via a digital highway to an electronic device, either digital television or hand held, or other developed personal communication device.

In order for these hugely popular mass and narrowcast print vehicles to be delivered into a different media, certain fundamental objectives must be achieved. Firstly, whatever device receives and displays these new forms of magazines and newspapers must present them in such a way that the devices themselves become "invisible" so that the print product appears in a thoroughly familiar and non-threatening way. The transfer, of course, may require certain reorganization of the data, but for the emotional response of the reader seeing their favorite product this way will be similar to the feeling evoked by the print product.

When this is achieved, it is then possible to transfer the loyalty and strong attachments readers have to print media over to new electronic forms. Once this is achieved, all of the elaborate and dreamed for manipulation of this data can evolve. Perhaps to be in "sync" with the nomenclature of the Information Age, the software that delivers the audience over from the Industrial Age to the Information Age might be called "Moses."

The internet began in the late nineteen sixties as a system of communication developed by the U.S. government to keep the nation linked in the event of a nuclear war. Today it has evolved into an "information superhighway" with the capacity to transmit an endless supply of information that allows people from all reaches of the globes to communicate. The internet has found its way, seemingly overnight, into the everyday life of America, forever changing the way we communicate as a nation and with the rest of the world.

Businesses were the first to embrace the "Net" because it allows companies and their executives to become increasingly mobile. With a high speed laptop and a modem, business can literally be conducted from all corners of the earth and in any environment, turning the world into anyone's marketplace. But the global reach of the internet is by no means limited to the business world.

With high speed personal computers becoming economically feasible for the average American family, the internet has increased the average citizen's connection with the world. No more waiting for the five o'clock news. Now all one has to do is type in a few key words and whatever information you choose comes right to your computer. Users have the freedom to instantaneously access one of more than one million sites that serve as forums to present, exchange and debate ideas on news, politics, or even check the weather in a far off land. In the future the internet may even replace the shopping mall as America's number one place to shop. The possibilities of the internet are only limited by the scope of one's imagination. Grammar schools have even conducted classes on the internet, allowing an expert in California to speak about the details of the Mars Pathfinder landing. Nearly every college campus in the U.S. and most public libraries house internet stations or plan to do so.

The ease of communication via the net has raised numerous questions about ethics and free speech on the web. Since the internet is growing exponentially (the number of sites nearly double every fifty days) it makes monitoring the content of sites very difficult for the government, and regulating the net becomes nearly impossible. The most the government can do is place pressure on the "hosts" of the site to keep the material within certain boundaries.

Notwithstanding occasional technical glitches and, for the present, deficit financing, the internet continues to expand, becoming more worldly in its scope it will continue to generate new markets, and newer means of communication, faster and more far reaching than we can possibly imagine. It will surely challenge and enrich the world as we know it today.

To which Professor Steven Isaacs, addressing the future of media in his class at the Columbia University Graduate School of Journalism, in effect says Amen by stating: "Clearly what's happening is the merger of all media, the *convergence*—the merging of print and video and audio and whatever else may come."

Professor Isaacs adds that in reply to his question what newspapers would be like in twenty years, he was told by a professional futurist, "given the speed of technological change nowadays, whatever it will be hasn't been invented yet."

Isaac's conclusions:

"What's clear is the ability of the computer to give each person exactly what that person wants.

"New magazines more than ever—five born every three days in the United States and contrary to what you hear, many of them stick.

"The continued growth of specialization, the nichification of media, narrowcasting.

". . . Three hundred channels on cable.

"Chaos, and who takes advantage: the trained, the swift, the ourageous."

Looks like a brave new world, doesn't it?

10

CHARITY, PHILANTHROPY, AND VOLUNTEERISM

by Ruth Stafford Peale

Ruth Stafford Peale is co-founder and co-publisher, with her husband Dr. Norman Vincent Peale, of Guideposts *magazine; chairman of the Peale Center for Christian Living; and vice-president of the American Bible Society.*

ONE OF THE GREAT GIFTS John Templeton has given the world is his study and listing of the world's universal values, which he calls "the Laws of Life." The driving force behind charity, philanthropy, and volunteerism is the "law" of giving. Simply stated: giving is using what you have, both time and resources, for the benefit of others, without regard to the consequences to yourself.

This giving impulse is uniquely human, and most certainly, spiritually motivated. Other species will fiercely care for their own young, but outside that small circle, the "law of the jungle" and "survival of the fittest" prevails. Only among humans will you find anything like the story of the prominent English physician who leaves his practice on a moment's notice to travel halfway round the world, at his own expense, to come to the aid of survivors of a Russian nuclear accident.

Such impulses can only be said to spring from our connection to the divine nature of God. It is well and concisely stated in the ancient biblical principle of being "our brother's keeper." Once basic survival needs are met in any group of people, the best and brightest of those people will turn a portion of their attention to the task of lifting others up.

Throughout history there have been periods of great spiritual awakening which in turn produce some of mankind's greatest progress. For instance, the great Methodist movement in England and America in the nineteenth century produced religious leaders like William Wilberforce, who worked to abolish slavery on two continents, and William Booth, who launched the worldwide Salvation Army movement, the predecessor to every successful human services agency.

This present time, at the end of the twentieth century, seems to be another in which we are seeing tremendous spiritual progress. My husband Norman Vincent Peale and I travel thousands of miles every year and meet hundreds of people. More than ever before, when we talk to people, we find a growing hunger for spiritual discussion and understanding. People are rediscovering the benefits of a life of faith and want to know how to apply it to everyday problems.

Perhaps this can be related to giving on a personal level by a story told to me recently by Lane and Annette Adams. Lane is an entertainer, and one summer he and Annette were traveling to different cities as he performed. One particular Sunday they attended a Methodist church. It happened to be "Layman's Sunday," and the speaker was a dentist, who talked on the spiritual principle of tithing.

Tithing is the biblical principle of giving away 10 percent or more of one's income. One of the best-known scriptural promises regarding tithing is found in Malachi 3:10, which speaks of giving away 10 percent of income: "Bring the full tithes into the storehouse . . . and thereby put me to the test, says the Lord, if I will not open the windows of heaven for you and pour down for you an overflowing blessing."[1]

Knowing they were down to their last dollar, Lane was put off by this talk on tithing. But he could see Annette was listening intently. He told me what happened next:

"I couldn't get out of that church quick enough. In my mind I already had a plan of action to divert Annette. From the moment we hit the front steps, I started an endless chatter on a world of subjects. We got in the car and I never stopped chattering. Finally I had to stop to take a breath and she started right in and said, 'I think we ought to start tithing.'

"Ruth, my worst suspicions were confirmed. This nut of a dentist had gotten to her. I could either get mad all at once or save that for the final stopper. I tried the reasonable approach. 'Honey,' I said, 'you realize of course that I borrowed money from my brother recently when we were short, and our car is a wreck, and we owe this, and we owe that and . . .' I really just rehearsed every debt we had and she said, 'But the dentist said our first debt is to God. He implied that God owns everything, and if you don't see your first debt as to God, then you are robbing God.'

"And I replied, 'Honey, I will agree tentatively with the idea that somewhere in the mysterious future, when our ship comes in, when everything gets right, then we will begin to tithe.'

" 'But,' she answered, 'the dentist said if you put God first, He will add all these things to you, and that the way out of a tough financial situation is to put God first.'

"Well, I tried fury and anger and all her answers were prefaced by that little phrase, 'But the dentist said . . .' This conversation went on through lunch and into the afternoon. She was sweet and patient. I tried my worst anger and she did not provoke. Finally I decided to give in and said, 'You will be sorry the day I cannot feed you because we have run out of money.'

"I told her exactly how much money we had and how we couldn't possibly live until the first paycheck from my new show if we lopped ten percent right off, because in the madness of the moment she was proposing we do it *now*. So I said, we'll do it tomorrow . . . thinking she would forget it then.

" 'That won't do,' she said, 'I'll tell you what, you get your money and I'll get mine and we'll pile it on the bed right here and we'll see how much the tithe is.'

"We got it all counted out and I continued to tell her how much we couldn't afford to give up one dollar, but she put the ten percent in an envelope and said we would go to the post office the next day and send a money order off to our parents' church.

"I hoped she would come to her senses with a good sleep, but the next morning the first order of business was to go to the post office. And something wonderful happened. When I put that envelope into the slot, I had to turn away from Annette so she couldn't see my face. I could not suppress what was beginning to erupt from within me, a sense of 'Hey, buddy, you did something right, something incredibly right.' I dared not let Annette see that because I was still convinced we were going to go hungry. I managed to get a gruff look on my face and said, 'You're going to be really sorry about this.' But all the while I had this great feeling growing inside and she just had a little smile on her face.

"That day we decided to go to lunch in the Brown Hotel. Now the last person I wanted to see was the theatrical agent, because the show I was to be in didn't open for several days. I didn't want him to know I didn't have anything else going until then. But just as we were seated for lunch, in walked that agent.

" 'Hey,' he called out, 'I didn't know you were in town, where are you staying?' I told him and he said, 'Move out and get over to this hotel because I have a free room for you.'

"I was stunned, but Annette whispered, 'But the dentist said . . .' and there it was.

"The next thing was even more amazing. How the government ever found us when we traveled around so much I'll never know, but a few days later a check arrived from the Veteran's Administration.

"Then the show I was in was held over for two extra weeks and that was great. These were hard times in the entertainment business and extending a show was something special. Next, the show was held over another six weeks. All the while I kept protesting it was coincidence, until that particular coincidence lasted forty-two weeks. By then I' had the message: when you put God first, God takes care of things."

This example of a spiritual awakening illustrates what can happen when one practices the law of giving. On the most basic level, that is the foundation of all charity, philanthropy, and volunteerism.

Norman and I arrived in New York City in 1932, where he was to be pastor of one of the oldest and most influential churches in that great city. It soon became apparent that this responsibility would consume him night and day. Becoming aware that the national and international offices of most major denominations were located in New York City, I decided to see if there wasn't a way for me to get involved in that work. My reasoning was simple. If my husband was going to be busy with a local church, I could give my time to the national and worldwide church and keep him informed of developments and programs in those realms.

This process started a life-long involvement for me with non-profit, philanthropic, and charitable organizations. After my beginning with church-centered organizations, I found myself working with diverse groups such as the Red Cross, Hope College, and the American Bible Society, among others. Along the way Norman and I founded Guideposts Associates, the Peale Center for Christian Living, and the Blanton-Peale Institutes, the latter a school and clinic dedicated to combining the spiritual and therapeutic disciplines.

During this almost sixty years of involvement with non-profit activities, there have been trends which define and distinguish the matters of charity, philanthropy, and volunteerism. Each of these three has a developmental pattern of its own, but each is also interconnected with the others. A good example of this interconnectedness is that all three subjects—philanthropy, charity, and volunteerism—are composed of two basic elements: individuals and institutions.

Philanthropy, for instance, is conducted and promoted by individuals who cause a portion of their wealth to be used for the good of others. Many times the individuals are directly involved in the process. But a major portion of philanthropic activity is conducted through institutions (foundations, trusts, museums, etc.), where the decisions are made by hired or appointed staff members carrying out the wishes and direction of a board of trustees.

To examine the trends and directions among these endeavors, it will be helpful first to define them. By necessity, the definitions will reflect my own interpretations and be fairly general in nature. But they should provide a useful framework for discussion.

Charity

Charity is giving away a portion of what you have for the benefit of others. For general definition, charitable giving is the smaller gifts that come from many people to add up to a larger amount that sustains a project or effort. Church collections and benefit events are good examples of this kind of giving. In the United States, charitable giving sustains several thousand people-serving organizations and is the basis for 80 percent of all annual giving.

Philanthropy

Philanthropy involves the giving of private or corporate wealth to projects or individuals. Most often, philanthropy is understood to involve gifts of larger amounts, covering the spectrum of a few thousand dollars to many millions. Substantial wealth is generally seen as the source for this giving, as opposed to the one-time gift that may come from a donor who has received a windfall such as a bequest or insurance settlement.

Philanthropy involves both individuals and institutions. An individual or corporation creates an institution (such as a foundation) to carry the philanthropic intent into future generations.

Volunteerism

Volunteerism is the giving of time to charitable causes. It often involves working with essential tasks—nursing AIDS babies, teaching illiterate adults to read, or taking responsibility to mentor a juvenile offender. A January 6, 1992, article in *The New York Times* reported that a 1990 Gallup Poll found that the number of volunteers among the adults surveyed had risen from 45 to 54 percent in a 1988 survey.[2]

If one believes, as I do, that these three expressions of the law of giving are entering an era of expansion worldwide, there are several interesting questions to explore: Who is involved? What changes are taking place? And Where are we going?

WHO IS INVOLVED?

It is incredible to see how individuals from all walks of life and all parts of the world are being swept into the worldwide experience of giving. Recently I attended the memorial service for a great friend who had been extremely generous in his giving throughout his life. While there I met an acquaintance who said, "It is sad to see such a generous soul pass away. There just aren't many like him anymore." I disagree with this statement. For more than fifty years I have been involved with charitable organizations and the people who support them. In the last ten years I have seen more five-, six-, and seven-figure gifts to various organizations than in all the previous forty years.

Moreover, I see an explosion of charitable interest and involvement from people in all walks of life, not just the wealthy. My husband is a founding trustee of a program called "America's Awards," which honors unsung heroes who personify the American character and spirit. A ceremony was held in the Kennedy Center in Washington, D.C., to honor the 1991 award winners. Among them was a Catholic nun who became a doctor and sought out the poorest county in America in which to serve. Another was a single black mother who took on the decrepit housing project where her family had lived and turned it into a community of hope. But my favorite of the 1991 honorees was seventy-year-old John Fling, who does every day what he has done every day for forty-five years: spend most of his waking hours helping those in need.

• One night in 1951, John accompanied the police to settle a domestic dispute. The couple had a small baby, but apparently the boy wasn't fathered by the husband. John asked if it would solve the problem if he took the baby. The couple readily agreed, signing a scrap of paper that gave John all rights to the boy. John and his wife Jane raised the child along with their natural son.

• They have never owned a home. They live on Social Security, in a rent-free cottage behind his mother-in-law's house. Though he has worked all his life, sometimes several jobs at once, John is almost without material possessions. The clothing he gives away is often better than what he wears. He doesn't have a television, or the time to look at one. Only recently did John get a telephone—to better serve those who depend on him. He has never owned a car, but he has bought cars for five others.

• For forty-five years, John Fling has spent most of his waking hours driving the streets of Columbia, South Carolina, looking for someone he can help. There has not been a single day that he hasn't done something to help someone in need. He delivers food, medicine, and laundry, helps with bills, repairs screen doors, mows lawns, unstops sinks, transports the needy to appointments.

He has an extended "family" that includes forty blind people, two hundred senior citizens, and four hundred children.

• John is caring, selfless, and limitless in energy. He is unincorporated and refuses to become a non-profit organization. There is no board to direct him, no committee to support his activities. Most of the money he hands out is either his own or is donated by local businessmen and friends around the country. He often takes the last dime out of his pocket to help someone.

• Once, while visiting a nursing home with two deacons from his church, John met an elderly woman who said she didn't know what time to take her medicine because she didn't have a watch. John pulled the watch from his own wrist, handed it to the woman, and walked on. As the three men left the nursing home, John met a one-legged man on the street who said he needed a raincoat. John took off his own coat and gave it to the man. One of the deacons said to John, "Let's get back in the truck before you give away your pants."

• When asked why he has lived this way, John's reply is simple, "I believe this is how the Good Lord intended us to live."

While John Fling is in his seventies, I also see many younger people finding and expressing the joy of giving. One organization I know recently launched a national advisory board. The youngest member is not yet thirty and the oldest is nearing eighty. The board includes a Korean-American immigrant, a Swiss expatriate, a midwestern executive, and an East Coast "WASP." One member still shy of forty years old has been a six-figure contributor to this cause for several years.

WHAT CHANGES ARE TAKING PLACE?

An exciting development in recent years has been the growth of international philanthropy. In the years preceding and following World War II it was rare that any nation other than the United States was involved in a major way with philanthropic efforts outside its own borders. Foreign aid was largely the province of the governments of Europe and Asia, and little of a private nature was developed. Largely as a result of the worldwide missionary efforts of American religious movements beginning to surge in the 1930s, Americans were confronted with the social as well as the spiritual needs of people in many other parts of the world.

It was during this period that many of the relief agencies began operations. Hand in hand with denominations and religious agencies, missionary efforts to spread the Gospel began to be coupled with medical services, relief of hunger, and efforts aimed at the preservation and enhancement of life for children. It was at this time that the term "social Gospel" was coined and hotly debated. From history's perspective, it seems an odd debate. One side hotly contested that the principles of religion must be the primary emphasis of any religious missionary effort. The other side countered that sick and dying people would have a hard time hearing any Gospel message. Better to feed and heal them with loving care and thus prepare the way for the message.

What was discovered is that neither side of the spiritual message can be separated from the other. Any consideration of God must include not only a discussion of His intent and purpose for mankind, but also His intense love and care for the practical needs of each individual.

By my rough estimate, however, the acceleration of effort began to expand outward from North America about the time of the Vietnam War. Suddenly it seemed the entire world became aware of the plight of many oppressed peoples from many nations. The swell of refugees from Southeast Asia was a problem that Europe, Africa, and South America began to perceive and confront.

Perhaps it was the ticking of the nuclear clock which began running after World War II that pushed people all around the world to begin discovering the spiritual resources necessary to deal with such a world. Perhaps technology had become a kind of "god," and when the ultimate "gift" of this god was the nuclear nightmare, people were driven to rediscover the universal spiritual values that always have and always will transcend technology.

Whatever the reason, during the 1960s and 1970s events began to unfold that drew the world closer around the theme of giving of ourselves for the benefit of others. International efforts were organized to combat hunger and oppression. Events like the global "Live Aid" concert series were conceived and conducted by a consortium of people not led by North Americans. Truly we see this encouraging trend continuing today as former neighboring enemies become mutually supportive while the Berlin Wall comes down and the Iron Curtain melts away.

There has been another phenomenon of involvement that has appeared and grown in my lifetime. Where once the giving impulse was largely an individual decision and effort, we have seen giving through charity, philanthropy, and volunteerism become organized and institutionalized. Once a band of neighbors would come together to replace a barn that had burned. They would gather for the task, finish it, and then disband until another emergency arose. But as we moved into the twentieth century these efforts became the inspiration for a move to create permanent agencies to carry forward certain work.

The nurses organized as volunteers for the Civil War became institutionalized as the Red Cross. The hunger and homelessness that prompted William Booth of England to act became institutionalized as the Salvation Army. Four ministers, faced with the crushing blow of mass unemployment in Denver, Colorado, founded the forerunner to the United Way.

And the pace of this development has accelerated in recent years. The number of non-profit organizations approved by the United States Internal Revenue Service to receive tax-deductible donations has nearly doubled in the last ten years. And the number of private foundations, where individuals set aside a portion of their personal wealth for charitable purposes, has nearly quadrupled in the same period.

With the recent turmoil at United Way and other organizations, many have questioned whether this proliferation is a positive development. Despite the problems, we must conclude that it has been very positive. Properly run, organizations can do so much more than individuals, and do it faster and more efficiently. A fine example of this is the organization Americares. Only a few years ago, it was nearly impossible to get relief supplies quickly to areas stricken by natural disasters or political strife. Then one man, Robert Macauley, sat down one day and asked: "Why does it have to be this way? Why can't we just load up an airplane and fly to needy people and handle the paperwork later?" In just a few short years, he and his colleagues have done exactly that—moving millions of dollars of donated food, medicine, and supplies around the world and into the hands of stricken peoples. Americares did not exist in 1980; yet in 1991 it airlifted nearly $104 million worth of supplies to seventy-five countries around the globe.

Americares' ability to respond quickly was highlighted by the emergency needs following the violence that occurred in Los Angeles in the spring of 1992. Grocery stores were among the worst affected businesses at that time. With transportation suspended and thousands of people out of work, an acute food situation quickly developed. Before the last of the fires were put out, Americares had a plane loaded with basic supplies leave its East Coast headquarters and head for Los Angeles. Within hours after landing, the supplies were brought right into the affected communities and distributed by churches and neighborhood organizations. No bureaucracy, no middleman, and most importantly, no waiting to get supplies to the needy families.

The process of formalizing giving efforts into organizational structures will continue to grow. This process can be made to serve the world even better, however, if we begin now to develop an understanding of how organizations are born, grow, and sometimes die.

I have spent nearly sixty years working in various charitable organizations. They range in size from a few volunteers and a budget in the thousands of dollars to hundreds of full-time workers and a budget in the hundreds of millions. The oldest was the Reformed church mission societies, founded 250 years ago, and the youngest is the Positive Thinking Foundation, started in 1989. The missions of these groups have been as varied as building a high-rise office building in New York City to serve religious organizations to organizing volunteers to fold bandages for World War II. In all of my experience, however, I have only found two types of organizations: the bureaucratic and the innovative.

In a word, bureaucratic organizations focus on policies and process; innovative organizations focus on ideas and visions. Both are vitally needed at any one time in our world and, indeed, most successful organizations go through the process of changing from a bureaucratic to an innovative posture and back again.

A wonderful example of this principle is the March of Dimes campaign. Launched in the 1930s to combat polio, its explosive growth demanded a smooth-running bureaucracy to coordinate the annual drive, which required thousands of volunteers to conduct the annual campaign each year in the same time period, using a common theme and spokesperson every time. Year after year the knock at the door and the cans at the checkout stands finally became almost synonymous with the coming of spring. If you drove across the United States and Canada in March of 1967, for example, you would pass hundreds of billboards, all unveiled on the same day, depicting the 1967 "Poster Child," and reminding you to give to the campaign.

Then came the blessed result: polio was wiped out. The achievement of their goal, however, presented the March of Dimes with a troubling dilemma: should they throw one last celebration, close the doors, and go home? Or could there be a different mission for the effective and efficient organization that had succeeded? At this point, they had only one choice. The bureaucracy had to give way to innovation in order to answer that one great question. Innovative thinking and research gave the March of Dimes a new mission—to eliminate life-threatening childhood diseases. The innovative spirit allowed the bureaucracy once again to be applied effectively to an important new problem, and in the process to reshape the bureaucracy itself by new techniques and methods in order to face the new mission.

Effective organizations

I would like to say a few other things about this matter of organizations and the law of giving. First, effective organizations are those which always remain secondary to the individuals who work in them and support them. There is no "chicken-and-egg" question here. The people always come first, and any organization that drifts from this reality is doomed to become useless. That said, I believe organizations are a good thing. People banded together can always accomplish more than an individual working alone. This is true whether we are speaking of the International Lions Clubs working to eliminate unnecessary blindness on a global scale or the deacons of the local church holding a tag sale to raise money to pay the heating bill. Millions of Lions Club members or dozens of church volunteers can do more together than one person can alone.

However, it takes the vision of one person to set the organization in motion. There would be no movement to eliminate blindness had not one doctor decided to do something about it and found a way to call others to the task.

A second point about organizations is that there are no specific patterns that work in every case. Some bureaucratic organizations are vitally efficient and effective; others are hopelessly mired with internal struggles and very little gets accomplished for their mission. Similarly, innovative organizations can respond well, but sometimes grow so fast that they cannot continue to simply bubble up ideas and act on them. Systems and procedures are needed in order to multiply the results of innovation and get more people involved.

Let me give you two quick examples. First in the United Way and the crisis faced at the national level in 1992. Simply stated, the bureaucracy became so insulated from the mission that some key individuals developed an arrogance and insulation from the grass-roots movement that supports them. Innovation was needed badly to deal with the situation and preserve the tremendous mission of United Way. In the first few months of the crisis, however, the leaders were not capable of innovation, only damage control. The only possible result was the steep and rapid decline in support for the national program.

Similarly, Covenant House International, based in New York City, faced a grave crisis in 1990. Again, insulation from the mission on the part of a few had led to mismanagement and scandal. In the case of Covenant House, however, the leaders responded quickly and decisively to affirm the mission and make the changes necessary to correct the problems. An open and frank examination of the entire organization was undertaken immediately with the help of very capable outsiders. The result was that by 1992, Covenant House was serving more runaway and desperate children than ever before.

WHERE ARE WE GOING?

This is a wonderful time to be alive, and especially to be involved in charity, philanthropy, and volunteerism. The opportunities opening before us and being accepted on a global scale could barely have been dreamed about five years ago. Only a handful of visionaries could have predicted the recent picture of Boris Yeltsin, president of Russia, standing before the United States Congress and asking for foreign aid to rebuild his region's crumbling economy. More important perhaps was the fact that Yeltsin came not only to the United States but to Germany and Japan as well, showing how the law of giving can and will be global in scope.

However, it is the very nature of this rapidly changing world that presents us with our greatest challenge. Before we can operate in tomorrow's world, we must begin to understand it, and it will be very different from today's. Both individuals and organizations involved in giving must stop to think about the future and the changes that will occur. Then they must change, or they will find themselves not fading over time, but vanishing overnight.

In the organizations Norman and I have helped to lead, we have always enjoyed what I call "idea sessions." People from every part of the operation, and some volunteers, will gather in a room and ask "what if" questions about any problem or project. I believe this type of thinking is vital to the future. One book I have found particularly helpful here is *The Art of the Long View,* by Peter F. Schwartz. He puts the need for creative thinking like this:

> How can people, businesses and institutions plan for the future when they do not know what tomorrow will bring? A deep and realistic confidence is built on insight into the possible outcomes of our choices. . . .
>
> To act with confidence, one must be willing to look ahead and consider uncertainties: "What challenges could this world present me? How might others respond to my actions?" Rather than asking such questions, too many people react to uncertainty with denial. They take an unconsciously deterministic view of events. They take it for granted that some things just can't and won't happen; for example, "oil prices won't collapse," or "the Cold War can't ever end." Not having tried to foresee surprising events, they are at a loss for ways to act when upheaval continues. They create blind spots for themselves. . . .
>
> To operate in an uncertain world, people need to be able to *reperceive*—to question their assumptions about the way the world works, so that they may see the world more clearly. . . . The end result, however, is not an accurate picture of tomorrow, but rather better decisions about the future.[3]

We need to be looking for new ways to perceive charity, philanthropy, and volunteerism in the future. What signs are appearing today to guide us? I believe there are several.

Growing individual involvement

The involvement of individuals with the spiritual principles of giving is definitely increasing. One only has to look at the growth of individual giving in the United States, which has increased markedly in the years 1989–92, despite the pressures of recession. The United States has long been an indicator for the charitable patterns of other nations.

The new involvement of other countries is also a growing trend that will affect the future. Twenty-five years ago, *Guideposts* magazine began publication in Chinese from a base in Hong Kong. Soon the magazine's expansion found us with a growing level of net revenues that were difficult to convert and transfer to the United States. This gave us the idea of using these funds to give back something to the Hong Kong community. After careful research we discovered that there was a lack of kindergartens for children three to six years. So we began a series of *Guideposts* kindergartens.

At the time, this was an amazing development in the city of Hong Kong because we cared and would take problem children. Here was an operation that was being set up, not to make money but to assist with a need. We found that this practice was not at all common among the citizens of Hong Kong and therefore somewhat of an oddity.

Late in 1991 we traveled to Hong Kong to open a third kindergarten. While there, we met with various business and official groups in the city. And we made a happy discovery. Starting with the events that brought thousands of "boat people" to Hong Kong, members of the community began to see and accept responsibility for the caring of others less fortunate than themselves. Dozens of agencies, both governmental and private, have sprung up to deal with the problems and opportunities these refugees bring. Innovation abounds; in just one example we saw how housing was obtained in a country where vacant land is almost nonexistent. The space set aside for earthen dams and power plants has been used to set up temporary housing for families that have spent years without a home.

Giving on a larger scale is also growing, both in the United States and abroad. One example is the S. C. Johnson family, known for the Johnson Wax products in grocery stores worldwide. Philanthropy is taught as a part of family history as well as corporate practice. The generosity of the great-grandfather of this remarkable family has been multiplied many times through his descendants. This passage from *The Essence of a Family Enterprise*, a history of the family and company by chairman Samuel C. Johnson, reveals why:

> My great-grandfather, a true church-going man, believed in corporate philanthropy. He held the notion that businesses should put back something into the community in which they are located. By various extensions and indirect methods, a corporation also should give back something to the broader group of consumers from which it has earned profits. Providing jobs in a community, he believed, while certainly important, was simply not enough.
>
> His concept is, of course, in the tradition of the Carnegie, Mellon, and Rockefeller families. And although Johnson Wax—then a little Midwestern parquet flooring manufacturer—could not be philanthropic on so grand a scale, my grandfather carried on his father's notion and set the tone for the company's tradition of giving "something" back. As founder of the United Fund, he even gave an endowment to the charity which is used to provide money for the volunteers' campaign luncheon and dinner report meetings. . . .
>
> My father gave away most of his money during his lifetime, to varied causes including Cornell University and The Johnson Foundation. The Johnson Family has long believed that basically one should give money away as it is made, rather than passing funds along in an estate. After all, it is a lot more fun to give it away while you are alive than to have trustees do it after you are gone.
>
> My father was very active in giving—a practice I have followed— right up to the maximum the Internal Revenue Service allows an individual to deduct. This has become something of a family tradition. Accumulated wealth really isn't very important. If it just sits there, what good does it do? Personal wealth should be reinvested in productive enterprises, just as a corporation does with part of its earnings, or it should be put to use in a philanthropic way. I find the thought of sitting on a pile of money, a passive investor in a portfolio of managed funds, utterly boring.
>
> Corporate philanthropy and social responsibility are imprecise concepts: We are dealing with complex issues, emotions, people and cultures. The most creative ideas can fail. And money often is not the only solution. Still, by providing creative ideas, and both human and financial resources, we believe we can make a difference.[4]

Larger-scale giving is growing worldwide as well. When the recent upheaval in Los Angeles left the Korean community without access to a basic dietary staple, rice, the first response came by airlift from Seoul, Korea. It was collected, funded, and delivered completely by Korean donors.

But perhaps the greatest area of growth will come in the area of volunteerism. The *New York Times* article mentioned earlier on charitable volunteering gave a few of the reasons why. First, as donors become more sophisticated and aware of how charitable organizations work, they want more involvement to ensure that their contributions are having the greatest possible effect. Also, a baby-boom generation raised on activism is finding out that much can be accomplished through the systems that exist, saving the enormous amounts of energy required to set up new systems. Also, as people lose jobs, the need to keep busy leads to volunteerism, as does the decision by a growing number of women to leave the career workforce for a time to raise a family. Just a few short years ago, schools and churches were desperate to find adults available during normal workday hours to staff volunteer positions. That shortage is rapidly becoming a surplus.

Another important factor quoted in the *Times* comes from Carol Stone, president and chief executive officer of the Volunteer Center of Greater Orange County in California: "In the 60's people tried to make a better world through political change, outside the system. Now they are working within the system and working hands-on, one-on-one with the people who need help."[5]

To these indicators, I would add a few personal observations. We are all aware that the baby-boomer generation represents a huge bulge in population. As these people mature and the economy keeps changing, more and more will be taking early retirement and, in just fifteen years, will begin to retire naturally. Better health care means they will have vigorous and active lifestyles well into their seventies and even eighties. They will want to find activities to stay busy. The spiritual movement that is raising their awareness of the law of giving will cause them to volunteer in ever-increasing numbers. Already several organizations I know have top-notch personnel who work for little or no pay, giving their years of experience and wisdom in exchange for a meaningful activity. Surely this is a trend that will grow.

Increasing worldwide needs

Our world seems headed for years of economic upheaval and rebuilding. The struggles of the United States to eliminate its deficit are matched by the monumental task for Germany of re-unification and for former Soviet bloc nations of developing market economies. Even the economic powerhouse that is Japan faces an aging workforce and limited access to natural resources. The exploding inflation among nations of the Southern Hemisphere is declining, but still exceeds 30 percent in many nations.

All of these pressures mean that governments will continue to reduce the money they spend on social programs. What just a few short years ago seemed an unending fountain may well diminish to a token trickle for all but the most basic crisis life support.

These government reductions will mean that enormous needs will have to be filled by charitable, philanthropic, and volunteer efforts. Those needs represent the vast opportunities ahead of us.

Another area of need is much more serious, however. When I was involved with the Salvation Army in the 1940s, poverty meant hunger and a lack of clothing and toys. Today, we know that poverty raises the threat of child abuse, drug abuse, violent crime, and other problems. These darker issues were certainly present a generation ago, but the social structure kept them hidden. The openness of our society will continue to reveal our deepest needs.

THE IMPORTANCE OF ORGANIZATIONS

Because the task ahead will be a growing one and because the numbers of people wanting to face those tasks will continue to grow, organizations will be very important in future charitable work. However, only those with the ability to find the balance between efficient bureaucracy and creative innovation will be truly useful. In fact, it is highly likely that some of our larger organizations today will pass from the scene as a result of their inability to adjust. And, given that inability, they should not be preserved. Others can and will rise to take their place.

Organizations able to be useful in the future will likely share some common characteristics. Among these will be:

1. The ability to find the emerging core needs of people and to meet them successfully. This is presently seen in the realm of

American churches. For years, the major denominations have experienced declining memberships. However, at the same time, overall church attendance is growing rapidly. Why? Because the machinery of the denominations has not been retooled to find and meet contemporary needs. Churches that are finding those needs are often independent "superchurches"; and others, patterned on them, are free from national influence and able to innovate.

Interestingly, the decline of major denominations is not a worldwide phenomenon. Often the structure and resources of denominational ties are just what is needed for churches in emerging nations. A good example is Young Nak Presbyterian Church, in Seoul, South Korea, the largest Presbyterian church in the world. Its founding minister, Dr. Chik Han, received the Templeton Prize in 1992 for his innovative methods and ministry.

2. The ability to involve donors in the organization. The donor of the past is not the donor of the future. Future donors want to get involved in partnership with the organization, not just write a check. They are interested in hearing about results, not only responding to appeals for need. Peter Drucker, the famous management consultant, has devoted the last few years to helping non-profits look ahead and better prepare themselves for the future. He has written extensively about the need for organizations to begin talking about their results, as opposed to their needs.

One new concept targeting this need for involvement is "annual donor meetings." Many of the elements of communication and accountability that are seen at stockholders' meetings apply to non-profit organizations as well. Offering the donor public a chance to gather and meet the leadership of the organization is a trend that will grow in the future.

3. Another trend is the movement away from charismatic leaders and toward teams that are more accountable to their boards and donors. These leaders will in turn trend away from the "hired guns" who move from one organization to another and toward individuals committed over the long term to the mission they serve. These men and women will be devoted, innovative, imaginative, and spiritually directed. This last factor, spiritual direction, will become more common at both "secular" and "religious" groups. The general spiritual awakening mentioned at the begin-

ning of this essay will spread its influence across all types of charitable, philanthropic, and volunteer organizations.

In summary, the future is challenging and bright on the frontiers of the human endeavor to follow the law of giving. I firmly believe that many among our next generation will be drawn to the principle taught by Jesus Christ when his disciples asked him: "Lord, when did we see you hungry and feed you, or thirsty and give you drink? When did we see you a stranger and take you in, or naked and clothe you? Or when did we see you sick or in prison, and come to you?" . . . "The king will answer and say to them, 'Assuredly, I say to you, inasmuch as you did it to one of the least of these My brethren, you did it to Me.' "[6]

REFERENCES

1. *Holy Bible, King James Version.*
2. *The New York Times,* January 6, 1992.
3. PETER F. SCHWARTZ, *The Art of the Long View,* pp. 3, 9.
4. SAMUEL C. JOHNSON, *The Essence of a Family Enterprise* (Indianapolis: Curtis Publishing Co., 1988), pp. 127, 134.
5. *The New York Times,* January 6, 1992.
6. Matthew 25:37–40. *Holy Bible, King James Version.*

11

RELIGION

by Robert L. Herrmann

*Dr. Robert L. Herrmann is executive director of the
American Scientific Affiliation, and the author, with John
Marks Templeton, of* The God Who Would Be Known.
*A molecular biologist, he was a member of the biochemistry
faculty of the Boston University School of Medicine for
seventeen years and is presently a trustee of the National
Institute for Health Care Research.*

I. INTRODUCTION

It is my conviction that any discussion of the religious future must
be set in the context of the scientific age of which we have been a
part for the past several centuries. Our knowledge of our world
has changed dramatically in this century, and now the pace of
accumulation of new data has quickened to a gallop. More than
half the scientists who ever lived are alive today. More than half of
the discoveries in the natural sciences have been made, and more
than half of the books ever written have been written in this
century.

But in the past decade or two a remarkable thing has happened.
Scientists have begun to ask religious questions, stimulated by the
enormity and intricacy of the physical world and the degree to

which physical reality shouts for a deeper explanation in terms of design and purpose. Indeed, God seems to have chosen science, a discipline often misused to deny His existence, to reveal Himself in His staggering immensity and creativity as the Light-giver who brings illumination to all who would seek Him.[1]

II. RELIGION IN A SCIENTIFIC AGE

Looking back

Living in a scientific age, it would seem that science has made religion irrelevant for many modern persons. Yet it has not always been so. Indeed, there is strong support for the thesis that Western science arose in significant part as a consequence of a Judeo-Christian theology that viewed God as Creator and Supreme Ruler of nature, one who had not only brought the cosmos into being, but governed it by laws that reflected His faithfulness and consistency. The pioneers of science adopted the attitude that God had given them a world to be understood and appreciated through science in much the way that theologians understood and appreciated God through the study of the Scriptures. This reverential attitude is seen in Francis Bacon, Isaac Newton, Clerk Maxwell, and the vast majority of their contemporaries.

Given this attitude among its practitioners, the first centuries of Western science were euphoric. Scientists explored the creation with humility and wonder, understanding that everything they observed was under the hand of Providence and thus contingent upon the divine will.

Walter Thorson tells us:

> Francis Bacon epitomized this attitude when he insisted that if a man wishes to know reality, he must abandon the dogmatic confidence of his pride in reason alone and sit down humbly before the revelation of God, whether that were the book of Scripture or the book of nature. This parallel between scientific and religious knowledge, both of which are to be acquired by "reading the revelation of God," and not by *a priori* reason, is a favorite and important emphasis of the early scientists. . . . These early thinkers thought of themselves as "empiricists" with respect to Scripture as well as with respect to creation.[2]

It may seem surprising then that this sense of humility on the part of scientists did not continue, but the very success of science led to the gradual separation of scientific and theological categories. For, as the idea took hold that the universe could be explained as a clockwork, with each phenomenon separated into cause and effect, under the operation of natural laws, there seemed nothing left for God to do.

The changing character of twentieth-century science

At the beginning of this century, a surprising shift began to occur. The physicist Werner Heisenberg demonstrated a profound physical phenomenon: the uncertainty of the simultaneous knowledge of both position and momentum of elementary subatomic particles. The upshot of this was that events studied with individual subatomic particles seemed to have no bearing on the aggregate of particles in the macrocosm. The sum of the parts appeared to equal the whole, but without explanation. Cause and effect were decoupled.

Then the emerging field of cosmology revealed that the universe was bigger by many orders of magnitude than we had ever dreamed, and that it had come to be by way of a "big bang," a singular electromagnetic detonation which was reminiscent of the first verses of the Book of Genesis.

On the biological side, study of the origin of life was growing increasingly intriguing. There seemed to be a delicate and intricate balance in the structure of the cosmos necessary for the emergence of life. The collection of constraints was so striking as to be given a name: the anthropic principle. If life came about by purely mechanistic means, then it was on the basis of a special sort of circumstance.

There have also been some remarkable findings on the human brain. The combination of all the neurons in a human brain and the multitude of connections between neurons makes for a level of complexity that rivals the number of stars in the universe. In effect, there is a universe of complexity in our heads! Such complexity appears to be arising everywhere. And along with baffling complexity and the sheer enormity of the cosmos has come humility. There is really no room left for arrogance or pride over what science has achieved. We begin to understand how little we know. Timothy Ferris has given us some idea of the extent of our ignorance in his book *Coming of Age in the Milky Way:*

> We might eventually obtain some sort of bedrock understanding of cosmic structure, but we will never understand the universe in detail; it is just too big and varied for that. If we possessed an atlas of our galaxy that devoted but a single page to each star system in the Milky Way (so that the sun and all its planets were crammed in one page), that atlas would run to more than ten million volumes of ten thousand pages each. It would take a library the size of Harvard's to house the atlas, and merely to flip through it, at the rate of a page per second, would require over ten thousand years. Add the details of planetary cartography, potential extraterrestrial biology, the subtleties of the scientific principles involved, and the historical dimensions of change, and it becomes clear that we are never going to learn more than a tiny fraction of the story of our galaxy alone— and there are a hundred billion more galaxies. As the physician Lewis Thomas writes, "The greatest of all the accomplishments of twentieth-century science has been the discovery of human ignorance."[3]

Yet, as Ferris goes on to point out, this realization carries with it a new awareness of the open-endedness of learning, of the vast storehouse of discovery and opportunity which is ours.

The character of science has also changed sociologically, based upon the powerful critique among scientists interested in the philosophy of science who were joined by a large number of sociologists and historians of science. A forerunner in this critique of science is Thomas Kuhn, whose *Structure of Scientific Revolutions,* published in 1970, proposed a new interpretation of the history of science.[4] Kuhn argues that science goes through periods of normality during which an accepted paradigm—a broad conceptual framework—is employed and applied, and periods of revolution in which a given paradigm is shattered and replaced by a new one. This new emphasis on the sociological factors influencing the development is described by Arthur Peacocke as follows:

> Science came to be seen as a continuous social enterprise, and the rise and fall of theories and the use and replacement of concepts as involving a complex of personal, social, intellectual, and cultural interactions that often determined whether a theory was accepted or rejected. Theories are constructed, it was argued, in terms of the

prevailing world view of the scientists involved: so to understand them one must understand the relevant world view. A new emphasis was therefore placed on the history of science, especially the sociological factors influencing its development. Thus a new area was opened up for the application of the expanding enterprise of the sociology of knowledge in general and of scientific knowledge in particular. However, it turns out that the world view of the scientist is an exceedingly complex and elusive entity—even more so when a *community* of scientists is involved.[5]

Out of this debate between extremists arguing for scientific truth as purely social construction and those arguing for science as final truth has come what is referred to as "the critical realist position." The philosopher Ernan McMullin has suggested that the basic claim for scientific realism is that "the long-term success of a scientific theory gives reason to believe that something like the entities and structure postulated in the theory actually exist."[6] He proposes four qualifications for his definition:

(1) The theory must be a successful one over a significant period; (2) The explanatory success of the theory gives some reason, though not a conclusive warrant, to believe it; (3) What is believed is that the theoretical structures are *something like* the structures of the real; (4) No claim is made for a special, more basic, privileged, form of existence for the postulated entities.[7]

Even here we see the extent of provisionality assigned to theories. Terms like "significant period," "some reason," and "something like" are the essential elements of a valid approach to scientific truth in the new scientific era. This cautious approach, now accepted by a majority of working scientists, ought to instill in all of us a greater openness to the more philosophical and theological questions of meaning and purpose in our universe. There simply are no exclusive pathways to truth. Add to this the baffling questions of interpretation of quantum uncertainty at the subatomic level, and the staggering size of the universe at the cosmic level, and we marvel at the unreasonable effectiveness of scientific study to comprehend nature and nature's laws.

The changing character of twentieth-century theology

Arthur Peacocke has pointed out that, just as scientific realism has gone through a transition from the naive realism of the positivist to the critical realist position of the socially sensitive scientists, so also theology has experienced a healthy reassessment of the nature of theological doctrine, and has acquired a valuable perspective on the use of theological language as model and metaphor. The naive realism of the scientist has its counterpart in the fundamentalist literalism of the theologian, and the critical realist position in science would be comparable to a theological viewpoint which regarded the doctrines and symbols of theology as partial and limited but nevertheless essential ways of expressing the reality that is God and God's relation to human beings.[8]

The recognition that religious and theological language is a form of expression which depends upon models was first emphasized by Ian Ramsey in his book *Models and Mystery, Models for Divine Activity, and Religious Language*.[9] What has been appreciated is that the Scriptures make extensive use of models. God is described as Father, Creator, King, Shepherd, Judge. Jesus is described as the Christ, the Second Adam, the Great Physician, the Son, the Lamb. The third person of the Trinity is figured as Holy Spirit, Holy Ghost, Comforter. And the Trinity itself is a quite metaphorical construction—God as Creator, Incarnate as the Son, and Immanent as the Holy Spirit. God's relationship to the world is often depicted by monarchical models (God as King, Sovereign, Maker), or by organic models (the created order as a garment worn by God, or as the work of a potter, or as the emanation of life-giving energy, or as the spoken Word). The atonement through Christ's death is described in terms of models such as sacrifice, redemption, ransom, and substitution.

Just as in the case of scientific models, theological models are analogical and metaphorical, rather than attempting to be explicitly descriptive or literal. The idea of discovery and increasing intelligibility is again involved, but the subject is the relationship nature–man–God. The context for discovery for both scientific and theological models is a community with what Peacocke calls "a living tradition of reference back to originating experiments and experiences, and one that has developed and is still developing language to maintain this continuity of intelligibility."[10]

Peacocke points out that, in science, the continuous linguistic community provides the essential social structure through which discovery of entities and establishment of terminology occurs. By comparison, in the Christian community, for example, key terms and concepts relate back to statements in the biblical sources or statements by church councils convened to formulate—often after heated debate—the valid interpretation and language (the appropriate models) of theology. Furthermore, these experiences of God continue to occur and to be the subject of interpretation as new findings of a historical or scientific type impact on theological models.

It is within this framework of growth of theological understanding that one can see a powerful future for religion.

A new understanding of the creativity of the cosmos

The incredible events of evolution are punctuated, we now know, with quite miraculous emergences and extinctions. The extraordinarily complex origin of life, the sudden early appearance of multicellular animals in great profusion in the Cambrian,[11] and the proliferation of mammals following the sudden extinction of the dinosaurs 65 million years ago argue for a marvelous creativity and connectedness. The process seems to seethe with new innovations and a superb timing that dispels any notion of blind chance. And the end result? Matter has become mind, and now contemplates its origin and its reason for being.

There is here no knock-down argument for design and purpose, but certainly there are strong hints of ultimate realities beyond the cosmos. One of the strongest hints, in my opinion, relates to the new understanding of the capacity of the cosmos for so-called self-organization. For, following the big bang, a most astounding story of creativity unfolds throughout time, from the void of space to galaxies, planets, crystals, life, and people. Science has previously been ruled by the Newtonian and thermodynamic paradigms, viewing the universe as either an unchanging and static machine, or as a process moving inexorably toward degeneration and decay. But current science leads us to pursue a new paradigm, wherein the universe appears driven creatively in the direction of cooperative and organizational processes. The gradual growth of complexity has been noted throughout the history of science, but it was given powerful support through the theory of biological evolution proposed by Charles Darwin and Alfred Russel Wallace. Subsequent developments in cosmological science have demonstrated that the increased complexity and diversity inherent in biological evolution have also been characteristic of the entire universe from its origin. Indeed, there appears to be a continuity of organization into novel and increasingly complex structures and relationships throughout the spectrum of transitions from stardust to thinking human beings.

Paul Davies, in his book *The Cosmic Blueprint*,[12] says that the discovery of the self-ordering character of nature has brought physicists to feel that their subject is poised for a major revolution. On one side are the unifiers, those who seek to reduce all phenomena to a single explanation, to search out the ultimate principles that operate at the lowest and simplest level of physics. For the unifiers, the ultimate goal is a "theory of everything." The other side is represented by the diversifiers, who see the universe as a holistic phenomenon, with the emphasis on organization and function as integrated wholes. The key ideas are complexity and connectedness rather than simplicity. The big question is whether the propensity of matter to "self-organize" is explainable by the known laws of physics or whether a completely new set of principles is involved. I agree with Davies that some scientific explanation is forthcoming, but would give even more emphasis to his plea that the concept of organizing principles in nature not be simply dismissed as "mystical" or "vitalistic."

From a theological perspective, it is indeed tempting to see this self-organizing tendency as an expression of the intimate nature of the Creator's activity and identification with our universe. It certainly hints at purpose, and, together with many other "signals of transcendence," makes a rather strong case for a higher purpose for our world. Certainly the cosmological evidence for a very special set of circumstances for the origin of living systems, and eventually mankind, fits in this category. The enormous diversity seen also in the arts, in business, and in the various religious manifestations of our modern culture is testimony to a highly creative principle at work.

III. FUTURE AREAS OF INTERACTION BETWEEN RELIGION AND SCIENCE

Evolutionary theory has struggled with two major scientific problems: the origin of life and the mechanisms of macroevolution.

Some of the religious community who oppose evolution as a god-less system have taken comfort in the scientific difficulties. And indeed, when we face the fundamental issue of what is known about the biochemical mechanisms for the origin of living sys-tems, we have to confess along with Dean Kenyon, author with Gary Steinman of *Biochemical Predestination*,[13] that there are seri-ous reasons for doubting that any straightforward naturalistic ex-planation will be readily forthcoming. Kenyon, writing in the preface to a book entitled *The Mystery of Life's Origin: Reassessing Current Theories* by Charles Thaxton, Walter Bradley, and Roger Olsen,[14] argues that most recent studies of biogenesis are so ar-tificially simplified as to be useless; potentially interfering cross-reactions and the presence of optical isomers in pre-biotic systems have been ignored. Kenyon also expresses concern for the enor-mous gap between the most complex "protocell" model systems of the laboratory and the simplest living cells, such as *Mycoplasma*. Progress has been very limited in this area of research. However, given the past history of scientific endeavor, we have no reason to believe that an explanation for life's origin will not gradually be fashioned. What might be anticipated is that the explanation will argue strongly for a remarkable informational input, which will suggest the design and intimate involvement of a Creator.

The second problem, the paucity of mechanisms for macro-evolution—the sudden production of new groups of plants and animals and the structures unique to them—is probably much closer to a scientific explanation. This is because several fields of biology are beginning to merge, pooling their resources and con-cepts in a new "developmental synthesis."

According to Scott Gilbert, writing in his third edition of *Devel-opmental Biology*,

> a new developmental synthesis is emerging that retains the best of the microevolution-yields-macroevolution model and the macro-evolution-as-separate-phenomenon model. From the latter it de-rives the concept that mutations in regulatory genes can create "jumps" from one phenotype to another without necessary inter-mediate steps. From the former, it derives the notion that genetic mutations can account for such variants and that selection acts upon them to delete them or retain them in populations. It also retains a multiplicity of paradigms. In some instances (such as the creation of

neural crest cells) a qualitative change occurs, whereas in other cases (such as the formation of the pocket gopher pouch) quantity becomes quality when a threshold is passed.

We are at a remarkable point in our understanding of nature, for a synthesis of developmental genetics with evolutionary biology may transform our appreciation of the mechanisms underlying evolutionary change and animal diversity. Such a synthesis is actually a return to a broader-based evolutionary theory that fragmented at the turn of the past century. . . . See Figure 1.

. . . In the late 1800's, evolutionary biology contained the sciences that we now call evolutionary biology, systematics, ecology, genetics, and development. By the turn of the century, the "question of heredity," i.e., genetics and development, separated from the rest of evolutionary biology. Genetics eventually split into (among other rubrics) population genetics and molecular genetics, while embryology became developmental biology. During the mid-twentieth century, population genetics merged with evolutionary biology to produce the evolutionary genetics of the modern synthesis, while molecular genetics merged with developmental biology to produce developmental genetics. These two vast areas, developmental genetics and evolutionary genetics, are on the verge of a merger that may unite these long-separated strands of biology and that may produce a developmental genetic theory capable of explaining macroevolution.[15]

The future may see a plethora of new genetic mechanisms, especially in the processes of embryonic development, which may explain macroevolutionary change. It therefore should caution us to maintain a position of openness to evolution as the process the Creator may have used to bring life and mind into being. Fundamentalists may once again find themselves isolated from the mainstream of modern thought and divorced from new theological perspectives which have the potential for bringing science and religion together.

IV. A THEOLOGICAL PERSPECTIVE

God's action in the world

One of the major contributions of very recent science has been to give a strong sense of the dynamic and intimate involvement of

FIGURE 1.

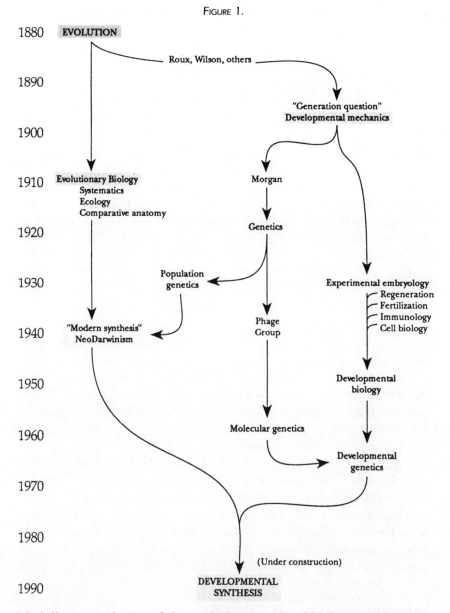

Disciplinary road map of the evolutionary side of biology, 1880 to the present. For sake of clarity, other paths (such as those from genetics to human genetics or from evolution to immunology) have not been shown.

SOURCE: From Scott Gilbert, *Developmental Biology* (3rd edn., Sunderland, MA: Sinauer Associates, 1991).

the Creator in the processes of this world. One view of God's action has been given by the neurophysiologist Donald MacKay, who describes God as the Divine Artist who fashions a constantly changing panorama of unfolding events, actually "holding in being" the whole multipatterned drama of the universe.[16] The emphasis in this analogy is on the sovereignty of God and on His direct involvement in His creation. And the consistency and regularity of the pattern are the proofs of His faithfulness. God is thus the arbiter of the entire sweep of creation, from the big bang, through the formation of star systems and supernovae from which heavy elements were made, to the origin and evolution of life.

The difficulty with this view of God's role is that there is much that is apparently flawed about this process, and Louise Young, in her book *The Unfinished Universe,* is quick to say that this is hardly what one would expect for the unfolding work of an Almighty Creator.[17] How could an omnipotent God design a world so full of happenstance and struggle, and with the wholesale extinction of large groups of plants and animals?

The physicist-theologian John Polkinghorne has addressed this question in terms of a second view, in which God's activity is more open and experimental. He proposes that two of God's salient characteristics, love and faithfulness, are consistent with the world we see—a world of random events operating within a structure of natural law, a world of chance and necessity. God's love gives freedom to His creation for trial and error through the operation of chance, while His faithfulness is expressed in the natural laws, which act to select and retain useful innovations. Polkinghorne readily admits that this concession on God's part to give freedom to His creation does open the way for disorder as well—earthquake, famine, epidemic, and the like—as consequences of genuine freedom. But that same freedom allows the creation to seek out its full potentialities in a truly free creative interaction of its parts. And the result has been an unimaginably fruitful and dynamic process.

The changing picture in theology

There has been common misunderstanding in our scientific culture that a scientific understanding makes any other explanation superfluous. It is now clear that science owns no such exclusive position; that the best that we can do is to adopt a scientific realist position which accepts the theories and models of science as only approximations of the structures of reality. And the degree to which a given theory may provide any sense of confidence that we are approaching reality is dependent upon how well that theory functions in prediction and control and in the design of new experiments.

If science's grip on reality seems to be loosening, so also is religion's. The view of reality which religion provides and theology interprets has undergone marked changes in attitude toward Scripture and the various religious traditions. Arthur Peacocke sees this as a healthy reassessment of the nature of theological reality, regarding the doctrines and symbols of theology as partial and limited but nevertheless essential ways of seeking to express the reality of God.[18] He points out that theology carries a special distinction because of its highly integrative character, bringing together God, man, and nature. The models and metaphors of theology are therefore of necessity more complex than those of the sciences, and its view of reality highly integrative and anthropomorphic. And just as with the sciences, the fact that theology is studied and articulated within a historical community or tradition makes its description of reality more susceptible to cultural and linguistic influence. In fact, the community seems to exercise an even greater restraint in theology than in the sciences, and new ideas and concepts are less easily considered by the theologian than by the scientist. It is probably for this reason that the current interest in natural theology shown by scientists is not matched by theologians, despite the fact that these new concepts could provide enormous benefits to religious communities.

As an example of the opportunities, John Polkinghorne has been writing about the important contribution which chaos theory can make to our notion of divine action.[19] We have been considering in our examination of the evolutionary process a new arrow of time, pointed in the direction of ever more developed and elaborate states of matter and energy. The mediators of this evolutionary process are complex and irregular non-linear reactions, which under far-from-equilibrium conditions can give rise to spontaneous order. Reactions of this kind also display chaotic behavior, shifting back and forth between states of order and disorder as energy either becomes available or is dissipated.

Polkinghorne points out that chaos is not limited to highly complex reactions, but is even seen in simple equations such as that which describes population growth in biological systems. The relationship appears perfectly deterministic, yet the population at any time is found to be extremely sensitive to the choice of starting value of population size. As he says, "It is characteristic of chaotic systems generally that unless one knows the initial circumstances with *unlimited* accuracy, one can only project their behavior a small way into the future with any confidence. Beyond that they are intrinsically unpredictable."[20] And he confesses his own surprise:

> The general picture resulting from these considerations is that of deterministic equations giving rise to random behavior; of order and disorder interlacing each other; of unlimited complexity being generated by simple specification; of precise equations having unpredictable consequences. That there are these possibilities is very surprising to those of us who were brought up on the study of those "tame," predictable mathematical systems on which we cut our mathematical teeth and which provided the standard teaching examples for generations of students. The recognition of structured chaos has been hailed as a third revolution, worthy to be set alongside the Newtonian and quantum mechanical revolutions which preceded it.[21]

As argued earlier, here is a world in which novelty and order are intertwined. It is the kind of open-ended world in which a God who is both loving and faithful can take an active role. His action can be mediated both through the interaction of law and chance and through introduction of new form and direction at the infinity of starting points and branching points in non-linear, chaotic processes.

All that we have said seems to shout for a God of marvelous creativity, who mediates a world in dynamic flux, a world moving in the direction of ever more complex, more highly integrated form—form set free to dance.

As Louise Young has suggested, everything is in a state of transition. Molecules, organisms, species are not fixed states of being, but rather stages of becoming. The current perspectives on reality of both science and theology seem dimly to grasp the edges of this grand paradigm of becoming. Perhaps in the end it is only God who expresses this ceaseless progression toward the highest integration and the greatest complexity. Perhaps in the end, the only reality is God.

V. THE FUTURE OF RELIGION

Science once again the handmaid of theology

God has placed remarkable signs in the heavens, on earth, and in our selves: signals of transcendence. This universe is here by divine plan, and science itself, for decades a bastion of unbelief, has once again become the source for humankind's assurance of intimate divine concern in its affairs. We have looked at the origin of the universe and our own remarkable evolution, and found the whole punctuated with the purpose of the Creator. In the words of the Nobel Laureate Sir John Eccles and co-author Daniel Robinson:

> We have the strong belief that we have to be open to the future in the adventure of human personhood. This whole cosmos is not just running on and running down for no meaning. In the context of natural theology we come to the belief that we are creatures with some supernatural meaning that is as yet ill defined. We cannot think more than that we are all part of some great design. Each of us can have the belief of acting in some unimaginable supernatural drama.[22]

Ralph Wendell Burhoe, in an article in *Zygon,* adds:

> It is my view that the sciences add more than vital new evidence for the credibility of the essential wisdom of ancient theologies in recognizing the reality of a system of superhuman power that created, sustains, and selects us according to how well we meet its requirements for human life and advancement. The sciences also add far clearer evidence than we have had previously that the essential reality of evolving human life includes much more than our bodies: something as "inner" to us as our genes and innermost "feelings" and also something as lasting as "immortal souls."[23]

We have observed the structure of the universe and concluded that it is pervaded with order and regularity, a theme repeated again and again even in the midst of seemingly chaotic events. The conviction that comes is that even in our science we arrive at truth through faith—faith in an objective reality that lies beyond our empirical measurements and our theorizing. It seems that the rational order and structure of the universe that we observe derives not from some present idea or insight of ours, but from the rationality and faithfulness of the God who yet creates and sustains it. On our part there must be a commitment to receive this truth as we look away from ourselves to the objective source of truth, the Truth-giver. The power and fruitfulness of this approach has been the key to science's remarkable success. It is a program from which theology can greatly benefit.

Humility and a future integration of science and religion

Bringing scientists and theologians together within this framework of exploration would be a source of tremendous opportunity for extending our understanding of ourselves and of the spiritual dimension. Science has proved a powerful tool for bringing us new concepts about our universe—its origin and its structure—and about our biosphere and its myriad manifestations of life. The sheer size and intricacy of what we study in science invokes a sense of awe and a feeling of humility. This expression of humility is fundamental to the success of integration—scientists and theologians alike humbled by the awesome majesty of the Creator and His creation, freed of their pride and self-centeredness, and open to the many theological challenges of the new science. The future will be open to the scientific exploration of spiritual subjects such as love, prayer, meditation, and thanksgiving. We may see the beginning of a new age of "experimental theology," which may reveal that there are spiritual laws, universal principles that operate in the spiritual domain, just as natural laws operate in the physical realm.

Such an experimental theology should be God-centered, and should recognize the inadequacy of our senses and our intellect to comprehend the Creator. Yet it will recognize that God also manifests Himself through a spiritual dimension, which not only speaks to each of us personally but seems to pervade the world we live in. Such an experimental theology will recognize that a new renaissance in human knowledge is coming, and that our religious traditions may need fresh interpretation, building on the powerful insights of the past with new data from the physical and human sciences. This future religious emphasis will encourage thinking that is open-minded and conclusions that are tentative. It will encourage diversity rather than syncretism, even as our universe has proved to be in constant change and progressive development.

The evolution of our universe would seem to be vast in its conception, yet curiously experimental and tentative, a truly creative work in progress. Its end product, up to this point, is a conscious being endowed with a remarkable brain, with a spiritual hunger for meaning and an overarching sense of purpose. We have come a long way from the cave shelters of the Ice Age, but it may well be, in God's great plan, that we have yet further to travel. Science has revealed a creation of awesome magnitude, intricacy, beauty, and order, and we sense that what lies beyond our instruments is vastly greater still.

With a new sense of humility derived from these experiences, the way is now open to examine the spiritual nature of human beings. Indeed, several researchers have already begun an extensive examination of religious variables in health care. Of special significance is the work of the psychiatrist David Larson and his colleagues in revealing the extent to which religious commitment is ignored or mismeasured in clinical medicine,[24] and the work of Herbert Benson, author of the best-selling book *The Relaxation Response*.[25] Benson, the director of the Mind-Body Medical Institute at Harvard Medical School and the New England Deaconess Hospital, is conducting research into the relationship between spirituality and health which demonstrates that spiritual experience is correlated with increased life purpose and satisfaction, a health-promoting attitude, and decreased frequency of medical symptoms.[26]

Several institutions are developing programs along these lines. The National Institute for Healthcare Research in Arlington, Virginia, is pressing forward with studies which include an examination of religious values in family life; and the John Templeton Foundation of Bryn Mawr, Pennsylvania, is developing a broad program to encourage experimental and statistical study of spiritual entities such as love, prayer, forgiveness, and thanksgiving. The foundation has established what Sir John Templeton has called a Center for Humility Theology, devoted to the encouragement of scientific research into the spiritual realm based upon the open and humble attitude engendered among theologians and scientists by the new discoveries of science.

It is also encouraging to see interest developing among prominent scientists like the Nobel Laureate Sir John Eccles and MIT's Professor Emeritus Frances O. Schmitt, both pioneer neurophysiologists. Schmitt, who was the organizer of the Neural Sciences Research Program in 1962 which has now grown into the 15,000-member Society for Neuroscience, has recently called for a new research program to study the mind–brain–spirit relationship and parapsychological phenomena such as psychokinesis and extrasensory perception with the same rigor and enthusiasm that has been applied to the study of brain mechanisms.[27]

Perhaps the future will see research foundations and religious institutions devoting huge resources to spiritual research, just as today we provide enormous amounts of funding for research into physical health. There could be great rewards in terms of increased human peace, harmony, happiness, and productivity as evidence accumulates that mankind's spiritual nature is the central aspect of our being. Even present research on physical health provides strong hints that major determinants of disease may be internal. The massive human genome project,[28] which proposes to map the entire 100,000 genes of human DNA, has revealed that the number and kind of possible disease conditions is much greater than anticipated. The most dramatic new diagnostic data relate to diseases that are expressed late in life. It has been possible to forecast the later development of a condition such as Huntington's chorea (Woody Guthrie's disease) and, more commonly, to describe genes which predict "susceptibility" or "vulnerability" to conditions like Alzheimer's disease and bipolar disease, the hereditary manic-depressive illness suffered by Winston Churchill. The latter illness is one member of what appear now to be a large number of "contingent" diseases whose expression in later life is quite variable.[29] In an article in the *Hastings Center Report,* Kathleen Nolan and Sara Swenson describe these contingent genetic conditions as common, and often coded for by more than a single gene. Furthermore, they are strongly affected by environmental factors—biological, psychological, and social—

which lead to wide variations in the expression of the underlying illness. As they describe these potential illnesses:

> One reason for substituting the language of "contingency" for that of "susceptibility" is that the latter tends to impute passivity and illness to those "cursed" with genes linked with the potential emergence of disease. Contingency implies malleability and a certain amount of independence from nature's dictates. A contingent condition may simply not occur, or may be prevented through early intervention. Hence, the contingent aspect of many common disorders may eventually inform our public imagination about genetic identity and determinism. We have always known that nurturing ourselves and each other could prevent the onset of certain conditions, but this power may be far greater than expected.[30]

Perhaps in the end we will realize how desperately we need each other. As an evangelical Christian, I am deeply saddened by the strife within my own religion in Northern Ireland and between religions in the Middle East and the Balkans. Admittedly, the struggles are as much political as ideological, but it is tempting to look hopefully at a future in which we might humbly seek reconciliation with our brothers and sisters around the globe. That could be the most powerful outcome of a theology of humility. Perhaps the Old Testament prophet Micah said it best:

> And what does the Lord require of you?
> To act justly and to love mercy
> and to walk humbly with your God.[31]

My prayer is that that will be the future for all of us.

REFERENCES

1. J. TEMPLETON and R. HERRMANN. *The God Who Would be Known* (San Francisco: Harper & Row, 1989).
2. W. THORSON. "Spiritual Dimensions of Science," in *Horizons of Science,* edited by C. F. H. Henry (New York: Harper & Row, 1978), pp. 241, 242.

3. T. FERRIS. *Coming of Age in the Milky Way* (New York: Morrow, 1988), p. 383.
4. T. KUHN. *The Structure of Scientific Revolutions* (2nd edn. Chicago: University of Chicago Press, 1970).
5. A. PEACOCKE. *Intimations of Reality* (Notre Dame IN: University of Notre Dame Press, 1984), p. 16 (italics).
6. E. McMULLIN. "The Relativist Critique of Science," in *The Sciences and Theology in the Twentieth Century,* edited by A. Peacocke (Notre Dame, IN: University of Notre Dame Press, 1981), pp. 301–2.
7. Ibid., p. 26 (italics).
8. PEACOCKE. *Intimations of Reality,* p. 40.
9. I. RAMSEY. *Models and Mystery, Models for Divine Activity, and Religious Language* (London: SCM Press, 1957).
10. PEACOCKE. *Intimations of Reality,* p. 42. See also Peacocke, *Science and the Christian Experiment* (London: Oxford University Press, 1971), pp. 12–28.
11. S. GOULD. *Wonderful Life—The Burgess Shale and the Nature of History* (New York: Norton, 1989).
12. P. DAVIES. *The Cosmic Blueprint* (New York: Simon & Schuster, 1988).
13. K. KENYON and G. STEINMAN. *Biochemical Predestination* (New York: McGraw-Hill, 1969).
14. C. THAXTON, W. BRADLEY, and R. OLSEN. *The Mystery of Life's Origin: Reassessing Current Theories* (New York: Philosophical Library, 1984), p. vii.
15. S. GILBERT. *Developmental Biology* (3rd edn., Sunderland, MA: Sinauer Associates, 1991), pp. 854–56.
16. D. M. MacKAY. *Science and Christian Faith Today* (London: CPAS Publications, 1960), pp. 8–9. See also Templeton and Herrmann. *The God Who Would Be Known,* pp. 20–21.
17. L. YOUNG. *The Unfinished Universe* (New York: Simon & Schuster, 1986), p. 92.
18. PEACOCKE. *Intimations of Reality,* p. 38.
19. J. POLKINGHORNE. *Reason and Reality* (London: SPCK, 1991), pp. 34–36.
20. Ibid., p. 36 (italics).
21. Ibid., pp. 37–38.
22. J. ECCLES and D. ROBINSON. *The Wonder of Being Human* (Boston: New Science Library, Shambala, 1985), pp. 178–79.
23. R. BURHOE. "The Human Prospect and the Lord of History." *Zygon: Journal of Religion and Science,* 10 (1975), 299.
24. D. LARSON, E. PATTERSON, D. BLAZER, A. OMRAN, and B. KAPLAN. "Systematic Analysis of Research on Religious Variables in Four

Major Psychiatric Journals, 1978–1982." *Amer. J. Psychiatry*, 143 (1986), 329–34. See also F. Craigie, D. Larson, and I. Liu, "References to Religion in the *Journal of Family Practice." J. Family Practice*, 30 (1990), 477–80.

25. H. BENSON. *The Relaxation Response* (New York: Morrow, 1975).

26. J. KASS, R. FRIEDMAN, J. LESERMAN, P. ZUTTERMEISTER, and H. BENSON. "Health Outcomes and a New Index of Spiritual Experience." *J. for the Scientific Study of Religion* (in press). See also S. Myers and H. Benson. "Psychological Factors in Healing: A New Perspective on an Old Debate." *Behavioral Med.*, 185 (1992), 11.

27. F. O. SCHMITT. "Generating a New Paradigm in the Context of Science and Theology." 1991 Templeton Foundation Symposium on "Human Viability and a World Theology," Chicago Center for Religion and Science, Chicago, IL, November 16, 1991.

28. "GENOME ISSUE—MAPS AND DATABASE." *Science*, 254, no. 5029, October 11, 1991.

29. R. HERRMANN. *Genetic Engineering* (Washington, D.C.: Council of Independent Colleges, 1990), pp. 13–20.

30. K. NOLAN and S. SWENSON. "New Tools, New Dilemmas: Genetic Frontiers." *Hastings Center Report*, 18, no. 5 (October–November 1988), 40–46.

31. MICAH 6:8, *Holy Bible, New International Version* (Grand Rapids, MI: Zondervan, 1978).

INDEX